The Scottish Political System

First published in 1973, Professor Kellas's account of Scottish government and politics has long been recognised as the standard textbook in the field. Its scope includes a definition of the Scottish political system, and critical descriptions of Scottish administration (central and local), parliamentary activity, parties, electoral behaviour, and pressure groups. Scottish nationalism is given a wider interpretation than usual, covering not only the support for the Scottish National Party, but the manifestations of national feeling in Scottish life generally.

The General Election of 1987 provided further evidence of the distinctive character of politics in Scotland, with the Conservative party reduced in strength to ten MPs, barely sufficient to fill the existing Scottish ministerial posts. In a new postscript Professor Kellas looks at the principal political developments of the period since 1983, and examines the political and constitutional developments posed by the current imbalance of forces as between Westminister and Scotland.

Some reviews of earlier editions

'Everyone concerned with the future of the United Kingdom should read this book.'

The Economist

'This is a guide to the central and local institutions of government in Scotland and to political activity in that country . . . a mine of information on Scottish social, economic and political affairs . . . a useful and informative guide.'

British Book News

The Scottish political system

Fourth edition

JAMES G. KELLAS
Professor in Politics, University of Glasgow

CAMBRIDGE
UNIVERSITY PRESS

Published by the Press Syndicate of the University of Cambridge
The Pitt Building, Trumpington Street, Cambridge CB2 1RP
40 West 20th Street, New York, NY 10011-4211 USA
10 Stamford Road, Oakleigh, Melbourne 3166, Australia

First published 1973
Second edition 1975
Third edition 1984
Fourth edition 1989
Reprinted 1990, 1992, 1994, 1995

Printed in Great Britain by
Athenæum Press Ltd, Gateshead, Tyne & Wear

British Library Cataloguing in publication data

Kellas, James G.
The Scottish political system—4th ed.
1. Civics, Scottish
I. Title

Library of Congress cataloguing in publication data
Kellas, James G.
The Scottish political system / James G. Kellas—4th ed.
  p.   cm.
Bibliography.
Includes index.
ISBN 0 521 36319 5. ISBN 0 521 36864 2 (pbk)
1. Scotland-Politics and government-20th century. 1 Title.
JN213   1988
320.9411-dc19 88-11894

ISBN 0 521 36864 2 paperback

SE

Contents

Illustrations and tables

Abbreviations

BBC	British Broadcasting Corporation
CBI	Confederation of British Industry
CNAA	Council for National Academic Awards
COSLA	Convention of Scottish Local Authorities
DEA	Department of Economic Affairs
DES	Department of Education and Science
EEC	European Economic Community
EIS	Educational Institute of Scotland
GCE	General Certificate of Education
GTC	General Teaching Council
HIDB	Highlands and Islands Development Board
IBA	Independent Broadcasting Authority
IDC	Industrial Development Certificate
IDS	Industry Department for Scotland
ITV	Independent Television
MSC	Manpower Services Commission
NCB	National Coal Board
NOP	National Opinion Polls
ORC	Opinion Research Centre
SCE	Scottish Certificate of Education
SDA	Scottish Development Agency
SDP	Social Democratic Party
SED	Scottish Education Department
SEPD	Scottish Economic Planning Department
SNP	Scottish National Party
STUC	Scottish Trades Union Congress
STV	Scottish Television
TUC	Trades Union Congress
UGC	University Grants Committee
UN	United Nations

Geo-political glossary

In this book an attempt is made to use geo-political terms in as precise a manner as the language allows. Although this may at first appear to be pedantic, it is in fact essential to the nature of the argument, which depends on distinctions being made between the different parts of the United Kingdom.

United Kingdom (UK)	United Kingdom of Great Britain and Northern Ireland (the British state)
Britain	Short version of the above
Great Britain (GB)	England, Wales, and Scotland (i.e. the UK excluding Northern Ireland)
England, Wales, Scotland	Component nations of the above

One unresolved problem of terminology is the adjective 'British'. This can be derived from 'United Kingdom' or from 'Great Britain', although the territories involved are dissimilar. If it is important to make the distinction, the text does so.

Some authorities (e.g. the *Shorter Oxford Dictionary*) do not distinguish between Britain and Great Britain (excluding Northern Ireland from both), but this is not in accord with normal or official usage. In *Britain: An Official Handbook*, Britain (the UK) is distinguished from Great Britain (England, Wales, and Scotland).

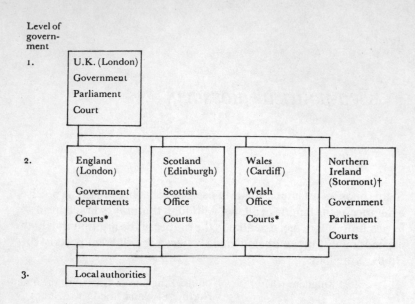

Level of
govern-
ment

1.
U.K. (London)

Government

Parliament

Court

2.
England
(London)

Government
departments

Courts*

Scotland
(Edinburgh)

Scottish
Office

Courts

Wales
(Cardiff)

Welsh
Office

Courts*

Northern
Ireland
(Stormont)†

Government

Parliament

Courts

3.
Local authorities

*The courts of England and Wales form part of one judicial system. Strictly
the only U.K. court is the House of Lords (Law Lords).
†The political system of Northern Ireland has changed several times
since 1972.

The territorial governments of the UK.

Preface

I should like to record my thanks to the many people who have helped me during the writing of this book. In particular, to my wife, who undertook the laborious task of compiling a card-index of Scottish Office administrators.

Interviews granted to me by politicians and civil servants were, of course, invaluable, as was advice from colleagues, particularly Professors W. J. M. Mackenzie and A. M. Potter. I must also thank Charlotte Logan for coping so well with the typing and editing.

Glasgow   J.G.K.
September 1972

For the third edition, the text has been completely revised and a new chapter added on devolution. Since the first edition appeared, a great deal has happened in Scottish politics, and the study of the subject has expanded to include a large number of publications. This edition attempts to bring these developments together in an academic analysis covering the whole range of Scottish politics and government during a period of great importance in the evolution of the Scottish political system.

I should like to acknowledge help received from Richard Parry, Christopher Hood, Michael Ewart, and Fred Craig in preparing this edition. The considerable task of preparing the manuscript for this edition was undertaken mainly by Barbara Fisher, with the assistance of Avril Johnston and Elspeth Shaw, to whom I express my thanks.

Glasgow   J.G.K.
September 1983

Map of the local government boundaries.

1

Scotland as a political system

Political scientists now realise that the British political system fits rather uneasily into the conventional categories by which it is usually described (see, for example, Rose 3). The concepts of unitary state, nation-state, political homogeneity and sovereignty of parliament, for example, are now being re-examined to see whether they are in fact applicable to Britain. Firstly, the unitary character of the British state is restricted by the existence of various forms of devolution or decentralisation which exist above the level of local government. The most extended of these was the government of Northern Ireland, which from 1920 to 1972 included a separately elected parliament at Stormont, an executive responsible to it, a local government structure and a system of courts. In this period, Northern Ireland was governed partly from Stormont and partly from London, the division of powers being laid down in the Government of Ireland Act of 1920 and subsequent statutes. This was a sort of federal relationship between the government of the UK and that of Northern Ireland. The Ireland Act of 1949 stated that Northern Ireland would not cease to be part of the UK without the consent of the Northern Ireland Parliament. In 1972, however, the Stormont system was suspended by the British Government, and replaced by 'direct rule', pending the establishment of a new constitution. Between 1973 and 1982 several attempts were made to establish a reformed Stormont system with a 'power-sharing Executive' including both Protestants and Catholics. Such a 'consociational' device of government is unknown in the rest of Britain. So too is the right to vote to remain in or to leave the state. This right was transferred from the Northern Ireland Parliament to the people of Northern Ireland by the Northern Ireland (Border Poll) Act 1972. The Poll took place in 1973, and 98.9% voted to stay in the UK, on a 58.7% turnout.

Wales is also treated as a distinct area in British central government. The development of various administrative bodies exclusive to

1

Wales led in 1964 to the establishment of the Welsh Office, with a Secretary of State for Wales in the British Cabinet. In the House of Commons, a Welsh Grand Committee has existed since 1960 to discuss Welsh affairs, and legislation relating exclusively to Wales is occasionally passed by Parliament. There is no Welsh legal system, however, and the identity of Wales rests more on language, education and religion than on political institutions. Although it has increased vastly in scope since 1964 (e.g. gaining health and education in 1969 and 1970 respectively), the Welsh Office has not the range of functions possessed by the Scottish Office, and the Welsh Grand Committee is not as important as the Scottish committees of the House of Commons, since it cannot discuss Bills or Estimates.

Scotland comes somewhere between Wales and Northern Ireland in political status. While possessing neither a government nor a parliament of its own, it has a strong constitutional identity and a large number of political and social institutions. The Act of Union of 1707, which is the 'fundamental law' joining Scotland with England, laid down that Scotland would retain for all time certain key institutions such as the Scottish legal system, the Presbyterian Church of Scotland (the Established Church), the Scottish educational system, and the 'Royal Burghs' (local authorities). These became the transmitters of Scottish national identity from one generation to the next.

Political institutions in Scotland were not encouraged. Scottish MPs were to be an integral part of the House of Commons, and Scottish peers could elect representatives to the House of Lords. There was initially a Secretary of State for Scotland in the government, but this was dropped in 1746, leaving the chief Scottish law officer, the Lord Advocate, as the principal 'spokesman' for Scotland in the executive. In the nineteenth century, the development of Scottish administrative boards and rising national feeling led to the demand for the creation of a Scottish Office headed by a Secretary for Scotland. In 1885, this Office was established, and the Scottish Secretary soon gained a permanent place in the Cabinet. His department grew in size and range of functions, so that today it is the equivalent in Scotland of several Whitehall departments. Its estimates amounted to over £6,000m in 1982–3, about four times the expenditure of the Home Office, and twice that of the Department of Education and Science.[1] There are also a large number of Scottish agencies of government that are loosely related to the Scottish Office, or to Whitehall departments. And there is a separate structure of local authorities, in part derived from the historic 'Royal Burghs'. A Royal Commission on Local Government in Scotland reported in 1969, and a reformed structure has been introduced to meet the special needs of Scotland.

In the legislative branch, the Union of the Parliaments did not mean the unification of the laws of Scotland and England. As long as there was a separate legal system in Scotland, there was a need for separate legislation for Scotland. The Act of Union attempted to divide the spheres of 'British' and Scottish law, broadly along the lines of public and private law. In the former, Parliament would legislate for the whole of Britain, while in the latter, Scotland could have its own arrangements. This division has never been strictly adhered to in practice, and the 1707 settlement did not provide for 'judicial review' of legislation, which could determine which sphere, Scottish or British, an Act properly belonged to. Nor was there any supreme court which could undertake such a task (the nearest was the judicial committee of the House of Lords). Even more remiss was the absence of any machinery for revising the Act of Union, other than by an ordinary Act of Parliament. Nevertheless, the doctrine of the 'sovereignty of Parliament' has been challenged in Scotland by some Scots lawyers, who regard the terms of the Union as more than ordinary legislation to be lightly repealed.[2] Moreover, it is claimed that the Scottish Parliament did not possess the 'sovereignty' attributed to its English counterpart, and so could not transmit this quality to the Parliament of the United Kingdom.[3] These arguments are largely academic, and the relationship between Scotland and England depends more on mutual accommodation and working the Act of Union in a proper spirit.

The process of passing laws separately for Scotland became troublesome, both for the Scottish MPs and for their English colleagues. Scottish Bills took up the time of the House of Commons, yet only the Scots were really interested in them. By the 1880s, parliamentary time was becoming a valuable commodity, and Scottish Bills were getting squeezed out. It was therefore decided to set up a special committee, the Scottish Grand Committee, to relieve the House of this burden. This dates from 1894, and today there are several Scottish committees of the House, dealing with the various stages of Scottish legislation. There are usually between five and ten purely Scottish Bills passed during each parliamentary session.

The legal system of Scotland is one of the strongest clues to the existence of the Scottish political system. The people of Scotland are subject to many laws which are exclusive to Scotland. They have a

3

system of law courts which are, with one exception, different from, and independent of, the law courts of the rest of Britain. The exception is that the final court of appeal in civil cases is the House of Lords, in its judicial capacity. All other cases, whether under Scots Law or law applying to the whole of Britain, must be decided in Scottish courts. Legal procedures in these courts differ from those in English courts. This gives the Scottish legal system more independence than the legal systems of federal states. In the USA, for example, federal (national) courts are found in all states, and federal law applies throughout the nation. State law and state court decisions are subject to federal judicial review under certain circumstances (e.g. conflict with the Constitution or laws of the United States), in civil and in criminal law. Both federal and state courts have jurisdiction over the population, while in Scotland there is essentially one set of courts, the Scottish courts.

The Scottish legal system is represented in the government by the Lord Advocate and the Solicitor-General for Scotland. But the Lord Advocate is not quite the equivalent of the Lord Chancellor in England and Wales. While the Lord Chancellor heads the English judiciary, in Scotland that position is held by the Lord President of the Court of Session (the supreme Scottish court). The Scottish legal profession is recruited separately from that of England, through the Scottish universities, the Law Society of Scotland and the Faculty of Advocates, and has its own qualifications and traditions.

Scotland then has its distinctive institutions, in the executive, legislative and judicial branches of government. It also has a whole host of party organisations, pressure groups, and advisory bodies as satellites to the institutional structure. All of these have somehow to be fitted into the concept of the British political system, which encompasses them. It might be possible to call Scotland a 'sub-system' of the British system, but this would be vague and ambiguous. It could, for example, be said that any territorial local authority was a sub-system of the central authority. Since Scotland is not a local authority in British terms, it would have to be a 'super-sub-system' of the territorial type. The contention here is that the concept of system is more appropriate since it does justice to the scale and nature of the phenomena which are found in Scottish politics.

This view is not accepted by all political scientists. Keating and Midwinter state that 'it is doubtful whether Scotland can be considered a political system when the main Scottish political institutions are UK institutions and authority and power are still

4

retained and concentrated at Westminster and Whitehall'.[4] Only devolution would provide Scotland with a political system in this sense, and even then it would still be the case that ultimate power was retained in London (see also Ch. 14).

A political system is not solely defined by political institutions and organisations, and can be supported by other criteria. Here the description of Britain as a 'nation-state' comes into question. If Britain were truly a nation-state, then it might be difficult to establish the existence of strong political systems within it, such as the Scottish. The USA is a nation-state, however, and yet contains fifty separate states which are political systems. But Britain is a special form of nation-state, just as it is a special type of unitary state. The criteria for nationhood are never easy to determine, and vary from nation to nation. But they ought to satisfy two broad requirements: that the members of the nation think of themselves primarily as such, and not primarily as members of another nation; and that the nation should have some objective characteristics of its own, such as language, 'complementary habits and facilities of communication',[5] religion, territory, previous statehood, a history of common action, and so on.

The first requirement is well fulfilled in the case of Scotland, and for Wales and Northern Ireland too. In these areas of Britain people today think of themselves primarily as Scots, Welsh, or Irish, not British. It is also likely that most Englishmen regard themselves as such and not as Britishers (see Ch. 7, p. 125). This national consciousness in Britain, which does not correspond to *British* national consciousness, is a fact which has rarely been taken into account in works on British politics. Of course, it came to the surface during the late 1960s with the rise of political nationalism in Scotland, Wales, and Northern Ireland (the last a quite separate variety). But in reality it was always there. The absence of attitude surveys on the subject before the period of political nationalism makes it difficult to document with any degree of precision, but all the other evidence points to such national consciousness having existed over a long period. To take one indicator, the teaching of history in Scottish schools lays stress on the nation-building process in Scotland and the historic warfare with England. Scottish school-children frequently play games of the 'Scots versus the English' type. While this national identification is much less emphasised in secondary education, the early experiences are important in shaping nationalist feeling.

Can we then say that Scots do not feel British at all? If their subjective identification with Scotland were translated into politics, they

5

would apparently be Scottish nationalist and disdain cooperation with the 'English' political parties. That they do not (usually) shows that subjective nationality can be a weak indicator for voting behaviour. But it can be called upon, in certain circumstances, to give a nationalist form to such behaviour. Most of the time, however, the political nationalism lies dormant, and the 'British' pattern of political behaviour prevails. Scots feel British as well as Scottish, and so they should, since Scotland is an integral part of the UK, a situation accepted by the vast majority of Scots. But their consciousness of 'Britishness' is much less clear than their consciousness of 'Scottishness'. Geographical separation, a separate educational system, and the other 'objective' criteria of nationhood account for this, and reinforce the institutional basis of the Scottish political system.

What is the extent and significance of the other 'objective' criteria of the separateness of Scotland? The differences in political institutions have already been summarised, and it should be emphasised that social institutions such as those of religion and education are as important in determining the nation as are the politico-legal ones.[6] In religion, for example, Scotland's characteristics are markedly different from elsewhere. Presbyterianism is dominant, with the Church of Scotland the principal and Established Church. Its regular communicants amount to around one quarter of the adult population. Its influence on the political culture of Scotland has always been strong, for its emphasis on democratic organisation and individualism, coupled with puritanism, have encouraged the application of these principles to government. Scots have shown greater enthusiasm for democratic institutions and equality of opportunity than the English, and they have been less inclined to relax old moral standards in favour of 'permissiveness'.

The Roman Catholic Church shares much of this morality and is proportionately stronger than in England and Wales. (16% of the Scottish population are baptised Catholics, compared with 8% in England and Wales.) It is particularly concentrated in the Glasgow region, as a result of Irish immigration, where it amounts to about one quarter of the population.

In general, religion plays a greater part in Scottish life than it does in English life, since there is a higher proportion of church membership and attendance. The churches are involved in politics in a different way, with the Church of Scotland General Assembly claiming to be a 'Scottish Parliament', and the Roman Catholic schools built and maintained entirely by the state, thus constituting

6

part of the public provision of education. There is also some evidence that religion and voting behaviour are more closely connected in Scotland than in England (Budge and Urwin, pp. 60–3, and Bochel and Denver[7]).

The educational system of Scotland is of course closely involved in socialisation, and we have seen that it has a direct bearing on national consciousness. Its influence permeates Scottish society, and the public sector is stronger than the public sector of education in England. In higher education there is a greater proportion of the population in Scotland at university than in England, and the schools and universities are organised (on the whole) along different lines. Scottish educational principles stress equality of opportunity, a liberal education over a wide range of subjects, and a somewhat didactic pedagogy. These approaches have left their mark on the Scots and the structure of Scottish society, for good or ill. As far as politics is concerned, it may be pointed out that the resilience of the educational system in Scotland makes the administrative boundary between Scotland and England a strong one in this field. Scottish schools are the responsibility of the Scottish Education Department, not the Department of Education and Science. Scottish universities are principally subject to the (British) University Grants Committee and so to the British Education Minister, but student grants are provided by the Scottish Education Department, and take account of the differences in course length and content in Scotland. These differences mark most Scottish universities off from their counterparts in England, and help to identify the Scottish nation, or at least its more educated stratum.

A more pervasive influence than the universities on the people is mass communication. Most of the theorists of 'British political homogeneity' point to the power of London-based communications media as evidence that Britain is one nation politically. It is said that the great majority everywhere read London newspapers or consume London broadcasts. But the evidence in Scotland is clearly at variance with regard to the press, and ambiguous about broadcasting. No newspaper published in Fleet Street is read by more than 17% of Scottish adults on weekdays and 12% on Sundays.[8] The most popular papers in Scotland (*Daily Record* (52%), *Sunday Post* (69%) and *Sunday Mail* (54%)) are distinctly Scottish in content. So are the 'quality' papers, the *Scotsman* (6%) and the *Glasgow Herald* (9%), which in Scotland partially replace the *Daily Telegraph* (2%), *The Times* (1%), the *Guardian* (1%), and the *Sunday Telegraph* (2%). No English region (and

7

not even Wales or Northern Ireland) varies so much in readership from the British average, and this is reinforced by the fact that total daily newspaper readership is greater in Scotland than elsewhere in Britain.

In broadcasting, the BBC recognises the existence of the 'national regions' of Scotland, Wales, and Northern Ireland. Scotland and Wales have National Broadcasting Councils which are supposed to control the policy and content of their regions' broadcasts, while Northern Ireland has an Advisory Council whose chairman is a member of the BBC's Board of Governors. English regions are less strongly organised, and with the advent of local radio the BBC's English radio regions were abolished in 1970. The BBC's Scottish radio service was retained, however, and the National Broadcasting Council for Scotland 'felt strongly that Scotland, as a nation, must continue to enjoy a national output'.[9] In 1978, a separate programme, BBC Radio Scotland, was established, and in 1982 it broadcast for 90 hours a week. BBC television from Scotland had an output of around 10 hours a week. While this is a small share of total output, Scottish programmes are often politically relevant and deal with Scottish political issues.

ITV broadcasting is shared between Scottish Television (Central Scotland), Grampian Television (North-east) and Border Television (English and Scottish borders). STV's own programmes amount to about 10 hours per week, Grampian's to 6 hours, and Border's to 4 hours. In the case of Border, very few programmes are specifically Scottish in content, for they rely on creating a 'Border community'. This, and the division of Scotland into three for the production of programmes goes against a strong Scottish identity in ITV broadcasting. Instead, there is a regional flavour, more marked than in the BBC, which considers itself Scottish-national. STV, however, since it covers 80% of the Scottish population, regards itself as 'Scottish' rather than regional. Independent local radio is provided by Radio Clyde (Glasgow), Radio Forth (Edinburgh), Radio Tay (Dundee), North Sound (Aberdeen), Moray Firth Radio (Inverness), and West Sound (Ayr). Local BBC radio comes from Radio Highland, Radio Nan Eilean, Radio Aberdeen, Radio Orkney, Radio Shetland, Radio Tweed, and Radio Solway. The hours of broadcasting range from 'round-the-clock' on the major independent stations to about an hour a day on the small BBC stations.

The mass media in Scotland have to strike a balance between a Scottish- and a British/American-derived output. It seems that the

8

consumers of newspapers in Scotland are more favourable to a Scottish content than is the broadcasting public. But this is partly because it is easier, for economic and professional reasons, to make newspapers than to make broadcasts. Scots are often highly critical of the quality of Scottish broadcasting, while cheerfully accepting lower standards in some of their popular press. At the same time, they support two quality newspapers and a wide range of weeklies and other journals.

Scottish sport is strongly nationalist. There is a separate Scottish Football Association and Scottish Football League, and football-loyalties in Scotland are entirely to Scottish teams. Football 'internationals', involving Scotland against, for example, England, Wales, or a European team, arouse fierce partisanship. Other sports are also organised on a Scottish rather than British basis, and the combined effect of these arrangements is to reinforce national consciousness. It also affects the composition of newspapers and broadcasting in Scotland, for these must pay great attention to reporting Scottish matches.

It is possible to seek for other 'objective' criteria of Scottish nationhood, in the mass of social and economic statistics relating to Scotland. Here some caution should be exercised. In the first place, such statistics are inherently rather weak indicators of nationhood, since it is possible for different nations to be similar in socio-economic structure and yet remain distinct culturally and in their desire for self-government. Countries such as Norway and Sweden, or many of the developing countries in Africa, are similar in socio-economic terms, yet possess strong national characteristics which differentiate them. In the context of the UK, the profile of Scotland is closer to England in many respects than it is to any 'foreign' country, or indeed to Wales or Northern Ireland. And some regions in England (e.g. the northern) deviate more from the UK than does Scotland.

Secondly, only some of the statistics are relevant to politics (but which ones are is not very clear). Considerable differences exist in the eating and drinking habits of Scots, as compared with Englishmen. For example, Scots consume more starch and less vitamin C than any region of the UK,[10] and (of course) drink more whisky and less beer. The latter fact leads to a high level of alcoholism, and a correspondingly strong temperance or anti-drink movement. Until the Licensing (Scotland) Act 1976, licensed premises closed earlier than in England, but now local licensing boards can (and often do) sanction 'round-the-clock' drinking. Drink issues dominated Scottish politics in the

Table 1. *UK population (1981 Census)*

	Population (millions)	% of UK	Land area (% of UK)	Density per sq. mile (persons)
UK	55.7	100	100	598
Scotland	5.1	9.2	32.0	172
England	46.2	83.0	53.8	923
Wales	2.8	5.0	8.6	350
Northern Ireland	1.5	2.8	5.6	297

Note: For populations of local government regions, island authorities, and city districts, see Table 23, p. 164.

late nineteenth and early twentieth centuries, but are much less important today.

Scotland is well served with demographic and other vital statistics. It is listed separately in the UN Demographic Year Book as a subdivision of the UK, along with Wales and Northern Ireland. It also comes into the UN Statistical Year Book in the population, housing, education, health, and motor transport tables. No other subdivisions of sovereign unitary states are thus listed, and very few constituent states of federations. One reason for this is that Scotland produces its own Census, and operates a Statistical Unit, so that such information is readily available. It is thus possible to compare Scotland directly with the other countries of the world, and, more extensively, with other parts of the United Kingdom.

The indicators selected here include most of the key ones for comparative purposes, and for the understanding of Scottish politics in its own terms. There is, firstly, the population (size, distribution and density). The UK and Scottish profiles are shown in Table 1.

Scotland has about one-tenth of the population of the UK, yet it covers one-third of the land area. The density of population is therefore much smaller than the UK average, although within Scotland this varies considerably from the heavily populated central belt to the northern and southern divisions, which have very few people indeed. The contrasts in density are in fact much greater within Scotland than within England, which makes a uniform structure of local government very difficult to devise. According to the area, authorities will be very large territorially or very great in population if they are to be viable. Another striking difference with England is the absence of large towns. Scotland has only four cities with over 100,000 in population, and three of these are in the central

Lowlands. Although three-quarters of Scotland's population is urban, the typical Burgh (town) is small, and there is only one conurbation, that of Central Clydeside (1,713,287, or one-third of the total population).

Emigration has always been heavy, and net migration was 170,400 between 1971 and 1981, more than the natural increase in population. While England and Wales gained 262,000 people from 1971 to 1981, Scotland lost 111,817. Scots are less inclined to move far within Scotland than they are to move out of Scotland altogether, and this can be considered a 'safety-valve' or a potential source of national frustration.

Immigration to Scotland has not greatly altered the ethnic composition of the country in recent years. Apart from the population of Irish origin (about a sixth of the whole, and concentrated in the west central division), there are no large minorities. Those born in England and Wales are about 5% of the population, while coloured immigrants form a much smaller group than in England.

The 'Scottish minority' of Gaelic speakers ($1\frac{1}{2}$%) is important for its influence on Highland education and broadcasting, but it does not compare in strength with the Welsh speakers in Wales (20%). Scottish nationhood cannot be strictly defined on linguistic grounds, for nearly all Scots speak only English. They speak it with a Scottish accent, however, and many use a large number of 'Scots' (dialect) words in everyday speech. There is thus a division in speech between Scotland and England, which sets up something of a communication barrier. Some writers have sought to increase this separation by adopting an artificial Scots dialect, 'Lallans', but unlike linguistic nationalists in other countries, they have made very little impression on Scottish life. When set alongside the general pattern of communications and transactions of various kinds in Scotland, the linguistic situation confirms the nationhood of Scotland: in Karl Deutsch's words, 'Membership in a people essentially consists in wide complementarity of social communication. It consists in the ability to communicate more effectively, and over a wider range of subjects, with members of one large group than with outsiders.'[11] This seems true of the Scottish nation, even when the division between Highlanders and Lowlanders is taken into account.

The drastic migration of population from Scotland is related to the economic structure of the country (see Table 2). While this is broadly similar to that of Britain as a whole, it is more heavily dependent on agriculture and declining industries. The number employed in

11

Table 2. *Industrial distribution of employees in employment, 1978*

	UK %	Scotland %	England %
Agriculture, forestry, fishing	1.7	2.3	1.6
Construction	5.6	7.7	5.2
Mining, quarrying, gas, electricity, water	3.0	3.3	2.9
Distribution	12.2	11.6	12.4
Professional and scientific services	16.2	16.9	15.9
Food, drink and tobacco	3.1	4.4	3.0
Coal, petroleum, chemical products, metal manufacturing	4.1	3.5	4.0
Engineering and allied industries	14.6	12.3	15.2
Textiles, leather and clothing	4.0	4.4	3.9
Other manufacturing	6.1	4.6	6.4
Other industries and services	29.4	28.9	29.6

Source: Calculated from *Regional Trends 1982*, Table 7.5, p. 110, Central Statistical Office, HMSO (London, 1982).

agriculture is, however, small compared with Wales, and much smaller than in Northern Ireland. Scottish agriculture is somewhat different from agriculture elsewhere, having special interests in hill farming, crofting and stock-raising. It is administered by the Scottish Office, not the Ministry of Agriculture, Fisheries and Food, and Scottish farmers have their own union, the National Farmers Union of Scotland. Politically, agriculture and fishing are much more important in Scotland than in England, although they have been declining in both countries since the 1960s. In the early 1960s, twenty-one of the 71 constituencies in Scotland could be called agricultural (i.e. with more than 15% of the male employment in agriculture), while the total in England was 80 out of 516.[12] In 1979 this number had declined to 11 in Scotland and 20 in England (Butler and Kavanagh, pp. 359–83). Agricultural issues affect the parties in Scotland to a considerable extent. Crofting is separately regulated by the Crofters Acts and the Crofters Commission, and fishing is protected by the Sea

Fish Industry Authority. Although the last is a UK body, it works in close liaison with the Scottish Office.

Categories other than agriculture which vary by 0.5% or more from the figures for the UK are: (higher) food, drink and tobacco, textiles, construction, and professional and scientific services; (lower) chemicals, distribution, engineering, other manufacturing industries, and services.

The most serious aspect of the Scottish economy is the decline in the level of employment, especially in the older industries of coal, iron and steel, shipbuilding and textiles. Such employment has fallen sharply in the last decade, and the influx of new industry (largely from the USA and England) has not been able to compensate for the resulting unemployment. Unemployment in Scotland between 1971 and 1981 ran at 20% to 40% higher than the UK average. Gross Domestic Product (GDP) per head in 1980 was 4% lower in Scotland, though manual workers earned as much as the average for the UK (non-manual somewhat lower). The cost of living is generally higher in Scotland.

On these counts then, the Scottish economy differs substantially from that of the south of England, though not from the north of England, nor, since the late 1970s, from the West Midlands. Politically, Scottish economic problems are of the utmost importance, and much of Scottish politics is devoted to the problem of righting the imbalance of the Scottish economy through regional economic policy which will provide financial incentives to new industry. This involves action by the British government departments, the Scottish Office, Scottish pressure groups, local authorities, and industry itself. It also involves the three Scottish banks (with their own note-issue) and the Scottish Stock Exchange, which together form an autonomous group of financial institutions.

A big change, economically and politically, since 1972 has been the rising importance of North Sea oil for Scotland. With tax revenues anticipated to yield over £15,000m per annum by 1985, and the creation of over 50,000 new jobs, oil has transformed the Scottish economy and the Scottish political system. It has shifted the focus of attention of the British Government to Scotland, and it has boosted the fortunes of the Scottish economy. There is, however, an imbalance between the prosperous east of Scotland, nearest the oil developments, and the declining west, which does not benefit so directly. Moreover, since most of the economic gains in the long run will be in

13

Table 3(a). *Occupational group of head of household, 1979–80*

	UK %	Scotland %	England %
Professional and technical	7.5	7.9	7.6
Administrative and managerial	8.5	7.2	9.0
Teacher	2.7	2.3	2.8
Clerical, shop assistant, armed forces	7.2	6.2	7.5
Manual	37.4	42.7	36.8
Self-employed (manual and non-manual)	6.5	5.4	6.6
Retired and unoccupied	30.2	28.3	29.7

Source: Regional Trends, op. cit., Table 7.3, p. 109.

Table 3(b). *Occupational class by nation, 1979*

	Scotland %	England %	Wales %
Upper middle class (AB) (Professional; businessmen)	12	13	9
Lower middle class (C1) (office workers)	21	23	21
Working class (C2, DE)	67	64	70

Source: Rose 5, p. 43, using opinion polls.

the form of revenues rather than employment, Scotland would benefit only insofar as the UK Government is prepared to channel revenues back to Scotland, or to give a Scottish parliament some share of them. Thus the new oil wealth does not necessarily guarantee economic or political power to Scotland, though it has certainly stimulated demands that such power be established.[13]

Related to the economic structure is the social class structure of the population. As might be expected, this too is roughly the same as for Britain as a whole, but it is rather more weighted to the working class (see Table 3).

Subjective class assessment from social surveys supports the 'objective' class position. In a 1964 survey of Great Britain and a 1968 survey of Northern Ireland, 60% in Scotland assigned themselves to the working class, compared with 50% in England, 54% in Wales, and 31% in Northern Ireland. For the middle class, the figures were Scotland 33%, England 42%, Wales 39%, and Northern Ireland 47% (Rose 3, p. 18). Social class and voting behaviour are correlated in different ways in the various nations and regions of the UK, with Scottish working-class voters less favourable to the Conservative Party than working-class voters in most of England. Wales is more working-class/Labour than Scotland, and so is north-east England and Yorkshire (Butler and Stokes, pp. 140–4; Rose 5, pp. 40–2). Trade union affiliation is connected with this pattern of behaviour, for Wales and Scotland are more strongly unionised than England (Rose 3, pp. 18–19).

An important social and economic difference between Scotland and the rest of the UK is housing tenure. About half the population of Scotland rents its housing from a local authority, whereas in England and Wales the proportion is a quarter. Such 'council' housing in Scotland is much more heavily subsidised by government grants and local rates than its counterpart elsewhere. Rents are correspondingly lower. Scotland generally has bad housing conditions, although in the council sector the standard amenities are provided. General 'amenity' does not go much beyond this, however, and some council estates are notoriously run down.

The origins of the Scottish housing situation must be traced well back in Scottish history. A tenement type of house was common in Scottish towns in early modern times, and seems to have been copied from continental (especially French) practice. The feudal system of land tenure encouraged such development, as did shortage of land. But the nineteenth-century industrial revolution, and the large-scale Irish immigration to Glasgow, provided the dreadful legacy of urban slums which are only now being eradicated. Rural slums, such as the Highland 'black houses', are also a thing of the past, but Scotland's housing stock is still well below the average in England for overcrowding, and outside the council-house sector, amenities are deficient. Housing is a major political issue in Scotland, and no political party can afford to offend the large number of 'council-house' voters. Most local politics is dominated by the need to placate either council tenants or owner-occupiers (depending on the social composition of the community), and Scottish housing is given specially favoured treatment within British housing policy.

The picture which can be built up of Scottish society from such indicators is not nearly as sharply defined as the picture derived from

15

Scottish institutions. In terms of crude social and economic indicators, Scotland is perhaps not greatly different from the rest of the UK, nor indeed from England alone. It is certainly not as 'deviant' as Northern Ireland in economic structure, where unemployment and a lower standard of living interact with religion, politics and nationalism to reinforce the institutional separation. Scotland's economic problems differ from those of England in degree rather than kind, and the trend is towards assimilation in industrial structure, earnings and level of employment. Such assimilation requires government action which will discriminate in Scotland's favour, in economic development and house-building, and political pressures are readily mobilised in Scotland to this end. There is usually a response in London to these demands, largely because the Scottish political machinery is so strong and active. This activity depends on the very existence of the Scottish political system, which acts as a means of communication with the larger British system, as well as affording a communications and decision-making network within Scotland itself in those areas of politics where 'British' considerations are not so involved.

The concept of a 'political system' as applied to Scotland must take account of these two 'activity areas' (the Scottish and the British), and it is obvious that the 'boundaries' of the system are different in each case. Where the Scottish system acts as a communications 'input' to the larger British system its boundaries are most clearly related to the function of communication. Thus in the 'British' sphere of taxation, monetary policy, principles of regional economic development and departmental appropriations, the Scottish political system serves to make known the demands and needs of the Scottish people. As a communications medium the system is sophisticated, institutionalised, and powerful. It is not a 'pressure group', but rather an 'arena' of politics which takes the form of a nation and its organised groups.[14] Within that arena, there are many voices, interests, and opinions, but they show their common origins and concerns, which derive from the characteristics of the Scottish political system.

The decisions in the British sphere are of course taken within the British system, which is itself the principal arena of politics. Just as it is possible to be 'Scottish' and 'British' at the same time, so it is possible for Scotland to participate in the Scottish and British arenas simultaneously. Some Scots become political 'brokers' or go-betweens linking the two arenas. Such men are the ministers and administrators of the Scottish Office, the Scottish MPs and the leaders of the Scottish sections of British pressure groups. Their function is to communicate the demands of each arena to the other, and to arrive at a settlement.

In the other activity area of the Scottish political system (i.e. Scotland itself) the boundary is sharper and covers more than the function of communication (though that is included). It ranges from the boundary set by the Scottish legal system to the administrative functions of the Scottish Office. All these activities act *solely* on the population of Scotland, and in the sphere of criminal law the *judicial process* is contained entirely within the system. So in effect is the function of law reform, though it is formally within the British system (i.e. it must pass through Parliament). The distinction between the *effective* and *formal* boundaries of the Scottish system must thus be made, and there is no constitutional way of doing so. The Act of Union of 1707 is of little help, for reasons already stated. What has to be discovered is the range of activity which is effectively Scottish, despite the formal necessity for legislation or executive decision at the British level. This range gives us a sliding scale of boundaries rather than one boundary, but all in this sector should be clearly Scottish rather than British. For example, the activities of the Scottish Office, the *decision-making* in Scottish law reform, Scottish education, housing, and local government are predominantly within the Scottish system (some are almost wholly within it). As for the *outputs* of the system, these act as a defining boundary between Scotland and the rest of the UK: those in Scotland are the system's subjects, those elsewhere are not.

There are elements both of clarity and obscurity in this concept. But the case of Scotland cannot be fitted neatly into any of the existing categories of political science. If it fits the concept of 'political system', that may well be because that concept is flexible enough to contain any relatively independent political structure or set of political elements which move together in interaction. David Easton identified the essential activity of the political system as 'the authoritative allocation of values' in a society,[15] but he said that such systems can vary in size from 'the smallest bushman band to the most complex industrial society'.[16] Karl Deutsch defines a political system as 'a collection of recognizable units, which are characterized by cohesion and covariance', and he identifies ten system levels in politics, from the individual to the UN.[17] Another approach is that of Talcott Parsons, who sees the political system as a 'sub-system' of an all-embracing social system.[18] This stresses the 'functional' character of the system, as opposed to the organisational definitions of Easton and Deutsch. All systems theorists are concerned about the feasibility of

17

drawing a boundary round a system, and about the need to establish the interdependence (rather than random contact) of the elements composing it. Finally, most are interested in the processes by which a system is maintained or altered, and seek to discover the functions which must be performed if a system is to survive.

Taking these points in turn, we find that Scotland has a political system composed of many institutions and organisations, which are 'characterized by cohesion and covariance' (i.e. they act and move together). It can be seen (in Parsons' terms) as a sub-system of Scottish society, or (in Deutsch's terms) as a lower level of system than the British. Easton's condition that the system should authoritatively allocate values is clearly met by the different content of Scots Law, religion, education, and much else in Scottish life. That this content derives primarily from the 'political system' may be argued. It is, however, maintained by Scottish legislation, administration, etc., which are political in character.

The only problem is that of defining the boundary: it is not clear in all cases whether it is the *British* system which is allocating Scottish (i.e. applying only to Scotland) values, or the Scottish. Nor is it clear how important *Scottish* (as opposed to British) values are in Scotland. The Scottish system is both dependent and independent within the British system, and the latter emerges as a less homogeneous entity as a result, since it is modified by the existence of the Scottish and other systems within it. Moreover, the way in which the systems are maintained is given a new perspective by the altered view of their constituent elements and functions. The British system can only be maintained by accommodation with the national systems within it. Thus nationality and national interest become important props of the 'multinational United Kingdom'. At the same time, such centrifugal forces can only go so far if the system is to survive.

As a corollary, the Scottish system also seeks to maintain itself. The vested Scottish interests are numerous and powerful. They include the institutions of church, law, education and government. These hope to preserve Scotland, and through it themselves. But it is not so obvious that Scots outside these groups wish whole-heartedly to maintain or strengthen the system. The forces for change pull in opposite directions: a considerable body of Scottish opinion would like further autonomy in decision-making, but an equal tendency is towards assimilation with England, or with general 'British' standards. Many MPs for Scottish constituencies see themselves as members of a British party first and as Scottish MPs second (though

18

they usually take an interest only in Scottish matters). So too do members of British trade unions, whether affiliated to the Labour Party or not.

Scots in general maintain the system by their national consciousness, but the intensity of such feeling is modified by British aspirations of 'equality-all-round'. Political man in Scotland stands on two legs, one Scottish and one British, and both are needed if he is to remain upright. His cousins in England, Wales, and Northern Ireland are also two-legged in this sense, although they may prefer to walk on one leg, dragging the other behind them. Walking or limping, British political man is usually a good traveller, and it is to his journeys within Scotland that we now turn.

2

The constitutional inheritance

Scotland and England came together as a political unity in 1707, as a result of the Act of Union passed by the Parliaments of the two countries. After that date, the separate Parliaments of Scotland and England were abolished and were replaced by the Parliament of the United Kingdom of Great Britain. Since 1603, the Crowns of Scotland and England had been united, but while this gave England and Scotland the same king, it did not merge these kingdoms nor give them a joint Privy Council, joint state officials, or a joint Parliament. Each country retained its own institutions, and the arrangement was essentially a 'dual monarchy', illustrated by the title 'James VI of Scotland and I of England'.

The Union of 1707 has been subjected to much historical analysis, and legal discussion. Only part of this discourse has definite relevance to the study of the political system today. For example, the question of how the 'Treaty' was negotiated and passed, involving such matters as bribery and secret diplomacy, is of little importance in explaining its position today.

But the fact that it was not (overtly) imposed on Scotland gives Scotland a *locus standi* in the UK, unmatched by Wales or Ireland. Scotland was apparently guaranteed certain institutions and rights in 1707 as a result of a freely negotiated bargain. This was (and is) psychologically important to Scots, who have never considered themselves annexed by England, although some think they were tricked into signing away rights which could have been retained.

The principal provisions in the Act are union of the Scottish and English parliaments, the guarantee of freedom of trade within the UK and its possessions, and the perpetual safeguards given to the Presbyterian Established Church, to the Scottish legal system and courts, and to the universities. Thus the three bulwarks of Scottish culture (church, law, and education) are recognised as indestructible (in theory).

Just as important is the absence in the Act of any 'federal' features. There is to be no 'blocking mechanism' in the UK Parliament, whereby Scotland can exercise a veto. Scottish MPs are to be an integral part of the House of Commons, and Scottish peers similarly in the House of Lords. Initially, a quota was given to Scotland in each House (45 and 16 respectively), but Acts of Parliament have subsequently altered the proportions. Today there are 72 MPs and as many Scots as have been created peers (around 100).

Another feature which denotes the lack of federalism is the absence of any special law court to interpret the Constitution. In the USA, and in some other federal countries, this is the function of the Supreme Court. In Britain, on the other hand, no court (Scottish or English) has ruled an Act of Parliament unconstitutional, and it is generally accepted that Parliament is 'sovereign' and can by ordinary legislation 'amend the Constitution'.

The contradiction posed between a simple 'sovereignty of Parliament' theory and the terms of the Act of Union has on occasion caused some anxiety. It does seem odd that something guaranteed 'for all time' should nevertheless be subject to amendment by Parliament. It is, however, a convention of the Constitution that some laws are more 'fundamental' than others, and cannot lightly be changed. Such a law is the Act of Union, and an attempt to alter its principal provisions would be the subject of constitutional and political controversy, even now.[1]

Nevertheless, changes have been made over the years, and many of these have gone unnoticed. For example, university professors in Scotland need no longer subscribe to the Westminster Confession of Faith, and the clause forbidding special inducements to trade in any part of the UK has been repeatedly breached. It is possible to distinguish these 'altered' parts of the Act from the more 'unalterable' parts, such as those relating to the principal law courts and Presbyterianism. Even here, by a process of consent of the relevant parties within the British parliamentary system, legislation has brought changes. Examples are the Acts altering the establishment of Court of Session judges, and the Church of Scotland Acts, 1921 and 1925. The latter make up the basic constitution of the Church of Scotland today.

The doctrine, propounded by the English constitutionalist A. V. Dicey,[2] and others, that in Britain sovereignty cannot be divided, has been challenged in the recent past by some Scottish lawyers. Lord Cooper, in the case of *MacCormick and Another* v. *The Lord Advocate*,

21

1953, maintained that the principle of the unlimited sovereignty of Parliament 'is a distinctively English principle which has no counterpart in Scottish constitutional law'.[3] He was commenting on the (unsuccessful) attempt by the Scottish Nationalist J. M. MacCormick to have the title 'Elizabeth II' made illegal. MacCormick considered that since there had never been a 'First' Elizabeth in the UK, there could not now be a 'Second'. He tried to show that the proclamation of the latter title was contrary to the Act of Union, but in this he failed. Nevertheless, he elicited from some of the Scottish judges various assertions about Scottish constitutional law which have remained tantalisingly enigmatic to this day. If Parliament cannot alter the Act of Union, who can? The original parties are no more, for this was an 'incorporating union'. If the UK Parliament inherits some of the features of the old Scottish Parliament, as was suggested, how are they to be recognised, let alone made the basis of action?

From time to time, other Scottish lawyers have followed some of Cooper's thoughts. Professor T. B. Smith has called for judicial review of Acts of Parliament,[4] and Lord Kilbrandon once hinted that the Act of Union might present difficulties in law for Scotland's entry into the Common Market.[5] In *Gibson* v. *The Lord Advocate*, 1975, however, it was held that European Community Law could not be challenged in Scottish courts as contrary to the Act of Union. Lord Keith reserved his opinion on what the position might be if the UK Parliament passed an Act to abolish the Court of Session or the Church of Scotland, or to substitute English law for the whole body of Scots private law, but he believed that such an issue was a political, not a justiciable, one.[6]

The mainstream of legal thought in Scotland does not regard these as practical issues. Acts of Parliament have never been successfully challenged in Scottish courts, nor are they likely to be. Moreover, Scotland has no *de iure* status in international law, though its separate legal system will have to be taken into account in the legal institutions of the EEC. Since it is derived from Roman Law, it is more akin to the laws of the European countries than is that of England. This may give it a useful function as a bridge between the English and Roman systems.

The significance of Scots Law for the present operation of the Scottish political system is very great. To lawyers, it represents the touchstone of Scottish nationality, without which Scotland would cease to be a nation. Churchmen and educationists make similar claims for their institutions. In a sense, the law has priority. It lays down the rights of the others, and the courts must uphold them. The

Table 4(a). *The law court structure in Scotland*

Civil	Criminal
House of Lords	Court of Criminal Appeal
Court of Session	High Court of Justiciary
Sheriff Court	Sheriff Court
	District Court

Table 4(b). *The judicial and legal-administrative establishment*

Judges		Government law officers and principal officials	
Court of Session and High Court of Justiciary	(22)	Lord Advocate	
		Solicitor-General for Scotland	
Sheriffs-principal	(6)	Crown Agent	
Sheriffs	(76)	Procurators-fiscal	(46)

Note: The head of the judiciary in Scotland is the Lord President of the Court of Session, and not the Lord Advocate, who is the chief law officer of the Crown. This is unlike the position in England, where the Lord Chancellor fulfils both functions. The Law Society of Scotland recommended to the Commission on the Constitution that Scotland should have the equivalent of the Lord Chancellor's Office (*Memorandum of Evidence of the Law Society of Scotland* (1970), p. 6).

Scottish courts form an autonomous group within Britain, the principal exception being that in civil cases an appeal can be taken to the House of Lords, where only two of the five Lords of Appeal are Scottish judges (see Table 4(a)). In nearly all cases, and in all criminal cases, the Scottish courts decide the law. This applies to law relating to Britain as well as to Scotland.

The highest courts in Scotland are the Court of Session (civil cases) and the High Court of Justiciary (criminal cases). The same judges officiate in both these courts, and the total number is twenty-two at present. Appointments to the Scottish bench are often given to the principal government law officers as a political reward (for these officers, see Table 4(b)). Eight of the eighteen judges in 1970 were in this category, the remaining being former sheriffs or advocates, including four deans of the Faculty of Advocates. This led to some criticism, especially as the Lord Advocate is in a position to elevate himself to the bench. In 1970, the heads of the Scottish judiciary, the Lord President of the Court of Session, and the Lord Justice Clerk, illustrated the link between politics and the law in Scotland.

Lord President of the Court of Session – Lord Clyde.
  Conservative MP for Edinburgh North, 1950–5.
  Lord Advocate, 1951–4.
  Lord President, 1955.
Lord Justice Clerk – Lord Grant.
  Conservative MP for Glasgow Woodside, 1955–62.
  Solicitor General for Scotland, 1955–60.
  Lord Advocate, 1960–2.
  Lord Justice Clerk, 1962.

Note: In March 1972, Lord Emslie succeeded Lord Clyde, and Lord Wheatley succeeded Lord Grant as Lord Justice Clerk in December 1972.

On the bench, Scottish judges see themselves very much as public figures. They man important government committees, and pronounce on topical questions. In 1968, one judge, Lord Avonside, accepted an invitation to be a member of the Scottish Conservative Party's Constitutional Committee, which was examining Edward Heath's proposal for a Scottish Convention. Pressure from the Labour Government, however, forced him to withdraw, under protest. His wife became National Governor of the BBC in Scotland. In 1970 a Scottish judge, Lord Wheatley, became a life peer, and was soon active as legislator in the House of Lords in Scottish legal matters, as well as an interpreter of the law on the bench. Lord Kilbrandon is another important public figure.

The principal territorial courts of Scotland are the Sheriff Courts, and they cover a wide jurisdiction in both civil and criminal cases. There is also the Scottish Land Court, for cases arising under agricultural law.

In Scottish courts, procedure is different from that in England. Public prosecutions, under the direction of procurators-fiscal, are the rule, and replace police and private prosecutions. This system has been commended to England by the lawyers' organisation, Justice.[7] Majority and 'not proven' verdicts are also used, and a modified version of the former was introduced in England in 1967.

Local courts in the districts can have elected councillors as magistrates, which bring politics in at a lower level. Called 'bailies' under the old system, they are now restyled 'Justices of the Peace'. Former Justices of the Peace are also appointed to these positions.

The personnel of the Scottish legal profession is quite distinct from that in England. Scottish solicitors, advocates (barristers), and judges are nearly always Scots, and have received at least part of their legal education in Scotland. Very few Scots lawyers are qualified to practise in England, and few become MPs because of the loss of earnings, which cannot be made up by legal work in London. This separation of the legal professions of Scotland and England is similar to that in schoolteaching, and greater than that in public administration. Scots lawyers are thus strongly interested in maintaining the autonomy of Scotland in matters which concern them, and some of these matters impinge on politics.

The difference between the substance of Scots Law and English Law is obviously relevant to the political system. In the first place, separate laws are often passed in Parliament for Scotland, and this has led to the establishment of special Scottish committees of the House of Commons. At the same time, clauses relating only to Scotland are often tacked on to British legislation. Between five and ten purely Scottish Bills are passed each session, while over seventy Acts which apply to Scotland are passed in the same period.

The decision to legislate separately for Scotland is most likely to be taken in matters relating to law reform, education, local government, and (to a lesser degree) agriculture. In the last, important provisions relating to Scotland are also found in British statutes. Most revenue, social security, and economic legislation is British. While this makes up the bulk of policy-making, the existence of separate Scottish legislation is important in strengthening the autonomy of Scottish politics. No region of England requires separate laws, and Wales rarely does. Scots lawyers complain that the differences between Scots and English Law are not adequately respected in the Scottish adaptation clauses in British Bills. They would like to see much more Scottish legislation. But the pressure on the Scottish committees would probably be too great for this.

Separate Scottish legislation affects the Scottish MPs in the House of Commons, and all government departments and local authorities in Scotland. Each must relate its activities to the existence of the separate legal system, and become part of the Scottish 'system'. Although a process of assimilation between the legal systems is taking place, enough differences remain to perpetuate this division at the political and administrative level.

The legal differences are more noticeable in private and property law than in public, commercial, and constitutional law. The existence of Scottish constitutional law, though asserted by Scots lawyers, does not seem to be much in evidence in practice, and the distinction between it and English constitutional law is not easy to draw.[8] The Church of Scotland, as the Established Church, is undoubtedly unique in its freedom from state control. Scottish courts have sometimes taken a stronger line in cases involving administrative discretion than have courts in England. But these differences have grown less important in recent years, and the powers of government departments and administrative tribunals are essentially the same in both countries.

Civil liberties (e.g. the freedom from arbitrary arrest, freedom of speech and assembly) are similar throughout Britain, even though in Scotland they derive from Scots Law. But Scottish 'permissive' legislation (relating to divorce, homosexuality, licensing and Sunday entertainments) has usually taken longer to be passed.

The relationship between the Scottish legal and political systems is perhaps the strongest single reason for the autonomy of the latter within the British state. Separate laws engender separate politics and administration. A whole host of vested interests is thereby established which cannot be easily assimilated with those in England. Thus while the laws of Scotland and England grow daily closer together in substance, the lawyers who operate them (including those in local authorities and others with a Scottish legal training employed by public bodies and business firms) remain as separated as before. So too, to a lesser extent, do the administrators and politicians, since they have to deal with the laws and the lawyers. To the administrators and politicians we now turn our attention.

3

The Secretary of State for Scotland and the Scottish Office

The Secretary of State for Scotland has been called 'Scotland's Prime Minister'. He is Scotland's representative in the Cabinet (although other Scots or Scottish MPs can be members – Sir Alec Douglas-Home (now Lord Home) was Prime Minister and Foreign Secretary while a Scottish MP). The Scottish Secretary's department is the Scottish Office, with its headquarters in St Andrew's House,* Edinburgh. There is also a small office in Whitehall at Dover House, which serves as a centre for liaison with Whitehall departments, and as a base for the conduct of parliamentary business.

The ministerial 'team' at the Scottish Office usually consists of the Secretary of State, a Minister of State, and three Under-Secretaries of State. The junior ministers are given 'subject briefs'. In 1982 these were: Minister of State (Agriculture and Fisheries; Highland and Islands affairs); Under-Secretaries (Health and Social Work; Industry and Education; Home Affairs and the Environment). If the Scottish Secretary is Scotland's Prime Minister, these men comprise his 'Cabinet'.

But is he really a Prime Minister in any meaningful sense? The title has been fondly used by Scottish Secretaries in the past, but no doubt with a heavy dose of wishful thinking. It might perhaps be an attempt to compensate for the rather minor status of the office in the Cabinet, where, for example, key committees sometimes do not include the Scottish Secretary. Seen from Downing Street, there is only *one* Prime Minister – the man or woman in No. 10.

Seen from Edinburgh, the view changes somewhat. With an official residence in Bute House, and a large establishment at St Andrew's House and elsewhere in Scotland, the Secretary of State personifies 'Scottish government'. It is partly a proconsular rôle: if he 'speaks for

---

*Since 1975, the headquarters of the Scottish Office has been in 'New St Andrew's House', also in Edinburgh. For the sake of brevity, 'St Andrew's House' in this book includes 'New St Andrew's House'.

Scotland' in London, he also 'speaks for London' in Scotland. He is not the chosen leader of the majority party in Scotland, but the Scottish spokesman of the majority party in Westminster. It sometimes happens that the two majorities do not coincide, so that Scotland is ruled by ministers whose party has a minority of the Scottish seats. In 1979, George Younger, a Conservative, became Scottish Secretary, although his party won only 22 of the 71 House of Commons seats in Scotland, and received only 31% of the votes. Such a situation could not arise if the Scottish Office were responsible to an elected Scottish Parliament, but it does occur under the existing system, where governments are formed from British majorities. It will also happen that a general election result can force England to accept a government for which it did not provide a majority, yet which had a majority in Scotland (for example, the Labour Governments elected in 1964 and February 1974). In these ways, the UK political system displays its primacy over the 'Scottish', 'English', and other systems within it.

This does not destroy the subsidiary systems, and they do not disappear through such quirks of fate. Just as Her Majesty's Opposition remains 'loyal' in defeat, and participates in the legislative process, so too the mechanisms of the territorial systems in the UK keep turning despite the possible incongruities of the representative situations in these areas. A Conservative Secretary of State for Scotland in a Labour Scotland must still 'speak for Scotland' in the Cabinet and in the House of Commons. His 'legitimacy' is accepted by the major parties, for they agree to operate on the basis of the unity of Parliament. A Conservative Secretary tries to shape Conservative policies for Scottish consumption, and thereby becomes an integral part of the Scottish political system, as the target of its pressures.

Not the sole target, however. 'Scotland's Prime Minister' has not enough *power* to justify that. If he really did govern Scotland, the position would be clear, and all demands could be channelled to St Andrew's House. But Scotland is subject to the British Cabinet, of which the Scottish Secretary is just a member. 'Collective responsibility' is the cardinal principle on which 'British Cabinet Government' is based, and so policies for Scotland (whether exclusive to it or not) are all in theory devised by the Cabinet. Scots are well aware that ultimate executive power resides there.

Yet the Cabinet has little time for Scotland as such. Scottish Secretaries may not object to this situation, for it means that they can avoid a lot of awkward questioning from their colleagues about Scottish administration. If policies for Scotland are to be different from elsewhere this may require some justification, especially if more money than in other places is to be spent there for the same services. To a Scottish Secretary these arguments are usually better kept at a lower level, in interdepartmental committees of civil servants, or in direct dealings with other ministers. So much of Scottish policy-making lies hidden from view, even from the Cabinet.

Why does the Scottish Office exist at all, and what does it do? In the organisation of British central administration, government departments usually operate on a functional, rather than a territorial basis, a principle generally accepted in Britain from the Haldane Report on the machinery of government (1918, Cd 9230) to the White Paper on *The Reorganisation of Central Government* (October 1970, Cmnd 4506). Thus education, trade and industry, agriculture, and so on, are administered by separate departments. The exceptions to this are the Scottish and Welsh Offices (Northern Ireland, of course, has its own departments but their position is different, since they were, and may be again, responsible to a separate Parliament at Stormont). While the Welsh Office under a Secretary of State for Wales is a comparative newcomer (1964), the Scottish Office dates from 1885.

Yet long before these departments were created, there were in Scotland and Wales administrative bodies whose jurisdiction was both functional and territorial. In the case of Scotland (to which we restrict our attention), such bodies or officials were found immediately after the Union of 1707 in the shape of the Secretary of State for Scotland and the Lord Advocate. The former minister was entrusted generally with the government of Scotland, while the latter was (and is) the chief government law officer in Scotland. In 1746 the Scottish Secretaryship was abolished, and the Lord Advocate assumed the responsibility for government business in Scotland. Thus the key position of Scots Law in preserving Scotland's identity in the government was emphasised.

During the nineteenth century, the functions of government increased, especially at the local level. Poor law relief, public health, road-building, and education became the responsibilities of bodies which were specialised local government authorities. At the same time, the main local authorities (i.e. certain Burghs, and, after 1889, the Counties) became active in various forms of 'improvement' such as water supply, drainage, hospitals, and town planning. Of course, much of this was inspired by central government policy, though local authorities themselves sought to increase their powers by Private Bills (one of the most famous being Glasgow's Act to bring water from Loch Katrine in 1859). The seat of administration was essentially local in Victorian times, and central government control was intermittent and seemed a long way off.

Yet some control was needed. Governments could not wash their hands entirely of local government, for clearly certain standards had to be maintained, since grants were being expended. There thus arose supervisory boards, such as the Board of Supervision for Poor Relief (1845–94) and the Scotch Education Department (from 1872). Their job was to superintend the activities of the parochial boards and school boards respectively. What is interesting about this development, from the point of view of the origins of the Scottish Office, is that where 'intermediate' authorities were established in Scotland, between local and central government, they took a Scottish form. Thus by 1885 there were several Scottish administrative bodies, whose main task was the superintendence of local government functions, and who were finally (though vaguely) the responsibility of the Home Secretary. This minister had, since 1828, been formally put 'in charge of Scotland', but since he usually knew very little about Scottish affairs, the Lord Advocate was still regarded as the voice of Scotland in the government, and took the lead in Scottish debates. The legal system of Scotland ensured his survival, while the Scottish local government structure led to the creation of the Scottish boards.[1] In this way, both legacies from the Act of Union paved the way for the Scottish Office.

These were practical considerations. Scotland could not be governed efficiently from London as long as Scots Law and 'the Burghs' survived. And London did not really mind their survival (though in the case of the law something of a war of attrition took place through House of Lords decisions and the development of 'British' law). But the system of boards had its faults: it was difficult to see who was responsible for them, in the absence of a Cabinet minister who knew Scotland, and they were staffed by amateurs, not professional civil servants. They increased government patronage, something which Scotland knew well and perhaps loved, but which offended against the liberal and democratic tendencies of the later Victorian age.

Scottish MPs were particularly restless, and in 1869 they sent a memorial to Gladstone requesting the appointment of a Scottish Secretary with responsibility for the boards. They disliked the power assumed by a lawyer, the Lord Advocate, over the general affairs of Scotland and felt that Scottish Bills were being neglected for lack of a proper government sponsor. This was particularly clear in the case of educational reform, which would have come much earlier than in 1872, if the Scottish MPs had had their way.

Such considerations (still of a practical nature) linked up with, or stimulated, the growth of Scottish nationalism. Partly inspired by the example of the Irish Home Rulers of the time, but also 'native' in origin, nationalism found support among many Scottish MPs, members of the Scottish aristocracy (Rosebery, Argyll and Fife), the Convention of Royal Burghs, and a large section of Scottish public opinion. By 1884, Gladstone found the combination of arguments in favour of setting up the Scottish Office, with a Scottish Secretary, irresistible, and a Bill was introduced in 1884 to this effect.

From its rather modest beginnings (ironically, it was the Conservatives who actually provided the first Scottish Secretary in 1885), the Scottish Office has grown continuously in size and scope, until today it covers the functions of several Whitehall departments. This outcome was by no means obvious at the start, and the Home Office jealously guarded its rights to interfere in Scotland. The Lord Advocate, too, was on the defensive, and resented any implication that he was subject to the Scottish Secretary (Hanham 2). In fact, the transfer of functions to the Scottish Office was at the expense of these ministers as well as the Privy Council, the Treasury, and the Local Government Board for England. Principal functions transferred were poor law, public health, Fishery Board, General Register House, police, prisons, roads and bridges, parliamentary divisions (from the Home Office); Board of Manufactures (from the Treasury); Public Works Local Commissioners (from the Local Government Board for England).

The Scottish boards came under the Secretary's authority, but somewhat indirectly, since they still retained their statutory duties. Scottish education, for example, was still administered by the Scotch Education Department, a committee of the Privy Council, although the Scottish Secretary was now made the minister answerable to Parliament on the subject. The problem of the executive functions of the Scottish Office was not finally settled until 1939, when the remaining boards were absorbed within the Scottish Office, and the Scottish Secretary made directly responsible for them. The Secretary for Scotland was not a member of the Cabinet between 1885 and 1892, but after 1892 his place there became assured. In 1926, he was dignified with the title of Secretary of State, although his salary remained £3,000 lower than other Secretaries of State. In 1937, the

Table 5. *Chronology of the Scottish Office*

1746	Office of Secretary of State for Scotland lapses; Lord Advocate thereafter chief Scottish minister.
1828	Home Secretary made formally responsible for Scottish affairs, but Lord Advocate in practice responsible.
1845	Board of Supervision for Poor Relief established (to 1894); thereafter Local Government Board for Scotland (to 1919).
1849	Fishery Board (established 1808) restricts operation to Scotland.
1857	General Board of Commissioners in Lunacy (to 1913); thereafter, General Board of Control (to 1962).
1872	Scotch Education Department (committee of Privy Council); 1918 renamed Scottish Education Department.
1877	Prisons Commission (to 1928).
1885	SCOTTISH OFFICE established taking most Home Office functions, and education. Scottish Secretary responsible to Parliament for Scottish boards.
1886	Crofters Commission (to 1911, and from 1955).
1892	Secretary for Scotland in the Cabinet.
1897	Congested Districts Board (to 1911). Responsible for Highland resettlement.
1911	Scottish Insurance Commissioners (to 1919). National Insurance.
1912	Scottish Board of Agriculture (to 1928).
1913	Highlands and Islands Medical Services Board (to 1919).
1919	Scottish Board of Health (to 1928), absorbs Insurance Commissioners, Highland Medical Board, and Local Government Board for Scotland. Parliamentary Under-Secretary for Health for Scotland created.
1926	Elevation of Secretary for Scotland to rank of a Principal Secretary of State. Parliamentary Under-Secretary for Health for Scotland becomes Parliamentary Under-Secretary of State for Scotland.
1928	Creation of Departments of Agriculture for Scotland, Health for Scotland and Prisons Department, replacing boards (1912, 1919 above) and Commission (1877, above).
1937	Gilmour Committee Report on Scottish Administration (Cmd 5563) recommends Edinburgh-based Scottish Office, and tighter control of Scottish administration by Scottish Secretary.
1939	Opening of St Andrew's House, Edinburgh, and vesting of powers of Scottish Office (now four departments of Agriculture, Education, Health and Home) directly in Secretary of State.
1939–84	Piecemeal transfer of functions to and from the Scottish Office, and successive Scottish Office departmental reorganisations. Main additions: electricity, roads, some transport; increased activity in economic planning, agriculture, health, social work, Highland development, aspects of oil and industrial development, manpower services. Main loss: social security (National Insurance). Present departments: Agriculture and Fisheries, Development, Home and Health, Education, Industry; Central Services Divisions. Two additional Under-Secretaries of State (1940, 1951);

Table 5.   *(contd)*

Minister of State (1951); Second Minister of State replaced one of the Under-Secretaries (1969–70), returned with three Under-Secretaries (1974–9). One Minister of State and three Under-Secretaries (1979–   ).

Ministers of the Crown Act gave all Cabinet ministers £5,000 a year and in 1982 their ministerial salary was £28,000 (the Permanent Under-Secretary, a civil servant, received £33,000).

This is not the place for a detailed history of the development of the Scottish Office (for this, see especially Hanham 2; and in Wolfe, pp. 51–70; and Milne), since we are more concerned with the situation which exists today, and which may exist in the future. But the general features of that history are of great importance in understanding Scottish politics. Table 5 shows the chronology of the Scottish Office.

There is first of all the question of the development of the range of functions exercised by the Scottish Office. It is normally assumed that such functions are determined by the degree to which Scotland differs from the rest of the country. For example, where Scots Law, local government, or education are involved, it is appropriate to place these under the Scottish•Office. But where there is no distinctly Scottish characteristic about a government function, it should be performed by a Great Britain (or United Kingdom, if Northern Ireland is also covered) department. This approach is sensible and convincing until one reflects that perhaps all administration in Scotland has to deal with 'distinctly Scottish characteristics', since these arise out of the separateness of Scottish society itself. In the words of a former Permanent Under-Secretary of State at the Scottish Office, Sir Douglas Haddow, in answer to Lord Crowther, then chairman of the Commission on the Constitution, 'This is of course the basic case for Scottish administration, that our decisions in Scotland are taken in full knowledge of all the surrounding Scottish circumstances – history, tradition, law, everything.' (Kilbrandon 4, p. 12.)

If this is so, then perhaps all government functions in Scotland should come under the Scottish Office. Yet one could argue that such knowledge is not the prerogative of the Scottish Office, and that British departments operating in Scotland are able to adapt their administration, where necessary, to Scottish needs, without incurring the

Table 6. *The principal functions of central government in Scotland, 1982*

British Departments	Scottish Departments

Treasury
  Taxation, interest rates
  Departmental appropriations
  Linked body: Department for National Savings
Board of Inland Revenue
Board of Customs and Excise
  Collection of import duties, excise duties, and VAT
Department of Trade*
  Regulation of imports and exports
  Regulation of companies and insurance
  Marine inspection and accidents
  Consumer Affairs
  Linked bodies: Civil Aviation Authority (Highland airports), British Airports Authority (Scottish airports). British Airways Board (Scottish Airways), Northern Lighthouse Board
Department of Industry*
  Promotion of industry (from July 1975 selective regional assistance was transferred to the Scottish Office)
  Relations with shipbuilding, engineering, vehicles, steel and aerospace industries
  Posts and Telecommunications (including technological aspects of BBC and IBA. The non-technological side comes under the Home Office with Scottish Office participation)
  Linked bodies: British Technology Group (National Enterprise Board), British Steel Corporation, Post Office, British Telecom Scotland, British Shipbuilders
	Scottish Office
	  Department of Agriculture and Fisheries for Scotland
	  Land settlement, estate management, regulation of crofting
	  Agricultural education, advisory service and research (three colleges)
	  Administration of UK and EEC price support and fisheries policies
	  Royal Botanic Garden, Edinburgh
	  Linked bodies: Crofters Commission, Red Deer Commission, Sea Fish Industry Authority, Intervention Board for Agricultural Produce
	Scottish Development Department
	  Local government
	  Town and country planning, urban renewal
	  Housing and building control
	  Roads and transport
	  North Sea oil infrastructure
	  Ancient monuments and historic buildings
	  Linked bodies: Scottish Special Housing Association. Countryside Commission for Scotland, Historic Buildings Council for Scotland, Scottish Transport Group
	Scottish Economic Planning Department**
	  Industrial and economic development (Regional Development Division, Economics and Statistics Unit)
	  North Sea Oil (North Sea Oil Support Group)
	  Selective regional assistance to industry and factory building

Department of Energy
Energy production
Linked bodies: Offshore Supplies Office for Scotland, British National Oil Corporation (Glasgow), British Gas Corporation (Scottish Gas), National Coal Board (Scottish Area), Atomic Energy Authority (Chapelcross, Dounreay).

Department of Employment
Industrial relations, industrial training and employment offices

Department of Transport
Transport (rail and Stranraer–Larne shipping)
Ports, docks, waterways, freight
Linked bodies: British Rail, National Freight Company, etc.

Department of the Environment
Public Buildings and Works
Linked body: Property Services Agency

Department of Health and Social Security
National insurance, child benefits and other cash benefits

Department of Education and Science
Universities and higher research
Linked bodies: University Grants Committee and Research Councils (Agricultural, Medical, Natural Environment, Social Science, Science and Engineering)

Ministry of Defence
Linked bodies: Service establishments and Meteorological Office

Ministry of Agriculture, Fisheries and Food
Animal health
Emergency food supply and sponsorship of food-processing industries

Manpower Services
New Towns
Electricity (two boards)
Highland and rural development
Tourism
Linked bodies: Scottish Development Agency, Highland and Islands Development Board, New Town Development Corporations, Scottish Tourist Board, North of Scotland Hydro-Electric Board, South of Scotland Electricity Board, Manpower Services Commission

Scottish Education Department
Control and development of schools and colleges (not universities). Includes research: teacher training, student grants
Public libraries
Youth and Community Services
Recreation and the Arts
Social Work Services Group (child care, probation, welfare and mental health)
Linked bodies: Royal Fine Art Commission for Scotland, Royal Scottish Museum, National Galleries of Scotland, National Library of Scotland, National Museum of Antiquities of Scotland, Scottish Sports Council, etc.

Scottish Home and Health Department
Law and order (police, fire, civil defence, civil and criminal law, prisons, Royal Prerogative of Mercy)
Representation of the people
Regulation of liquor licensing, betting, entertainment
National Health Service ('Scottish Health Service') (including school health, health education and public health)

Table 6. (contd)

British Departments	Scottish Departments

Home Office
  Aliens, immigration
  Explosives
  Vivisection, cruelty to animals
Foreign and Commonwealth Office
  Passports
  Attraction of foreign investment
Cabinet Office
  Relations with European Community
  Devolution
	Linked bodies: health boards, Common Services Agency and Scottish Health Service Planning Council
	Other linked bodies: Scottish Record Office (Keeper of the Records of Scotland), Department of Registers for Scotland, General Register Office (Registrar General for Scotland), Lord Lyon, Mental Welfare Commission, Lands Tribunal, Scottish Law Commission
	Central Services
	Establishment
	Solicitor
	Finance (including Rate Support Grant)
	Scottish Information Office
	Computer and statistical services
	Liaison Unit, London
	Scottish Courts Administration (partly responsible to Lord Advocate)
	Lord Advocate's Department
	Chief Scottish Law Officer of the Crown (public prosecutions, legal appointments, drafting of Bills, courts)
	  Linked body: Scottish Law Commission
	Crown Office (criminal prosecutions)
	Crown Estate Commissioners
	Forestry Commission (HQ in Edinburgh; under Scottish Secretary in Scotland)
	Scottish Economic Council (before 1970 called the Scottish Economic Planning Council)
	Scottish Industrial Development Advisory Board

*These departments were merged as the Department of Trade and Industry in 1983.
**This department was renamed the Industry Department for Scotland in November 1983.

expense and complication involved in setting up a separate department. In fact, Scottish administration is based on both these approaches, and the result is a compromise between London-based and Edinburgh-based government, whose relative merits are extremely difficult to establish.

How does the existing division of powers implement the case for Scottish administration? (See Table 6.) The largest category of Scottish Office functions derives from the need for the central government to supervise the activities of local authorities, and half of the Scottish Office budget is spent by these authorities. Over the past hundred years, local government has come more closely under the wing of the central government, and some local functions have been transferred entirely to the centre. But while for the most of Britain 'the centre' means London, in this respect it usually means Edinburgh. Thus the strengthening of the centre at the expense of local government in Scotland strengthened the 'middle tier' (the Scottish Office), not Whitehall. The middle tier is part of central government, but it is much more closely related to, and in touch with, local government than the London-based departments. In this way, the accession of power at the centre in Scotland has not affected local government so severely, since the distance between local and central government and the scale of the supervisory department is not as great as in England.

The Scottish Office functions which derive from local government include education, health, housing, road construction and social work. Apart from roads, these are essentially supervisory of local or health authorities, and the supervision is close and decisive. A function directly transferred to the Scottish Office from local government is health, while others have come to the Scottish Office from local government after having been exercised for a time by British departments (roads, transport other than rail, and electricity in the south of Scotland).

In the field of social security, unemployment benefits moved from local government to a British authority (the Unemployment Assistance Board) in 1934, and health and pensions insurance was transferred from the Scottish Office to the Ministry of National Insurance in 1945. The remainder of public assistance was transferred from local authorities to the National Assistance Board in 1948, which was an enlarged version of the Unemployment Assistance Board. When the National Health Service was set up in 1948 this was given to the Scottish Office, so that the administration of the welfare state was completely split between Scottish and British departments. This did, however, mean a net gain in activity to the Scottish Office, for its health functions expanded greatly.

The pre-1885 Scottish functions such as law, education, and registration remained part of Scottish administration, and the Scottish Secretary is still in varying degrees responsible for them. He shares responsibility for the legal system of Scotland with the Lord Advocate, and with the Registrar General for Scotland (a civil servant on the establishment of the Scottish Office) for the organisation of the Census of Scotland and other demographic statistics. Scottish schools, further education, education, art, and technical colleges are the responsibility of local authorities, or of governing bodies and the Scottish Education Department, but Scottish universities deal through the University Grants Committee and research councils with the Department of Education and Science. There are thus two education ministers for Scotland.

These functions are inherited from the legacy of the past independence of Scotland; many of them (law, education, local government) were mentioned specifically in the Union settlement of 1707. But there has been a vast increase in the functions of the Scottish Office, in directions not contemplated in the Union. They result from the increasing government intervention throughout Britain in economic and social affairs. Governments do far more today to regulate the economy and to provide social security than they did when the Scottish Office was set up in 1885, and it has been decided that some of this activity should be organised separately in Scotland. In agriculture, the Crofters Act of 1886 established a separate administrative structure for the seven 'crofting counties' (Orkney, Shetland, Caithness, Sutherland, Ross and Cromarty, Inverness and Argyll), and this is preserved today, with the addition since 1965 of the Highlands and Islands Development Board. The Board's function is 'to prepare, concert, promote, assist and undertake measures for the economic and social development of the Highlands and Islands' (SCSA 3, p. 2). The rest of Scottish agriculture is also partly governed by special legislation. The Scottish Board of Agriculture was formed in 1912, and its descendant is the Department of Agriculture and Fisheries for Scotland (established 1960). The agricultural policies during and after the Second World War unified British agriculture to some extent. There was no separate Scottish farm price review before entry to the European Community, and none since. Products receive the same level of support in Scotland as elsewhere in the Community. Yet the tradition that Scottish agriculture has its own problems persists, and agriculture and fisheries are important functions of the Scottish Office.

The non-agricultural sector of the Scottish economy must also concern the Scottish Secretary, although here he is more conscious of the interests and powers of his colleagues in the Cabinet. He has probably not shared proportionately in the great increase in the economic decision-making power exercised by the Treasury and the other large economic departments in London. Yet he must try to shape the Scottish economy as best he can. What he cannot do by persuasion of other ministers he attempts to do himself: he has functions of road-building, transport, electricity and housing – the 'infrastructure' of economic development – and he can try to attract industry to Scotland by promotion campaigns, investment, grants, and loans. In the 1960s, the Scottish Office pioneered the concept of regional economic planning, producing its own plans and administrative machinery to implement them (see pp. 218–25). More and more economic functions came its way, but the main powers (over taxation, fiscal policy, and distribution of industry) did not. Regional economic planning meant planning *for* the regions by the centre, not by the regions themselves, and so the dominance of the UK political and economic systems was maintained. Opinion was divided anyway as to whether you could plan the Scottish economy from Scotland itself, and it was generally accepted that only certain economic functions were proper to Scottish administration. The practical result of this is that coordination with other departments is a problem, for the Scottish Office has only limited authority over the execution of its economic plans. Since 1973, the division of responsibility on North Sea oil development between the Scottish Office and the Department of Energy has become a sensitive and confusing part of Scottish administration. In 1975, the establishment of the Scottish Development Agency in the Scottish Office to promote industrial development did nothing to solve the question of who was responsible for the Scottish economy, though it was a significant increase in the executive functions of St Andrew's House. Selective regional assistance now came under the Scottish Office, which represented about one quarter of all regional assistance in Scotland. So too did some public participation in industry, though the major policy decisions on regional policy and nationalisation remained with Whitehall, and the

National Enterprise Board (1975) was to operate throughout the United Kingdom. Once more, this seemed a recipe for confusion and overlapping jurisdictions.

Along with the increase in functions, the Scottish Office has greatly increased its complement of civil servants. The centre of gravity in the Scottish Office shifted to Edinburgh after the Report on Scottish Administration of the Gilmour Committee in 1937 (Cmd 5563). This recommended bringing together the Scottish Office staff under one roof in Edinburgh, and vesting all Scottish functions directly in the Secretary of State for Scotland. This was done in 1939, when St Andrew's House opened its doors, and under the Reorganisation of Offices (Scotland) Act 1939, the functions of the four administrative departments of the Scottish Office (Home, Health, Education, and Agriculture) came under the Scottish Secretary. Today, the five departments are Home and Health, Development, Education, Agriculture and Fisheries, and Industry. There is also a group of Central Services divisions (see Table 6).

The degree of decentralisation to Scotland, however great it might appear to be, has little effect on the consciousness of mass public opinion in Scotland. Scots know very little of it, and what they know they probably regard as a subsidiary part of British government having few independent powers of its own. Scottish Secretaries are not thought of as powerful politicians, though they might be seen to be hard-working administrators. The major British politicians are just as well known in Scotland, if not more so, than the Secretary of State, as a result of the focussing of the news media (especially television) on them.

Of course, this kind of generalisation does not bite very deep. Any Scot who has an interest in politics, especially if he is active in local government, trade unionism or in other interest groups, soon makes himself aware of what St Andrew's House can, or cannot, do. But there are areas of confusion. The division of functions between Edinburgh and London is often unclear, and 'Scotland's Minister', though charged with the oversight of all Scottish affairs, and not merely those functions vested directly in him, can be a poor substitute for the appropriate London minister when action is required. British Rail, British Shipbuilders, the British Steel Corporation, and the National Coal Board are perhaps more vital to Scotland's economy than any responsibility of the Scottish Office, and pressure from Scotland must be exerted in London if the appropriate ministers are to be directly reached.

40

To the Scottish Secretary this can represent the greatest frustration of the job. Tiring as the administration of multifarious functions may be to a minister, it is much worse to bear the brunt of criticism for actions taken by other ministers with which he may not agree. Unemployment, emigration, and industrial closures dominate the Scottish economy, but there is very little that the Scottish Secretary can do within his own department to check them. He can use his influence with other departments, notably the Treasury, but he must compete with other ministers for a favourable decision. Even in areas of administration less dependent on purely financial considerations, such as law, education and the structure of local government, the need to conform with a pattern established by the corresponding ministries in England is strongly felt. Scotland cannot diverge too far from the norms of the rest of the country if the general desire for equality before the law, social justice, and mobility of labour is to be satisfied.

What sort of man becomes Scottish Secretary, and how does he promote the interests of his department? Since 1885, when the office was created anew, there have been 35 Secretaries or Secretaries of State for Scotland. The office is virtually the prerogative of a Scot, although an Englishman, Sir George Trevelyan, held it in 1886, and from 1892 to 1895. Another was Ernest Brown (1940–1). In the early years, it was common to appoint a peer to the job, and on the whole Scottish Secretaries have not been noted 'House of Commons men'. This has probably diminished their prestige within their parties, and it results partly from the practical difficulty of making a mark in the Commons in Scottish debates, which are of little interest to English MPs. In addition, Scottish committee work and the need to spend a fair amount of time in Edinburgh during parliamentary sessions reduces the number of opportunities for effective parliamentary performance. These considerations work against the prestige of the Scottish Secretary, and make it difficult for him to establish popularity on a wide front.

Labour Scottish Secretaries have mostly not been prominent in the Party, though some of them proved effective ministers. It may be surmised that the job was treated by them as a sort of fiefdom, rather than as a stepping-stone to other (higher?) things. At any rate, none of them did move on to other departments, and for Labour ministers especially it has been something of a dead end. William Ross stayed in the Cabinet from 1964 to 1970, and from 1974 to 1976. His successor, Bruce Millan, was in office from 1976 to 1979.

Scottish Office duties are of course considerable, and an extended stay in the office may be almost essential if a Scottish Secretary is to become more than the tool of his civil servants. At the same time, such prolonged tenures do not make for flexible and dynamic policies, and the practice has tended to stultify Scottish administration.[2]

Conservative Scottish Secretaries have been rather more mobile. A. J. Balfour (1886–7) became Prime Minister (1902–5). Sir John Gilmour (1924–9) became Minister of Agriculture and Fisheries (1931–2), Home Secretary (1932–5) and Minister for Shipping (1939–40). Walter Elliot (1936–8) was Minister of Agriculture and Fisheries (1932–6) and Minister of Health (1938–1940). John S. Maclay (Viscount Muirshiel) (1957–62) was Minister of Transport and Civil Aviation (1951–2) and Minister of State in the Colonial Office (1956–7) before coming to the Scottish Office. Michael Noble (1962–4) became President of the Board of Trade in 1970, which office became Minister for Trade soon afterwards.

Junior Ministers (Labour as well as Conservative) in the Scottish Office differ from the position of the Secretary of State in that many do move to or from other departments.

It is probably true to say that the Conservative Scottish Secretaries have carried as much weight within the Cabinet as the Labour ones, despite the fact that Conservative MPs are relatively few on the ground in Scotland (at least since 1959). This may be because there are 'hidden Scots' in many Tory Cabinets: men like Iain Macleod, who always signed his nationality 'Scottish' in hotel registers. Harold Macmillan (Prime Minister, 1957–63) was also proud of his Scottish ancestry, as of course is Lord Home. Winston Churchill, though no Scot, gave his support to Scottish Secretaries such as Thomas Johnston (1941–5) and James Stuart (later Viscount Findhorn) (1951–7). With such allies, Scottish Secretaries in Conservative or Coalition Cabinets have carried disproportionate weight, and there has also been the political desire to 'do something for Scotland' in order to make up electoral lost ground there.

Labour Secretaries have faced a rather different situation. Their party's solid support in Scotland in recent years has sometimes led to complacency or intransigence, especially on the nationalist question. The advent of a Labour government usually heralds a revival of nationalism in Scotland (as in the late 1940s and mid-1960s), and Labour Cabinets until 1974 were notably unsympathetic to its demands. Clement Attlee did not understand the force of Scottish national sentiment, nor did many of his colleagues such as Aneurin

Bevan and Herbert Morrison. Their mission was to secure a uniform system of social justice for Britain, not to break that system into different parts.

For most of the period of his office as Scottish Secretary, William Ross stood opposed to the then-current wave of nationalism, and resisted any further decentralisation to the Scottish Office. Yet he resolutely campaigned for economic discrimination in Scotland's favour, and strengthened the machinery of the Scottish Office in economic planning. Other Labour ministers, such as Richard Crossman, and quite a few Labour activists in Scotland, Wales, and even England, were more sympathetic towards devolution than Ross, who at that same time saw the Scottish National Party as his chief antagonist and a serious threat to the position of the Labour Party in Scotland. Ross prevailed on his Scottish henchmen and the Prime Minister, Harold Wilson not to budge one inch in opposing nationalism, but at the same time to dampen its fires by remedial economic action. While he apparently succeeded here, if one can judge by the result of the 1970 election, the recurrence of nationalism was inevitable, since many of the problems it uncovered remain unsolved. Thus it was that after the second SNP upsurge in 1974, Ross and the Scottish Labour Executive were forced to concede that a Scottish Assembly should be established.

When one examines the educational background of Scottish Office ministers, one finds an almost complete contrast between the Labour and Conservative office-holders. Of the 15 Labour ministers between 1945 and 1982, 13 attended a Scottish day school, 6 a Scottish university, 2 English day schools, and 1 an English university. Of the 21 Conservative ministers, 13 attended English public schools, 10 English universities, and only 3 attended Scottish day schools and 3 Scottish universities. Four attended Scottish public schools, and one (Lady Tweedsmuir) was educated abroad. The comparison should not only be between the parties, however. The Scottish Office ministers in Labour governments are distinctly more state-educated than Labour ministers in other departments, especially since 1964. The dominance of Oxford and Cambridge in the Labour leadership since the 1950s reflected the central position of these institutions in the higher education system of England and Wales, but their pull has always been much less in Scotland. The state school system is also more pervasive there. Thus the Scottish Labour leaders do not share the educational background of their colleagues in the south.

The Conservative leadership, on the other hand, is far more

homogeneous, since the Scottish upper class often prefers an English or Anglicised upper-class education. The Scottish Office under the Conservatives is usually run by Anglicised Scots, who are of course untypical of the mass of Conservatives in Scotland. It often happens that a Scottish Secretary has been educated entirely in England, yet finds himself in charge of the Scottish educational system. Labour Scottish Secretaries, by contrast, have invariably been educated at Scottish day schools and universities.

These facts have several implications for the power of the Scottish ministers. In the case of the Labour Party, their Scottish MPs and ministers display such a distinctively Scottish character that they are in danger of being isolated from the rest of the party in the Commons and in the Government. They are seen at Westminster as Scottish specialists, and their ministerial immobility reflects this. The Scottish Conservatives are socially integrated with the rest of the party, and quite mobile as ministers. Within the Cabinet, the Labour Secretary commands respect for the solid Labour constituency he represents. The Conservative Secretary makes up for his lack of grass-roots support by the very good social contacts which he usually has with the Prime Minister and other leaders of his Party.

In Scotland, the party distinction has a slightly different effect. Labour Secretaries know their Scotland very well, but like the Scottish 'dominie' (schoolmaster), they want their pupils to keep their distance. They tend to think that they 'know what is best for Scotland' and to resent criticism. Conservative Secretaries are less sure of their ground, and find social communication more of a problem. But their contacts with business are good, and they soon learn the economic and political facts of Scottish life. They are flexible, and although Anglicised, show a surprising pride in many things Scottish. Much of the increase in the powers of the Scottish Office has come under Conservative governments. Examples are the additional functions of electricity (1954), roads (1956) and economic planning (1962), and the appointment of a Minister of State in 1951. The move to St Andrew's House in 1939 was accomplished under a Conservative Secretary of State for Scotland, D. J. Colville.

Just how the Secretary of State for Scotland goes about his task of 'getting the goods for Scotland' must remain something of a mystery, in view of the secrecy of Cabinet proceedings and administration generally in Britain. Occasionally the publication of memoirs throws some light on the situation, as does the evidence given to official bodies such as the Select Committee on Scottish Affairs and the

Commission on the Constitution. But one of the hallmarks of the present system of Scottish (or indeed British) government is that the public rarely gets to know all the factors which determine the decisions which are taken. It cannot tell what the Scottish Secretary has done within the privacy of the Cabinet, nor how Scottish Office civil servants have argued the Scottish case in Whitehall. The official consensus is that this system pays Scotland, since it prevents wider political pressures (presumably from England) raising objections to a favoured treatment for Scotland. A contrary view stresses that an open system of negotiation, in which a Scottish government bargained with a British government in London for resources, would produce much better results for Scotland.[3] It would certainly allow for a greater range of variation in policy-making between Scotland and England, since the necessity for Cabinet approval for purely Scottish matters would disappear.

How much does Cabinet approval for these matters bear on the situation under the present system? Here it is necessary to return to the old question, what is Scottish and what is British? The Cabinet spends very little time on purely Scottish affairs, but this does not mean that what it does decide will not affect Scotland equally with the rest of the country. A decision to raise taxes for example, or to extend the range of social services, will apply to the whole of the United Kingdom. In education, the raising of the school-leaving age, or a policy of comprehensive schools, will apply to the separate educational systems of England, Wales, and Scotland. Proposals to reform industrial relations, to negotiate for entry into the EEC, or to change the structure of the National Health Service (to mention some of the most important policy decisions of recent years) affect the whole country. Even such peculiarly Scottish arrangements as the structure of local government and Highland crofting depend on decisions taken on local government and agriculture generally in Britain.

All this means that the Scottish Secretary must play a full part in Cabinet discussions, and indeed be more widely briefed than the majority of his colleagues, whose departmental responsibilities are narrower. Decisions taken by English ministers may have immediate repercussions in Scotland – usually because Scots demand parity with England. Examples of this can be found in the level of wage increases for teachers (negotiated separately for Scottish and English teachers, but made 'comparable' by demand), the amount of road-building and the level of subsidy to public transport.

To be thus watchful in the Cabinet imposes a tremendous strain on a Scottish Secretary, and there is a danger that he will be known there entirely for his interjections 'But remember, Scotland is different' or 'Of course Scotland will need as much, or rather more' to everyone else's proposal. A sort of 'log-rolling' can develop in which the Scottish Secretary backs up the Minister for Agriculture or Education or Transport in the knowledge that increased expenditure for these departments will not penalise but help him in securing more for Scotland. He thus has many potential allies in the Cabinet, who will not resent Scotland getting perhaps more than its share of housing subsidies, schools and roads in return for support for their policies.

Not all such decisions will be taken at meetings of the full Cabinet. Many important policy decisions are taken by Cabinet committees and merely ratified by the Cabinet. Membership on such committees is a test of whether a minister rates highly in the Cabinet as a key decision-maker, and here some Scottish Secretaries have had a low score. William Ross (1964–70; 1974–6) was not a permanent member of the Economic Policy Committee[4] or of the 'Inner Cabinet',[5] despite its importance for Scotland, and most Scottish Secretaries are absent from the Foreign Policy Committee. Their attendance there may be thought to be unnecessary, since Scotland is not specifically involved, yet such subjects as fiscal policy and foreign trade (including policy towards the EEC) affect Scotland intimately, and the Scottish viewpoint may be lost in the Secretary's absence. The Minister of State, or an official of the department, may be present however. In the Conservative Government formed in 1970, the representation of the Scottish Office in Cabinet committees dealing with economic matters passed from the Minister of State to the Parliamentary Under-Secretary of State for Development. This meant that the Scottish Office was represented by a more junior minister than other departments.[6]

Michael Noble (1962–4) was able to sit on whichever Cabinet committee he chose, but he could not be on everything, and in practice some decisions of significance to Scotland were almost settled in committee without his knowledge. In these cases, objections could be raised in the Cabinet itself, as was done over the siting of the Post Office Savings Bank, which Noble got transferred at the last minute from Newcastle to Glasgow.

Occasionally a dispute takes place in the Cabinet between the Scottish Secretary and other ministers, the tenor of which is reported (rightly or wrongly) in the press. Such was the alleged struggle between William Ross and Barbara Castle over the Transport Bill of 1967. Ross was anxious to increase the power of the Scottish Office over transport by establishing a Scottish Transport Group covering passenger road transport and ships. This was resisted by the Ministry of Transport and the Transport Holding Company. He also battled against the clauses in the Bill which penalised long-distance private hauliers, since the alternative of rail haulage was not available in large areas of Scotland. He won his Transport Group, but achieved only minor concessions on the road haulage levy (see *Glasgow Herald*, 21 December 1967). Later, concessions were made in regulations under the Act.

Most cases involving the Scottish Secretary in a Cabinet fight have concerned government decisions on industrial matters. The siting of the steel strip-mill at Ravenscraig (Lanarkshire) in 1958 was a classic case of this kind. It was only after vigorous argument in the Cabinet and elsewhere that the unlikely decision was taken to divide the strip-mill between Scotland and Wales. Its threatened closure in 1982 revived the dispute. Other examples of such bargaining are found in the discussions relating to the siting of the Dounreay fast breeder reactor (1966), the Invergordon aluminium smelter (1968, 1982), aid to Upper Clyde Shipbuilders (1968–69), and its successor Govan Shipbuilders (1971). In these disputes, the whole weight of the 'Scottish lobby' comes behind the Scottish Secretary in his efforts, and he must hope to win the support of the Prime Minister and the Chancellor of the Exchequer if he is to succeed. Although the Scottish Office is not the department primarily responsible for such decisions, its interests are so involved that it must take an active part in influencing them. So too, since 1964, must the Welsh Office, leaving the British department the duty of 'remembering England', which it no doubt does as a matter of course.

The spread of functions in the Scottish Office means that the Scottish Secretary is less specialised than many of his Cabinet colleagues. To them, subjects like education or agriculture or industry are the main interest, and they use most of their energies in promoting their department's point of view. There is a danger that a Scottish Secretary will neglect an area within his responsibilities that he is not personally attracted to, or knowledgeable of. Conservative Secretaries, for reasons already mentioned, seem unlikely to be greatly concerned with the details of the Scottish educational system. And few Secretaries are grounded in Scots Law, although part of their responsibility lies in this field (the same can be said of Home Secretaries and English Law). Some delegation of responsibility to the junior ministers in the Scottish Office is essential and the four junior ministers specialise in different areas of administration. They are usually put in charge of legislation in these areas during the committee stage, and they develop close relations with the appropriate departments of the Scottish Office.

The junior ministers do not detract in any way from the constitutional responsibility of the Secretary for all the affairs of the Scottish Office, and he is answerable for them to the House of Commons at question time. In practice, however, junior ministers take some of these question times. Scottish Office oral questions are answered in rotation with questions to other ministers, and Scottish question times are not as frequent as the range of the Secretary's responsibilities might demand. In 1982, these came up once every four weeks. Scottish MPs sometimes complain that their opportunities to ask questions are limited by these infrequent appearances, and they contrast their position with that of English MPs, whose questions can be directed at a greater number of ministers. But ample use is made of the opportunity to obtain written answers, which are unrestricted by the timetable of the House.

A demand is heard that the number of ministers at the Scottish Office should be increased, with a division of the Secretary's responsibilities between more than one minister. This has always been resisted on the grounds that it is essential that the Scottish Secretary be a member of the Cabinet, and if two or more ministers were responsible for the Scottish Office only one could be a member. Thus the heavy administrative responsibility of the office is the price paid for a seat at the Cabinet table.

The Lord Advocate is also a responsible minister, and is the chief law officer of the Government in Scotland. Yet he was outside Parliament completely from October 1962 to June 1970, and after 1979 was in the House of Lords. The Solicitor-General for Scotland may answer in the Commons, but some questions to him have been ruled out of order by the Speaker as falling outside his responsibilities and within the responsibilities of the Secretary of State. The confusion arises from the fact that the administration of justice, and law and order, have been brought more closely under the Scottish Secretary's control in recent years. The reform of the Sheriff Courts (1971) strengthens his position in this respect, for the Scottish Office now has its own Sheriff Courts Administration. The Lord Advocate retains much of the day-to-day administrative power over the courts, including the effective power to nominate judges and sheriffs (Kilbrandon 4, p. 48).

But since he is also the chief public prosecutor (a key position under Scots criminal law) it is considered inequitable to assign to him the constitutional responsibility for the courts as well. If the Lord Advocate were to transfer his prosecuting function to the Solicitor-General for Scotland, he could become a Scottish Minister for Justice in the manner of the Lord Chancellor in England and Wales. This would relieve the Secretary of State of some of his legal burden, and clarify the Lord Advocate's position as the chief law officer of the Crown in Scotland. The written evidence of the Lord Advocate's department to the Constitutional Commission in 1969 stressed that the Lord Advocate is independent of the Secretary of State as a minister and retains all the powers which he possessed before 1885 (Kilbrandon 2, pp. 65–6). But the practice, and public understanding, of the office has been rather different, and some modification of the situation is desirable in the interests of responsible government. In December 1972, ministerial responsibility over most judicial matters was transferred to the Lord Advocate.

Reforming the structure?

The Scottish Office has not been subject to the frequent and fundamental reorganisations of government departments which have taken place in Whitehall. Its stability rests largely on the solid foundations of nationalist vested interest and the flexibility accorded to the Secretary of State for Scotland in matters of departmental organisation. National sentiment has made it very difficult for any functions to be removed from the Scottish Office once they are granted. And any additional functions can be grafted on to the existing structure with ease, since the range of functions already operating within the Scottish Office is so great. It is difficult to think of any function which could not conceivably become part of the Scottish Office, especially as the Secretary of State is informally held to be responsible for all government in Scotland (Gilmour, pp. 25, 65; Kilbrandon 2, p. 4). This would, of course, require the agreement of other ministers. Such agreement is not required for a reorganisation within the Scottish Office, however. In 1962, the Scottish Development Department was created by taking some of the functions from the Scottish Home Department and the Department of Health for Scotland and giving them to the new department. What was left of the two original departments then became the Scottish Home and Health Department. In 1973, a similar rearrangement produced the Scottish Economic Planning Department.

The history of the Scottish Office would seem to point to two main influences in its development. One is nationalism, which demands that more administration be conducted in Scotland. The other is the pressure from within the administration to decentralise functions to Scotland, on grounds of convenience and efficiency. It is of course possible for the latter to be a disguise for the former, especially as the civil servants of the Scottish Office are themselves the important administrative pressure for decentralisation. In their case, nationalism may be confused with the vested interest which any administrative organisation has in furthering its own power. The wider nationalism helps to strengthen their position in relation to Whitehall, but it weakens it in Scotland. Scottish Nationalists attack the Scottish Office as the stooge of London government, and see an increase in its powers as a sham. Many other Scots distrust its complexity and secrecy, and would prefer a more open form of Scottish government. But a large residue are probably indifferent to how the machinery of government is shaped – they are concerned only with the results of policies. The Kilbrandon Report revealed that more than half of the respondents questioned in a survey in Scotland had not heard of the Scottish Office, and the remaining respondents were largely ignorant of its responsibilities (Kilbrandon 6, para. 379).

One could argue that the range of functions exercised by the Scottish Office is both too great and too small. Too great in that it means that one man, the Scottish Secretary, is made constitutionally responsible for subjects as varied as law and order, education, agriculture and economic development. Even under the new super-ministries in Whitehall, such diversity is not reached. The Scottish Secretary must, of necessity, leave a great deal of policy formulation to his civil servants or to his junior ministers, who could suffer from a lack of strong direction. The machine is so big that it threatens to become the master.

But in another sense it is not big enough. There are curious gaps in the Scottish Office's powers where it shares the responsibility for a function with another department. The principal divisions of authority occur in (1) education, (2) energy, (3) transport, (4) economic development, and (5) health and social security.

Finally, it should be remembered that devolution would involve a fundamental restructuring of the system to include a Scottish legislative, as well as an administrative, branch.

(1) Education. Universities and research councils belong loosely with the Department of Education and Science (DES), while schools and the rest of higher education belong with the Scottish Education Department. But the Scottish Secretary has responsibilities for the four ancient universities (St Andrews, Glasgow, Aberdeen, and Edinburgh) under the Universities (Scotland) Acts, and through his patronage of Principals (until 1981) and Regius Chairs. Student grants are administered by the Scottish Education Department, though their amount is principally determined by the Secretary of State for Education and Science.

It is argued for the status quo that since the universities are only loosely under ministerial control in Britain, and are subject to an intermediate body, the University Grants Committee (UGC), the position of the Scottish universities is one of greater independence than might at first appear from their relationship with the DES. The alternative of a Scottish University Grants Committee is claimed to be unsatisfactory in that its academic members would be unable to detach themselves sufficiently from the pressures of their own universities, something they can do in the UGC, since its 14 academic members represent 43 universities. The Scottish universities, it is argued, are part of the larger British system of university education (a fifth of the students are English) and therefore British administration is appropriate. There is a fear, even in Scotland, that the Scottish universities might become too parochial or politicised under Scottish control (Kilbrandon 4, pp. 101–10; W. H. Walsh in Wolfe, pp. 120–2; *Scotsman*, 5 March 1975).

On the other side, it is said that since the Scottish educational system is made up of interrelated parts it should all be brought under Scottish administration. The distinct pattern of Scottish schooling leads on to both sectors of higher education (university and non-university), for the Scottish SCE examinations, which differ from the English GCE in range of subjects and standard, are the basic entrance requirements. The rapid development of the non-university sector of higher education, which is subject to the Scottish Office, has increased the case for an integrated administrative structure, especially as some colleges of education are awarding degrees in collaboration with the universities.

But the demand for change is muted, with the universities largely satisfied with the present structure (but see R. E. Bell in Wolfe, pp. 108–19). The Scottish Office is represented on the UGC by the

Secretary of the Scottish Education Department (a civil servant), and on the Council for National Academic Awards (CNAA) by an HM Inspector. These bodies have not obviously affected the considerable diversity between Scotland and England in types of degree and diploma.

As for the schools sector, the close control by the Scottish Education Department (SED) seems to meet with general approval. It is at any rate one of the most autonomous parts of Scottish administration, for the English Ministry exerts almost no influence in Scotland at this level (see Ch. 12). Thus any impetus for reform of Scottish educational administration seems likely to come from the institutions of higher education other than the universities, for they feel that the Scottish Office, by increasing its control over the universities, could integrate higher education and avoid the 'binary' structure adopted in England. This structure has so far not been followed in Scotland, where 'polytechnics' on the English model have not been established. There are three types of higher education institutions in Scotland: (1) universities, under the UGC, DES, and SED, (2) central institutions (colleges of art, domestic science, and music, and technical colleges) and colleges of education under the SED, and (3) colleges of further education, and technical (etc.) colleges, under local authorities. In England, the system is binary, for there are no 'central institutions'. The independence of such institutions from local authorities in Scotland is especially noteworthy, given the tensions which have arisen on account of that connection in England.

(2) Energy. The post-1945 nationalisation of coal and gas placed these industries under a British ministry (Fuel and Power). Some decentralisation exists, however, through the Scottish area of the National Coal Board and Scottish Gas (which acts in conjunction with the British Gas Corporation). Atomic energy (other than some nuclear-powered electricity generating stations) is developed by the Atomic Energy Authority. All these now come under the Department of Trade and Industry.

Electricity, on the other hand, is totally under the Scottish Office (through two boards). This did not take place without a struggle. Thomas Johnston, the Secretary of State during most of the Second World War, secured for his department the North of Scotland Hydro-Electric Board (created in 1943), and the South of Scotland Electricity Board was transferred to the Scottish Office from the British Electricity

Authority in 1954 as a sympathetic gesture towards the devolutionist sentiments of the time (see the *Report of the Royal Commission on Scottish Affairs, 1954*, Cmd 9212, 'Balfour Commission').

There are obvious problems in the above arrangements. While the gas and electricity boards are autonomous in respect of pricing policies (Scottish prices are relatively high for gas but low for electricity), the price of coal is fixed for the whole country by the National Coal Board (NCB), and this also affects gas and electricity. The electricity industry is expected to sustain coal-mining by purchases of coal for power stations, although it is more expensive to do so than to use oil, thus leading to higher electricity prices. If all were under the same department, coordination might be easier. On the other hand, the development of natural gas from the North Sea, with a pipeline from source to consumer, supports a British administration and has led to further centralisation through the British Gas Corporation as supplier.

North Sea oil is much less clear in its implications for administration in Scotland. As the discoveries were made in the waters off the Scottish coast, the Scottish Office was immediately involved. It had, for example, to give final planning permission for onshore support bases, including construction sites, harbours, and refineries. It was also the department to supervise local government in providing 'infrastructure' (housing, roads, water, etc.).

After some hesitation, the Conservative Government in 1973 appointed Lord Polwarth as Minister of State in the Scottish Office with special responsibility for oil. He was also to chair an advisory body, the Oil Development Council for Scotland. The new Scottish Economic Planning Department soon busied itself with the question of onshore oil developments, and the Scottish Secretary had to sanction these, often after lengthy public inquiries.

But the Department of Energy had no intention of relinquishing its hold on oil, and the Offshore Supplies Office and British National Oil Corporation (though moved to Glasgow) were its responsibilities. There is thus the dilemma of divided departmental control over oil developments, with all the added political implications which flow from this in a period of heightened nationalism. Both the Labour and Conservative parties pledged themselves to use oil revenues to benefit Scottish industry, but the rate and conditions of oil exploitation seem to be firmly within the remit of Whitehall (though under strong pressure from Edinburgh).

(3) Transport. Transport in Scotland is a politically sensitive area of administration, and has distinct problems of its own. Large distances on land have to be covered by public transport over uneconomic routes, especially in the Highlands. There is the additional problem of sea and air routes to Orkney, Shetland and the west-coast islands, which emphasises further the special features of Scotland's geography. Related to the provision of transport is the building of roads, railways, harbours and airports.

The case for an integrated transport policy has been argued for many years, and in the case of Scotland it might appear to be imperative. Yet it is not easily obtained by the administrative structure. The Scottish Office has only recently entered the field, and it is by no means in control of transport policy for Scotland. It has been building roads and bridges since 1956, as a result of a recommendation of the Balfour Commission. Harbours, however, are not a Scottish Office responsibility, and are subject to the National Ports' Council and the Department of Transport. Airports are now built and maintained either by the British Airports Authority (Scottish Airports), or by the Civil Aviation Authority (the Highland Airports). BAA and CAA come under the Department of Trade and Industry.

The provision of transport itself is similarly split between different authorities. Railways belong to British Rail, and thus to the Department of Transport. State air services are provided by British Airways, which have a separate unit, Scottish Airways (established 1971), to run their domestic Scottish flights. These are all linked to the Department of Trade and Industry, in so far as ministerial responsibility is involved. Passenger road transport and sea transport (except Stranraer – Larne) were transferred from the Ministry of Transport to the Scottish Office by the Transport Act of 1968. The actual operating unit is the Scottish Transport Group, appointed by the Scottish Secretary. Freight transport does not come under the Scottish Office, but under the National Freight Company and the Department of Transport.

All this amounts once more to a confusion of functional and geographic administration. The function of transport is split between various authorities, and so is the operating area of these authorities. Much criticism has been levied at the system. The Scottish Council (Development and Industry) called for a Scottish Ports Authority at the end of 1969, and others have attacked the exclusion of the Stranraer – Larne shipping route from the Scottish Transport Group, especially since it is the only profitable public shipping line operating in Scotland. The closure of railway lines by a British Minister, although such lines often play a large part in the economic and social life of rural areas of Scotland, may be considered unsatisfactory. For example, the economic development of the Borders and the Highlands depends largely on the provision of good rail communications, and the closure of the Edinburgh – Hawick – Carlisle line in 1969 contributed to the failure of the Borders Plan, which the Scottish Office was promoting at the time. Similarly, the Dingwall – Kyle of Lochalsh closure was proposed in 1970 by British Rail at a time when no satisfactory road alternative was available.

The then Ministry of Transport told the Select Committee on Scottish Affairs that the division of responsibility for the various transport media was 'on the face of it not sensible' (SCSA 1, p. 35), but they considered that a transfer of railways to the Scottish Office would cause formidable administrative difficulties, notably in respect of investment in rolling-stock and interregional services and track. They did agree that there was maybe a case for making the Scottish Secretary responsible for payments of grants for unremunerative passenger services in Scotland. The Committee also thought this could be done, especially as local authorities might soon be asked to subsidise uneconomic services. The decision on whether to close a line or a service would then be taken in Scotland, and the subsidy found there. (Michael Noble, when Scottish Secretary (1962–4), had the power (subject to Cabinet approval) to delay rail closures in Scotland which he did not approve of.) But they concluded that on balance it was better for British Rail to deal with one government department rather than two since 'if British Rail are compelled to negotiate with different departments on what is basically the same problem, and if different criteria are to be used by different departments, it is unlikely that either British Rail or the users or the taxpayers will be satisfied with the fairness of the result' (SCSA 1, p. 38). So no change. These remarks, incidentally, do not square up with the practice of Scottish administration in other fields, and it is open to question whether British Rail does face 'basically the same problem' in Scotland as elsewhere.

Similarly, with air, ships and freight the Committee stood by the status quo. While deprecating the fact that only the airlines themselves had to look at the needs of the community for air services, they suggested that the Scottish Economic Planning Board and the Department of Trade and Industry could fulfil this function (although the airlines are not represented on the former). Despite the obvious ministerial struggles during the passage of the Transport Act 1968, and the difficulty of reconciling Scottish with English needs, no change was suggested on ships or freight. Behind much of the conventional wisdom on transport administration lies the assumption that transport between Scotland and England or Northern Ireland must come under a British authority (hence the solution for rail, long-distance freight, Stranraer – Larne, and the air services from Glasgow and Edinburgh to London and abroad). This must be balanced against the need to plan for an integrated transport policy to take account of Scotland's special needs.

(4) Economic development. For many years, the Secretary of State has been charged informally with the oversight of the Scottish economy. Scottish ministers speak in Parliamentary debates on the Scottish aspects of British economic legislation, although they are not constitutionally responsible for the work of other departments (except in the sense of the 'collective responsibility' of all ministers for government actions). Most matters of economic policy fall to non-Scottish departments, yet since 1962 the Scottish Office has entered the field of economic planning. It did so without actually increasing its executive functions. Economic plans (*Central Scotland*, 1963, Cmnd 2188; *The Scottish Economy, 1965 to 1970*, 1966, Cmnd 2864) have been produced and economic planning agencies (the Regional Development Division of the Scottish Office, 1964; the Scottish Economic Planning Board and Council, 1965; the Highlands and Islands Development Board, 1965 ; the Economics and Statistics Unit, 1970; the Scottish Economic Planning Department, 1973; and the Scottish Development Agency, 1975) formed. In this way, it has generally taken a much more active interest in the economic life of Scotland. An assessment of the policy-making process in this field will be found in Ch. 12.

Here the functional distribution will be briefly assessed. Most of the enquiries into Scottish administration have been exercised on this topic, but until 1973–4 very few material alterations were suggested. Taxation has nearly always been considered the prerogative of the Treasury, but regional allowances and investment grants (e.g. the regional employment premium from 1967 to manufacturing industries in development areas) are now standard practice. It is stressed that these are not given to Scotland as such, but to development areas throughout Britain.

The administrative problems of economic development have also become more controversial of late, and opinion has swung away from retaining the monopoly of Whitehall in this respect. Under the old system, the 'Board of Trade' functions relating to the distribution and support of industry (now in the Department of Trade and Industry) placed economic development largely outside Scottish administration. This was justified on the grounds that industry could not be steered to Scotland from England if the steering ministry were not British. Firms are diverted to Scotland and other development areas not only by the 'carrot' of grants and other allowances but by the 'stick' of being denied an industrial development certificate (IDC) in the prosperous south. A purely Scottish department could not wield the stick against English firms, and an English department would have no inclination to support a Scottish development area outside its jurisdiction. Since Scottish industrial development depends largely on economic policy in England, GB Departments of Trade and Industry are considered logical. The same is held to be true of the organisation of the large industries such as steel, shipbuilding, and aerospace engineering. In each case, a British strategy is required, and Scotland must not be seen as having its own steel, etc., industry.

Pressure during 1971 from the Scottish Office and the Scottish Council (Development and Industry), as well as from the other Scottish industrial organisations, convinced the government that some changes were needed in the administration of industrial incentives. A Scottish Industrial Development Office (SIDO) was set up in March 1972, with a director appointed from the private sector. Although it was within the Department of Trade and Industry, and not within the Scottish Office, the SIDO had powers to select firms for industrial grants, and to administer these grants in Scotland, without reference back to Whitehall.

The thinking behind this development was largely inspired by the Scottish Office, and by Scottish industrialists such as the late Hugh Stenhouse (who chaired Govan Shipbuilders, the successors of Upper Clyde Shipbuilders, for a few months). Their proposals went to the Cabinet, and were endorsed at the end of 1971 (*Glasgow Herald*, 24 March 1972). Although the devolved industrial offices were reproduced in Wales and the English regions, the superior resources of the Scottish Office in the government machinery once more gave Scotland the edge over the rest of the country. Perhaps one indication of this was the massive subsidy given to Govan Shipbuilders in March 1972.

Another major change in thinking about administration in Scottish economic development came in 1974, when the Labour Government announced the setting up of a Scottish Development Agency in the Scottish Office. This agency aids the regeneration of Scottish industry. Selective regional assistance also came under the Scottish Office in 1975. This marked an important acquisition of economic administrative powers for the Scottish Office, and anticipated economic powers for a devolved Scottish Government, although sections of Labour opinion wanted to keep such powers apart from the Scottish devolution structure, and under the Secretary of State for Scotland, who would remain a member of the UK Government.

(5) *Health and social security.* The creation of the Department of Health and Social Security in October 1968 brought about a new anomaly in British administration. This department combined the Ministry of Health and the Ministry of Social Security, so that in England the National Health Service and social services (comprising both personal care and cash benefits) now came together under one Minister. In Wales and Scotland, however, the National Health Service and personal care services were left under the administration of the Welsh and Scottish Offices, with the Department of Health and Social Security operating there in its cash benefits capacity only. Thus England enjoys a unified administration of health and social security while Wales and Scotland do not.

The reasons for giving the National Health Service to the Scottish Office in 1948 related to the existing tradition of health administration in the Department of Health for Scotland, the distinct local government structure from which many health services were inherited, the greater predominance of the teaching hospitals in the hospital system, and the problems of sparsely populated areas. National Insurance, on the other hand, was transferred to the Ministry of National Insurance from the Department of Health for Scotland in 1945, on the grounds that since cash benefits were uniform throughout the country, they should be administered uniformly. War and disablement pensions remained with the Ministry of Pensions, where they had been since 1916, until in 1953 these ministries were combined to form the Ministry of Pensions and National Insurance.

In 1968 the Government felt that it was desirable to integrate health and social security administration, and the Department of Health and Social Security was formed to achieve this in England. As

58

for Scotland, two alternatives for change were open. Either the Ministry of Social Security could lose its functions in Scotland to the Scottish Office, or the Scottish Office could lose its health and personal social services functions to the Department of Health and Social Security. In the event, no change occurred, largely because of London-based administrative vested interest in the case of the first alternative, and because of Scottish nationalism and Scottish Office administrative vested interest in the case of the second.

The result is another 'odd arrangement', in the words of the Secretary of the Scottish Home and Health Department (Kilbrandon 4, p. 43). While the system does not purport to give a 'different kind of service with a different objective in Scotland than in England and Wales' (loc. cit.), Scotland does come off better in terms of the ratio of GPs to patients, and of staffed hospital beds and health expenditure to the population than England and Wales. Much of this is due to the uneven distribution of the population and the different historical tradition (medicine is exceptionally well provided for in the universities, with about one quarter of all British medical graduates coming from Scotland). Some of the result can also be accredited to the Scottish Office, for successfully maintaining the differential.

On the social security side, the principle of equality of benefit may also work to Scotland's advantage. Despite the lower income level in Scotland, benefits are the same in London, Glasgow, or Stornoway (the unemployment rate in the last-named often reaches 30%). Earnings-related benefits and other personal payments have modified this situation, but there seems to be as great (or as little) a case for putting benefits under Scottish administration as having health there. A Scottish administration would mean that Scottish variations could be taken into account, and liaison made easier with the local authority social work departments, whose activities are coordinated by the Social Work Services Group of the Scottish Education Department. The integration of the health service (comprising hospitals, GPs, and local authority health services) into area health boards was engineered by the Scottish Office, and it would be desirable to take account of social services, both cash and personal, somewhere in the scheme. On the other hand, some would argue that a uniform standard in both health and social security is best achieved by one department operating over the whole of the United Kingdom. This is another area of Scottish administration in which the arguments have yet to be resolved, but where further decentralisation seems likely.

Conclusion

Scotland is governed by three levels of government: London, Edinburgh, and the local authority. It differs from England in having a strong middle tier, representing the central government decentralised to a region. The Scottish Office is more than a device of government, however, since its origins are historic as well as administrative, and the region comprises a nation. The previous statehood of Scotland and the provisions of the Union of 1707 are its heredity, and national consciousness provides its life-force. The Secretary of State for Scotland represents Scotland in the British government but he occupies a difficult position, in that his freedom of action is circumscribed by the need for collective policy-making by the British Cabinet. This inevitably means that he often merely administers British policies in Scotland. The major British departments usually carry more weight than the Scottish Office in such deliberations, and if a conflict arises 'Scotland's interests' may have to be sacrificed to a greater British interest.

But if it is suggested that the Scottish Secretary's wishes should always prevail, this would negate Cabinet government and the collective responsibility of the British Government for all its policies. It is also impossible, in the present system, to use the argument that the political representation of Scotland can on its own determine the policies for Scotland. A Labour Scotland must accept a Conservative administration.

The record of Scottish administration is surprisingly good, despite its built-in disadvantages. Scottish Secretaries have not ranked among the foremost politicians of the land, partly because they impose on themselves a self-denying ordinance in taking Scotland for their parish instead of the greater Parliamentary and Executive arenas, and partly because the work-load is so crippling, reducing them often to political shadows. It is also true that Scottish MPs have not provided a fertile field of recruitment to high office, for reasons to be discussed in Ch. 5.

The division of functions between the Scottish Office and GB departments, while defensible, is in many places illogical. Defining what is predominantly 'British' and what is predominantly 'Scottish' has led to notable impasses and anomalies. Short of independence for Scotland, there will always be this problem, but devolution would improve the structure and extend the area of Scottish decision-making. Scottish government should serve two purposes: to run those things which must be done differently in Scotland (e.g. law, education, housing, and industrial development), and to coordinate government activity on all fronts to take account of Scottish needs (e.g. economic planning). This already happens in some measure, and the signs are that Scotland will strengthen its grip on both fronts in the future.

4

The public service in Scotland

The full extent of the public service in Scotland, and indeed in the UK as a whole, is extremely difficult to determine with accuracy. It can be held to include not only the civil servants in government departments as popularly understood, but also a vast array of industrial civil servants, such as naval dockyard workers, employees of public corporations like the Post Office, British Rail, the National Coal Board and the British Steel Corporation, and the staff of the National Health Service. Numerous other bodies are in close relationship with the central public service and are publicly financed, such as the research institutes and councils, which employ many university graduates, and distinctively Scottish bodies like the Crofters Commission and the Scottish Tourist Board. Members of the armed forces and the staff of defence establishments must also be taken into account, from the rocket-testers on the Isle of Barra to the crews of submarines in the Gare Loch.

Local government provides another large sector of public employment, and encompasses not only the administrators of the local authorities, but also other employees such as schoolteachers, housebuilders, bus drivers, and conductors.[1] Further removed are nominally private bodies such as the universities, Govan Shipbuilders, and the Scottish Council (Development and Industry), which rely in part on public funds.

Taken together, these bodies are very important in the pattern of Scottish employment, and it may be that the public sector is disproportionately strong in Scotland.[2] Many of the heavy industries, such as coal, steel, and shipbuilding, which are particularly important in the Scottish economy, have been nationalised or are heavily subsidised by the state. The construction industry, transport, education, and medicine are also important in Scotland, and are largely dependent on public employment for funds.

If Scotland is thus heavily committed to the public sector, it is

Table 7(a). *Civil service staff in Scotland, January 1981*

Department	No. of staff (rounded off)	
Scottish Office		
Agriculture and Fisheries for Scotland	2,100	
Scottish Development	1,400	
Scottish Education	620	
Scottish Home and Health (including prisons)	3,950	10,910
Scottish Economic Planning	240	
Central Services	2,600	
Other Scottish departments	2,800	
Customs and Excise	2,600	
Defence	21,900	
Employment Group (including MSC)	5,800	
Environment	3,400	
Health and Social Security	8,200	
Inland Revenue	7,000	
National Savings	3,600	
Trade and Industry	1,100	
Other departments	1,400	
All departments	68,710	

Table 7(b). *Proportions of UK home civil servants employed in all departments in Scotland; all Scottish Departments (i.e. excluding GB, UK); and the Scottish Office, January 1981*

	No. of staff	% of comparable UK category
All departments in Scotland	68,710	9.9
All Scottish departments	13,700	2.0
Scottish Office	10,910	1.6

Sources: Civil Service Statistics, HMSO, 1981; *The Scottish Office* (Scottish Information Office Factsheet 20), Edinburgh, n.d.

relevant to ask what implications this has for the Scottish political system. Does it reinforce the autonomy of that system within that of the UK, or does it weaken it by setting up more numerous ties with London and overall British policy-making?

It is clear that only a small sphere of the employment in the public sector is taken up by purely 'Scottish' bodies. Most of the large employers, such as the public corporations and nationalised industries, are London-based, in terms of the location of their headquarters. And if one restricts one's attention to the civil service, the picture of London dominance is further maintained.

In Table 7(a), the category 'other Scottish departments' consists of departments, agencies and legal services whose headquarters are in Scotland. The principal ones are the Scottish Courts Administration (884), the Crown Office and Procurator Fiscal Service (820), the Registers of Scotland (514), and the General Register Office, Scotland (374). In Table 7(b), the category 'all Scottish departments' refers to all departments whose functions are confined to Scotland, and is thus a combination of the Scottish Office and 'other Scottish departments'.

Within Scotland, civil servants in 1981 were distributed between the principal groups in the following proportions: Scottish Office, 16%; all Scottish departments, 20%; GB/UK departments, 80%. This represented an increase over ten years of 3% in the share of the Scottish departments. Most of the staff in the Ministry of Defence are industrial civil servants employed in naval establishments such as Rosyth dockyard and Faslane submarine base. There was a total of 18,000 industrial civil servants in Scotland, and 50,800 non-industrial civil servants.

The fact that the Scottish departments are outnumbered by the non-Scottish in the ratio of five to one is not a good guide to the relative importance of the Scottish and non-Scottish parts of the civil service, nor can it be assumed that the non-Scottish bodies do in practice look more to London than to Edinburgh for guidance. In the first place, the position of the Scottish Office in the public service is pre-eminent on account of the range of functions it possesses and the responsibility of the Secretary of State for Scotland as overseer of all the affairs of Scotland. In some way, all departments are answerable to him for what they do in Scotland, and his voice in the Cabinet is heard on their activities as well as the voices of their respective ministers.

Secondly, the status of the Scottish Office civil servants is markedly higher than those of the other departments in Scotland. In 1970 there were about 160 members of the Administrative Class in the Scottish Office. This represented about 6% of the total of the former Administrative Class. Within the Scottish Office, the distribution was evenly shared among the constituent departments. Other departments in Scotland could muster only half-a-dozen between them (usually Scottish Controllers at Assistant Secretary rank). This is important, since the Administrative Class has traditionally represented that part of the civil service nearest to Ministers in the formulation and administration of policies. Although the Administrative Class was abolished in January 1971, the new classifications do not alter the superiority of the Scottish Office in this respect. The same is true of its strength in the establishment of professional and scientific civil servants, who, together with the senior members of the new Administration Group, constitute the higher civil service.

The Scottish Office's coordinating role, and its high status, lead it to dominate the public service in Scotland. This is partly because formal consultation is required between it and the GB departments, whose Scottish controllers must deal with St Andrew's House, and not Whitehall, on many subjects. Their counterparts in the English regions find such negotiations being carried on by the men at the London headquarters. This process of consultation, with its focus on Edinburgh, tends to give the Scottish Office the lead, and to bring the GB departments into 'Scottish' ways, which they would not follow in England. For example, the Department of Health and Social Security in Scotland is strongly influenced by the powers of the Scottish Office and the local authorities in social work, by the existence of Scots Law in their legal activities, and by the STUC and trade unions in their industrial injuries administration. Wherever local government or legal matters are involved in the work of the GB departments, the Scottish Office as supervising and grant-giving department is also concerned.

The non-Scottish departments are of course not necessarily non-Scottish in personnel. In fact, the overwhelming majority (about 90%) are Scots, and have been recruited in Scotland. There is, however, a greater tendency for the top jobs in these departments to be held by Englishmen, or by Scots who have worked in England, than is the case in the Scottish Office. (Only one of the six Scottish Controllers of British departments in 1970 was a Scot who had worked continuously in Scotland.) This may not be important, for most soon become Scots by adoption, partly as a result of pressure from other elements in the Scottish political system, and partly because they tend to play a Scottish role within their departments. In the words of the Regional Officer of the Ministry of Technology, giving evidence to the Select Committee on Scottish Affairs in 1969, 'I split myself into two persons, one the Ministry of Technology person nationally, the other the Ministry of Technology regional person, when I look at firms in Scotland' (SCSA, 2, p. 241).

Other British departments, such as the Ministry of Defence, tend to have a large number of non-Scottish personnel, although it should be remembered that Scottish regiments do much to stimulate a sort of Scottish nationalism (e.g. the campaign to 'Save the Argylls', 1968–70). On the fringe of the public service, the UGC and the research councils are more non-Scottish than the Scottish universities. These and other similar bodies give Scotland an international status and outlook, which is almost totally detached from the Scottish political system.

When one turns to the Scottish Office, the full 'Scottish' character of the public service in Scotland becomes evident. Its members are an integral part of the Home Civil Service of Great Britain, since that Service is governed by the conditions laid down by the Civil Service Department. The Civil Service Commissioners conduct the entrance examinations for the recruitment of 'established' (permanent and pensionable) staff in all departments, including the Scottish Office. Applicants from Scotland for the higher posts equivalent to those in the old Administrative Class go to London to be interviewed for a place in one of the departments. Strictly speaking, there is no freedom for an applicant to choose the department which he wishes to join, although he is asked to state his preferences. Some Scots will choose a British department as a first preference, while some English applicants may choose the Scottish Office.

These preferences are not published, and one must hazard a guess at their character from the actual placings, which show that the Scottish Office recruits Scots[3] overwhelmingly, but that they represent only half of the total number of Scots who are successful. This is because Scots are relatively successful in the Civil Service Examinations (see below), while only a few posts are filled in the Scottish Office each year. It may therefore be that as many Scots as wish to, go to Edinburgh, while the others go to England or the Diplomatic Service (entry for the latter is by separate tests, however). Under the new system, begun in 1971, recruitment of non-professional graduates is normally to the Administration Trainee grade (formerly the Assistant Principal grade), which may lead to appointment as a Principal after training. The number of administration trainees recruited to the Scottish Office annually in the 1970s was around ten (some graduates fresh from university, some graduate and non-graduate civil servants of Executive Officer or equivalent professional or scientific level). Around two-thirds of these trainees move out into the mainstream as Higher Executive Officers after 2–3 years, and the remainder will move into the 'fast stream' for another 2–3 years' training before becoming Principals.

As an illustration of a typical intake under the old system one may take that of 1968 (derived from the Civil Service Commissioners' Report for that year). This lists the successful candidates' names, the departments they are assigned to, and their education. Extracting the 'Scots', and those entering the Scottish Office, one gets this result:

C. J. A. Chivers (Treasury). Glasgow High School, Glasgow University, Cl. I Classics.

Evelyn Dobson (Public Building and Works), Bromley High School, St Andrew's University. Cl. I History. (Probably English.)

J. M. Currie (Scottish Home and Health), Blairs College, Glasgow University, Cl. II French/American Studies.

Elizabeth Graham (Agriculture and Fisheries for Scotland), Dunfermline High School, Edinburgh University, Cl. II(i) History.

B. V. Philp (Scottish Home and Health) Heriots (Edinburgh), Edinburgh University, Cl. II(i) Economics.

C. A. Munro (Inland Revenue), Watsons (Edinburgh), Edinburgh University. Cl. II (ii) French.

J. S. B. Martin (Scottish Education), Bell-Baxter (Cupar), St Andrew's University, Cl. I Chemistry.

G. Robson (no placing published; later in the Scottish Development Department), St Joseph's (Dumfries), Edinburgh University, Cl. II(i) Politics/History.

B. S. Morris (Treasury), Morgan Academy (Dundee), Dundee University, Cl. II(i) Politics/Psychology.

I. C. Orr (Diplomatic Service), Kirkcaldy High School, St Andrew's University, Cl. I Philosophy.

A. M. Layden (Diplomatic Service), Holy Cross Academy (Edinburgh), Edinburgh University, Cl. II(i) Law/Economics.

W. B. Sinton (Diplomatic Service), Kirkcaldy High School, Edinburgh University, Cl. II(i) French.

P. Morrice (Diplomatic Service – Limited Competition), Gordonstoun, Grade 9 Officer (1963–8).

In 1968, then, the Scottish Office recruited 5 Scots, while 6 went to other departments and 4 to the Diplomatic Service. During the 1960s, 6 out of a total of 30 recruits who entered the Scottish Office had been educated totally in England. At the same time 48 recruits with at least part of their education in Scotland entered other departments or the Diplomatic (Foreign) Service.

The Estimates Committee of the House of Commons in 1964 analysed the university degrees of the direct-entrant recruits to the Administrative Class between 1948 and 1963. They discovered that Scottish graduates made up 5.3% of the total entrants, while Oxford and Cambridge provided 81%, London 8%, and the other British and Irish universities 4.4%.[4] Although this is by no means proportional to

Table 8. *University background of the Administrative Class in the Scottish Office, May 1968*

	Oxford/Cambridge		Other universities		Non-graduates		Total
	No.	%	No.	%	No.	%	
DAFS	4	10	16	42	18	48	38
SDD	11	24	24	53	10	22	45
SED	4	14	20	69	5	17	29
SHHD	16	29	25	45	14	25	55
Total	35	21	85	51	47	28	167

Key:
DAFS: Department of Agriculture and Fisheries for Scotland
SDD: Scottish Development Department
SED: Scottish Education Department
SHHD: Scottish Home and Health Department

Note: This table includes some posts graded administrative, but held for the time being by Executive Officers. While it does not distinguish Scottish universities from the others, it may be safely assumed that the former predominate. Between 1949 and 1969, 72% of direct entrants from the universities had Scottish degrees.

the number of graduates from Scottish universities (who amounted to 15–20% of the UK total over the period), it is distinctly better than the contribution of the English and Welsh 'red-brick' universities (40–50% of the total). Scottish graduates at the time did extremely well in the 'Method I' examinations, which were of an academic nature (18.5% of candidates successful), but less well by 'Method II' which was based on interviews and practical tests (5% successful). The success rate for all candidates was 18.7% by Method I, and 9.5% by Method II.[5] Since 1969 Method II has become the only method of direct entry from the universities to the higher civil service. Under this, between 1971 and 1974, applicants from Scottish universities achieved a 12.5% success rate, compared with 34.5% for Oxford and Cambridge, 11% for London, 9% for other English universities, and 6% for Wales. Direct recruitment from university to the Executive Officer and equivalent grade in the same period gave a 61% success rate for Scottish universities, 56% for Oxford and Cambridge, 54% for London, 57% for other English universities, and 59.5% for Wales.[6]

Within the Scottish Office, the distribution of university degrees among the higher civil servants can be gleaned from a survey of the Administrative Class in May 1968. This gave the result shown in Table 8.

In the Scottish Office Administrative Class, 'Oxbridge' graduates amounted to around one-fifth of the total, while in that Class throughout the civil service they amounted to just under a half. Non-graduates in the Scottish Office were 28%, compared with 24% for the whole Class (Fulton 2, pp. 26–7). The difference between the Scottish Office and the other departments reflects the character of the Scottish educational system, for Oxford and Cambridge play only a marginal part in 'creaming off' the best pupils from Scottish schools. 'Oxbridge' graduates may feel reluctant to come to the Scottish Office, though it should be borne in mind that several of those who do come are in fact Scots, so that the total number of Scots in the posts equivalent to the Administrative Class is probably above four-fifths. In the other posts, a greater number are Scots, and entrance examinations for these, and for Executive Officers in other departments, are conducted by the Civil Service Commissioners in Scotland. Clerical Officers are recruited locally by the Scottish departments themselves. Professional and scientific staff are recruited from all over the UK to a greater extent than other civil servants. For example, the Scottish Office's Chief Architect, Chief Planner, Chief Engineer, and Director of Fisheries Research were non-Scots in 1981.

There seems to have been no problem in filling the administrative posts in the Scottish Office, and as far as can be ascertained, there is no marked difference in quality between Edinburgh and Whitehall in the higher civil service. Certainly there has been no recruitment problem such as faced the Welsh Office in its initial years after 1964, when it was found that Welsh university graduates were reluctant to opt for the Welsh Office (Kilbrandon 3, p. 108).

The early history of the Scottish Office gave little indication that the department would grow to its present size and be attractive to career civil servants. The dominance of the boards and the Lord Advocate's department meant that administrative posts were filled by ministerial patronage or by lawyers, rather than by graduate administrators (Hanham, in Wolfe, pp. 55–6). The total establishment in Scotland, including the boards, cannot have been much above 200 in 1885, and the Scottish Office proper (i.e. the Secretary for Scotland's staff) existed with under a dozen civil servants (Hanham 1, pp. 234–7). The only board run on civil service lines was the Scotch Education

Department, with a staff in London of 34 and a team of 40 school inspectors (Hanham 1, p. 237).

The growth of the Scottish Office is strikingly illustrated by its numerical strength at four dates: 1937, 1953, 1970, and 1981. The figures for non-industrial civil servants are:

1937: 2,400   1953: 5,500   1970: 8,300   1981: 9,900

These figures do not include the other Scottish departments, totalling 2,800 civil servants in January 1981.

The increase in the size of Scottish administration must be accounted an indicator of its now solidly entrenched position within the structure of British government. Things have changed greatly from the early days when the Treasury opposed all staff increases in the Scottish Office on the grounds that there was no work to do there (Hanham 1, p. 233). At that time the Scottish Secretary's base in Edinburgh consisted of a few rooms in Parliament House. Today the Scottish agencies are impressively housed in St Andrew's House, Edinburgh, and in offices throughout Scotland. They make up a distinct bureaucracy.

The careers of the top civil servants provide evidence of this distinctness from Whitehall, with whom they are nevertheless linked as members of one service. An analysis of the careers of the 544 Administrative Class or equivalent civil servants at the Scottish Office during the period 1946–82 shows how few have moved between Edinburgh and London. Table 9(a) gives the translations from the Scottish Office to Whitehall departments, and Table 9(b) the movements from outside to the Scottish Office. As some moved to London and back to Edinburgh again at a later date, the total number of movements recorded is greater than the number of civil servants who moved during their careers.

Table 9(a)(i) shows 25 movements from Edinburgh to Whitehall during the period 1946 to 1970, and Table 9 (a)(ii) 14 movements from 1971 to 1982. To this should be added the occasional secondment, for a period of two or three years, of Scottish Office personnel to the Treasury, the Cabinet Office, or the Civil Service Department (13 cases are recorded). Many of the movements are to high-ranking positions (2 Permanent Under-Secretaries; 2 Deputy Under-Secretaries of State; 4 Under-Secretaries, and 8 Assistant Secretaries, making 16 out of the 39). Thus a high proportion of these translations come to men well advanced in their careers, and it is

70

Table 9(a)(i). *Movements of Scottish Office Administrative Class* civil servants to Whitehall departments, 1946–70*

From	Home	Educ	Av/ C Av	T & C Trans Plg	Health/ DHSS	Agric	Others
DAS/ DAFS							1 (ARC)
DHS	1			2	1		
SDD						1	1 (Treasury)
SED		2	1	1		1	2 (Col. Off.; COI)
SHD	3		1	1			2 (Customs and Excise; Central Land Board)
SHHD					1	1	1 (CSD)
SO (AUSS)							1 (PBW)

Table 9(a)(ii). *Movements of Scottish Office Administrative (Principal and above) civil servants to Whitehall departments, 1971–82*

From	CSD	CO	DI†	Trans.	HMT	HO	MAFF
DAFS					1		1
SCA				1			
SDD	1	1					
SED		2			1		
SEPD		1	1				
SHHD						1	
SO		1	1	1			

*The 'Administrative Class' existed up to December 1970, and the tables for 1946–70 cover that 'Class' (Assistant Principal and above). The 'Administration Group' (January 1971–   ) is much wider than the old Administrative Class, and there are no Assistant Principals. For comparability, the tables for 1971–82 cover 'Principal' level and above.
†The Department of Trade and Industry applies for 1971–4, and the Department of Industry for 1974–82.

Table 9(b)(i). *Movements to the Scottish Office of Whitehall Administrative Class civil servants, 1946–70*

From	To DAS/DAFS	DHS	SDD	SED	SHD	SHHD
Agriculture	2					
Air			1			
Board of Trade			1		1	
Cabinet Office				1		
Central Land Board					2	
Colonial Office			1			
Education				1		
Health						1
Housing and Local Government			1			
Inland Revenue	1					
Labour					1	
Pensions		1				
Post Office		1			1	
Public Assistance Board		1				
PBW/Works		1	1			
Treasury					1	1
War Office		1				

Table 9(b)(ii). *Movements to the Scottish Office of Whitehall administrative (Principal and above) civil servants, 1971–82*

From	To SDD	SED	SEPD	SHHD	SO
Civil Service Department	1	1			1
Cabinet Office		1	1	1	1
Department of the Environment	1				
Department of Education and Science					1
Department of Industry			5		
Department of Trade and Industry			1		
HM Treasury	1				2
Ministry of Agriculture, Fisheries and Food				1	

Key to Table 9

Agric	Ministry of Agriculture to April 1955. Thereafter, MAFF
ARC	Agricultural Research Council
Av/C Av	Aviation/Civil Aviation
CO	Cabinet Office
COI	Central Office of Information
CSD	Civil Service Department
Col. Off.	Colonial Office
DAS	Department of Agriculture for Scotland (to 1960)
DAFS	Department of Agriculture and Fisheries for Scotland (from 1960)
DHS	Department of Health for Scotland (to 1962)
DHSS	Department of Health and Social Security (from 1968)
DI	Department of Industry
Educ	Ministry of Education to 1964. Thereafter Department of Education and Science
FCO	Foreign and Commonwealth Office
GRO	General Register Office
HMT	HM Treasury
HO	Home Office
MAFF	Ministry of Agriculture, Fisheries and Food
PBW	Public Building and Works
SCA	Scottish Courts Administration
SDD	Scottish Development Department (from 1962)
SED	Scottish Education Department
SEPD	Scottish Economic Planning Department (from 1973)
SHD	Scottish Home Department (to 1962)
SHHD	Scottish Home and Health Department (from 1962)
SO (AUSS)	Scottish Office (Assistant Under-Secretary of State)
T & C Plg	Town and Country Planning
Trans.	Transport

Sources: Imperial Calendars, Civil Service Yearbooks (HMSO). Whitaker's Almanacks. Additional information supplied by the Scottish Office, which does not, however, take responsibility for the overall accuracy of the figures.

unusual for the ordinary Scottish Office Principal or even Assistant Secretary to move to Whitehall.

Table 9 (b)(i) shows 23 movements (1946–70) to Edinburgh from Whitehall, and of these 9 were to high positions in the Scottish Office (1 Secretary of the Scottish Education Department, 1 Secretary of the Scottish Development Department, 1 Under-Secretary, and 6 Assistant Secretaries). From 1971 to 1982 there were 19 such movements (Table 9(b)(ii)) (1 Secretary of the Scottish Home and Health Department, 1 Deputy Under-Secretary of State, 4 Under-Secretaries, and 6 Assistant Secretaries).

Table 10(a). *Movements of Administrative Class* civil servants within the Scottish Office, 1946–70*

	To								
From	DAS	DAFS	DHS	SDD	SED	SHD	SHHD	SO	Others
DAS		(21)			2			5	
DAFS				3	1		2	11	1 (Registrar-General for Scotland)
DHS				(26)	2	1	(24)	8	2 (Registrars-General for Scotland)
SDD		1			2		7	17	1 (Scottish Commissioner of the Peace)
SED		3	1	3		1	1	7	
SHD		(9)	1	(9)	4		(25)	14	1 (Scottish Commissioner of the Peace)
SHHD		1		7	9			8	1 (Registrar-General for Scotland)
SO	5	7	5	7	7	15	5		

*See footnote to Table 9(a)(ii).

It must therefore be concluded that movements to and from the Scottish Office affect only a small proportion of the establishment of higher civil servants, and this fact serves to distinguish further the Scottish Office from the rest of the Service. The Fulton Committee on the civil service was worried by the high number and frequency of departmental translations taking place in Whitehall, which it felt was unsettling for administrators and bad for the development of specialist skills in particular areas of administration (Fulton 1, p. 40). These considerations do not apply nearly so strongly to the Scottish Office, where such major translations rarely take place.

What does happen, however, is that higher civil servants frequently move between the different departments of the Scottish Office (Table 10). Since these are the equivalent in function to several Whitehall departments, something of the same mobility appertains as in Whitehall. But the fact that these shifts take place usually within one

Table 10(b). *Movements of administrative (Principal and above) civil servants within the Scottish Office, 1971–82*

From	DAFS	GRO	SCA	SDD	SED	SEPD	SHHD	SO
DAFS		1		3	3	4	3	9
GRO					1	1	1	
SCA							1	
SDD	5				10	13	18	31
SED	3		2	7		5	16	19
SEPD	4			14	4		7	5
SHHD	6	2	1	11	14	5		25
SO	8	1	3	21	15	13	26	

Key: As for Table 9.

Note: Figures in brackets represent nominal movement to new departments. In Table 10(b) some of the movements to the SEPD (established 1973) are also of this kind. SO (Scottish Office) positions in Table 10(a) include private secretaries to ministers, which are short-term appointments, posts in the Regional Development Division, and the Permanent and Assistant Under-Secretaries of State. In Table 10(b) SO also includes Central Services.

building (and under one Secretary of State and one Permanent Under-Secretary) makes the change less noticeable. The civil servant can continue to use his specialist knowledge of Scotland in whichever Scottish Office department he serves. Since his clientèle is only five million people, with a fairly small number of local authorities and interest organisations, the principal political and official leaders will be known to him already. This is indeed one of the strengths of the Scottish Office as compared with Whitehall: personal contacts with the localities are good, making for frequent face-to-face contacts between central and local government.

Here, the professional and scientific civil servants play as large a part as the administrative men, and act as a leavening in the Scottish political system. Such Scottish Office officials as the Chief Social Work Adviser, the Chief Medical Officer, the Chief Planning Officer, and the Chief Engineer act as links between central government and local government, as well as with the organisations outside government altogether. The origins and careers of the 'professionals/scientists' vary in some measure from those of the 'administrators', although the picture is not very clear. Legal, educational, and medical officials tend to be Scottish because of the distinct Scottish institutions involved.

Architects, planning officers, social workers, and scientists are more likely to be non-Scottish or to have worked for some time outside Scotland. As in the case of those working in the GB departments, they soon become absorbed in the Scottish system, but their experience perhaps gives their work a broader outlook than the civil servants who are more rooted in Edinburgh.

The cooption of administrative personnel from outside occupations is perhaps not so marked in the Scottish Office as in Whitehall, although the large number of ex-teachers who are Inspectors of Schools and who sometimes move into administrative posts links the Scottish Education Department with the wider Scottish community. However, most top Scottish Office civil servants are a separate group in the community, joining the other élite groups of Edinburgh such as the lawyers, the churchmen, and the academics.

The leaders of the bureaucratic élite in Scotland are the Permanent Under-Secretary of State and the Secretaries of the five departments and Central Services within the Scottish Office. Brief biographical profiles of these men (derived from *Who's Who*) indicate their origins and careers. In 1982, 6 out of the 7 were Scottish, but 2 of the Scots were educated entirely in England, and another had a Cambridge degree. In 1975, 4 of the top positions were held by Englishmen, which illustrates the point made earlier that the very senior civil servants have greater mobility than the others.

> Permanent Under-Secretary of State: Sir W. K. (Kerr) Fraser. Born 1929 in Scotland. Educated, Eastwood School (Glasgow), Glasgow University. Scottish Office since 1955. Permanent Under-Secretary since 1978. Club: New (Edinburgh).
>
> Secretary, Department of Agriculture and Fisheries for Scotland: J. I. (Ian) Smith. Born 1924 in Scotland. Educated, Alderman Newton's School, Leicester; St Andrew's University. Scottish Office since 1949. Recreation: golf. Club: Royal Commonwealth Society (London).
>
> Secretary, Scottish Development Department: T. (Tony) R. H. Godden. Born 1927 in England. Educated, Barnstaple Grammar School, London School of Economics. Colonial Office, 1951–7. Cabinet Office, 1957–9. Scottish Office since 1961. Recreations: philately, photography, music. Club: New (Edinburgh).
>
> Secretary, Scottish Economic Planning Department: R. G. (Gavin) L. McCrone, Born 1933 in Scotland. Educated, Stowe School; Cambridge, Wales, Glasgow Universities. University teacher 1960–70. Scottish Office since 1970. Recreations: walking, music. Clubs: United Oxford and Cambridge University, Royal Commonwealth Society (London).
>
> Secretary, Scottish Education Department: J. A. (Angus) M. Mitchell. Born 1924 in India (son of Scottish Indian Civil Servant). Educated,

Marlborough College; Oxford University. Scottish Office since 1949. Recreation: maps. Clubs: Royal Commonwealth Society (London), New (Edinburgh).

Secretary, Scottish Home and Health Department: A. (Archie) L. Rennie. Born 1924 in Scotland. Educated, Madras College, St Andrews; St Andrew's University. Admiralty, 1944–7. Scottish Office since 1947. Recreations: Scottish literature, sailing, gardening. Club: Scottish Arts (Edinburgh).

Deputy Secretary, Central Services: William K. Reid. Born 1931 in Scotland. Educated, Robert Gordon's College, Aberdeen; George Watson's College, Edinburgh; Edinburgh and Cambridge Universities. Ministry of Education, 1956–60. Cabinet Office, 1964–7. Department of Education and Science, 1967–78. Scottish Office since 1978. Club: New (Edinburgh).

Of the five Permanent Under-Secretaries of State at the Scottish Office since 1946, four have been Scottish. Apart from the present incumbent (a Scot), they were:

Sir David Milne (1946–59). Born 1896 in Scotland; died 1972. Educated, Daniel Stewart's College, Edinburgh; Edinburgh University. Scottish Office, 1921–59.

Sir William Murrie (1959–64). Born 1903 in Scotland. Educated, Harris Academy, Dundee; Edinburgh and Oxford Universities. Scottish Office, 1927–44. Cabinet Office, 1944–8. Home Office, 1948–52. Scottish Office, 1952–64.

Sir Douglas Haddow (1964–73). Born 1913 in Scotland; died 1986. Educated, George Watson's College, Edinburgh; Edinburgh and Cambridge Universities. Scottish Office, 1935–73. Recreation: golf.

Sir Nicholas Morrison (1973–8). Born 1918 in England; died 1981. Educated, Cheltenham College, Cambridge University. War Office, Ministry of Defence and Civil Service Department to 1972. Deputy Under-Secretary of State, Scottish Office, 1972–3. Recreations: gardening, horseracing. Club: Athenaeum (London).

The organisation of the Scottish Office has federal features, in that the Secretaries of the five administrative departments report directly to the Secretary of State, not to the Permanent Under-Secretary. The Permanent Under-Secretary meets regularly once a week with the Secretaries of the five departments and the Deputy Secretary (Central Services) in a 'Management Group' to enable them to reach collective decisions on matters of common interest, but since they are the accounting officers for their departments and have direct access to the Minister, the Permanent Under-Secretary's power is somewhat less than that of the Permanent Under-Secretary of Whitehall departments, who is the sole accounting officer. The Permanent Under-Secretary at the Scottish Office is himself an accounting officer for the

Central Services of the Scottish Office, which comprise the Directorate of Establishments (personnel, organisation, management, office, and computer service), the coordination of finance work and statistical work, the Solicitor's Office, and the Scottish Information Office. He is of course the Secretary of State's senior adviser, and thus Scotland's 'chief bureaucrat'.

The federal organisation is a legacy of the former independence of the Scottish departments and boards, and was preserved in the 1939 reorganisation. It allows for considerable specialisation within the Scottish Office, and to some extent enhances career prospects there by opening up more positions of high responsibility. The minister has more channels of advice open to him than there are under the 'pyramid' departmental structure with one Permanent Under-Secretary at the top. The advantages of this type of structure were recognised by the Fulton Report, which recommended the establishment of 'accountable' units within departments (Fulton 1, pp. 51–2). Departmental changes in Whitehall since 1970 have in fact moved in this direction.

The nature of the work done in the Scottish Office, and the life-style of the administrators, is in many ways different from that of Whitehall.[7] In the first place, St Andrew's House is 400 miles distant from Parliament, where ministers must of necessity spend much of their time. Scottish higher civil servants find themselves constantly commuting between London and Edinburgh, and many will be posted for a time to Dover House, the Whitehall base of the Scottish Office.

During the passage of a Scottish Bill, or at Scottish question time, there will be some difficulty in briefing ministers, since most of the files have to kept in Edinburgh. Civil servants must prepare a formal submission to the minister, which is kept separate from the files and which gives the details of the case.[8] This is an added burden, and when unexpected matters are raised during a debate, telephone calls have to be made to and from Edinburgh to provide information. Other departments' files are usually within walking distance of Parliament. The strain imposed by constant travel and the difficulty of communications makes the job a hard one for the Edinburgh civil servant. Yet Edinburgh life has become relatively more attractive in recent years, as the living conditions in London have deteriorated. Long-distance travel to work is not required, and the facilities for recreation are good (many top Scottish Office men list golf or gardening among their hobbies).

Despite the frequent visits to London, there is surprisingly little

78

extended contact between St Andrew's House and Whitehall. The need to 'check out' any policies with opposite numbers in Whitehall does not loom so large as is sometimes assumed (as in Mackintosh, p. 131). In education, for example, the organisation and curricula of the schools, teacher-training, and the conditions of service of teachers are determined by the Scottish Education Department in conjunction with the local education authorities and Scottish educational organisations. There is practically no reference to the Department of Education and Science. Each department conducts its own educational system, and only very large issues such as the school-leaving age and comprehensivisation are determined on a British basis (even here Scottish differences persist). Much the same could be said of a large part of health and social work administration, local government, and legal matters. Where a matter appears to be 'political', or affects other departments, St Andrew's House will act more cautiously and Ministers and Scottish Office officials will consult their colleagues, but a great deal of what the Scottish Office does is not likely to affect the interests of other departments directly. This allows it a real freedom to go its own way with a different solution from England (for further development of these points, see Ch. 12).

Function for function, there are obviously fewer civil servants employed in Scotland than in England. For example, three times as many administrators are involved in the branches relating to teachers in the Department of Education and Science as are employed in the corresponding divisions of the Scottish Education Department. Thus it could be said that one man in Edinburgh covers the ground of three in Whitehall (he has of course only one-tenth of the clientèle). When it comes to research and policy-formulation there will be more specialists in the larger department, but the smaller will have the broader view. On the whole, this tends to favour the larger department taking the initiative, since the Scottish Office man spreads himself too thinly to make a real contribution in any one area. He may look to Whitehall for the latest ideas in his field, though he will not always accept them. This could explain why some educational and social welfare reforms have been adopted in England before they came to Scotland. But other reforms have come more quickly in Scotland (e.g. the Social Work Act of 1968) because the comprehension of the Scottish Office's organisation and viewpoint facilitated reforms, where Whitehall's separate empires and specialists hindered them (see Ch. 12).

Administration on the scale of the Scottish Office thus has its share of strength and weakness. It provides, for Scotland, a bureaucracy derived from, and knowledgeable of, its people and their special needs. For the men who staff it, it gives some technical problems not present in Whitehall relating to Parliamentary business and liaison with other departments. The type of work they do makes them generalists rather than specialists, although they probably remain within the same department to a much greater extent than do civil servants in Whitehall. This has given the Scottish Office in recent years an overall sense of direction lacking in much of Whitehall, and certainly in any region of England. The chief examples are the development of regional economic planning and of medical and social services. Nevertheless, 'the Scottish bureaucracy' may sacrifice depth and vision to a thin parochialism as a result of its 'isolation' in Edinburgh. Some of Scottish administration lacks the stimulus of continual interchange of ideas with the outside world, but the post-Fulton developments in the training of civil servants has to some extent altered this. Civil Service College courses are taken jointly by civil servants of all departments. In the 1970s, there was an Edinburgh centre of the Civil Service College, but it was not confined to Scottish administrators. Indeed, what is surprising is the lack of a course specifically related to the problems of Scottish administration, which is however the province of the Scottish Office Training Unit, and of courses on public administration at Scottish universities and colleges.

The strength of the Scottish bureaucracy in the Scottish political system lies partly in the relative weakness of the other parts of that system. Without a Scottish Parliament, the legislative checks are more remote, for the Scottish Grand Committee, the Scottish Standing Committees, the Select Committee on Scottish Affairs, and Scottish question time provide only an intermittent and largely ineffective threat to the administrators. The vast range of functions in the Scottish Office puts the Ministers at a disadvantage in acquiring expertise, while the other departments in Scotland cannot compete in the status of their administrators, and soon come under the influence of the Scottish Office. Scottish local authorities are financially subservient, and Scottish public opinion is docile (even a nationalist upsurge primarily attacks London government rather than the Edinburgh government which already exists). The only challenge to the Scottish Office comes from Whitehall, where the Treasury arbitrates between, or dictates to, all departments, and controls the civil service. The record here, as judged by favoured treatment for Scotland (see Ch. 12), and by the growth of the Scottish Office establishment, is that the Scottish bureaucracy can, at the least, hold its own against all comers.

5

Parliament

The Scottish MPs

In the Parliaments elected from 1950 to 1979, there were 71 MPs from Scottish constituencies in the House of Commons. A major redistribution of seats occurred in 1983, and the total number in Scotland rose to 72. This is an over-representation in terms of the ratio of seats to population. In 1885 Scotland had 72 seats, or 12.7% of the Great Britain total (i.e. excluding Ireland); in 1979 and 1983 it had 11.2% of the GB total. But in the meantime, its population proportion had fallen from 12.1% to 9.4%.

In the 1979 general election, the average electorate per constituency was 53,462 in Scotland and 66,301 in England. Fourteen Scottish constituencies had electorates of under 40,000, including four in the Highlands and six in Glasgow. At the same time, ten constituencies had electorates of over 65,000. The extreme range was from Glasgow Central (19,826) to Midlothian (101,482). In 1983, the average electorate per constituency was 53,985 in Scotland and 67,196 in England. The new constituencies are less disparate in the size of their electorates, although there is still a big difference between the four smallest with under 40,000 (the Western Isles remains the smallest with 22,822), and the largest (Ayr, with 65,010). More than half the new constituencies are within 10% of the mean, compared with only a quarter of the old.[1] It is politically difficult to merge Highland constituencies because of the immense area that would be involved.

Scottish MPs are a distinct group in the House of Commons. They have their own Bills to discuss; their own committees to sit on; and their own ministers to question. These activities set them apart from other members, who do not share these duties or interests.[2] Unfortunately for the non-Scottish MPs, however, the parliamentary system involves them in purely Scottish affairs, whether they like it or not. Scottish Bills are sometimes taken on the floor of the House; until

81

1981 the Scottish Grand Committee had English MPs coopted to it to preserve the party balance; and Scottish question time takes place in the House as a whole. In these ways, therefore, the workings of the House of Commons display the interaction of the Scottish and British political systems in a concentrated form.

The parliamentary segment of the Scottish political system consists primarily of the Scottish MPs (Scottish peers in the House of Lords play a less important role). Of the 72 MPs elected in 1983, 41 were Labour, 21 Conservative, 5 Liberal, 3 Social Democrat (SDP), and 2 Scottish Nationalist. In the whole House there were 209 Labour, 397 Conservative, 17 Liberal, 6 SDP, and 21 other MPs. Scotland was thus committed to the Labour Party in terms of seats, although the Labour vote was only 35%. The Conservatives were much weaker in Scotland than in England with only 28% of the votes, compared with 46%.

In 1955, the party distribution among the Scottish MPs was more like that of the whole House. There were then 34 Labour, 36 Conservative, and 1 Liberal MPs, out of a total of 277 Labour, 344 Conservative, 6 Liberal, and 3 other MPs. Thus from 1955 there was a massive swing away from the Conservative Party in Scotland, which was unmatched in any other part of the UK (for statistics for 1955–70 see Butler and Pinto-Duschinsky, pp. 356–7).

The characteristics of the Scottish MPs have accordingly changed (see Table 11). In 1955, there were more non-Scots sitting for Scottish seats. There was also a wider range of occupations. The Tory ranks consisted mainly of ex-army men, landowners, and businessmen. But there were also strong politicians such as Walter Elliott, Sir Robert Boothby, James Stuart, and Sir William Anstruther-Gray, chairman of the back-bench 1922 Committee from 1962 to 1964. Labour was nearly all working class or professional, and its 'politicians' included such figures as John Strachey, Hector McNeil, Emrys Hughes, Tom Fraser, Jean Mann, and Margaret Herbison.

By the 1970s, the Scottish representation had become much more indigenous. Scottish seats were being reserved for Scots, and Scottish affairs were more of a specialism in the House. The decline of the Tories in the 1960s, and their retreat to the hard-core rural areas, gave them more of an aristocratic or landed image. Many of their MPs had English public school educations and spoke with 'English' accents. Few were natural politicians. To some extent this changed after 1979, when businessmen and lawyers made up a good proportion of the still-depleted (21 MPs after the election of 1983) Conservative representation.

Table 11. *Scottish MPs, 1955, 1974 (October), 1979, and 1983*

	1955			1974 (October)				1979				1983				
	Con	Lab	Lib	Con	Lab	Lib	SNP	Con	Lab	Lib	SNP	Con	Lab	Lib	SDP	SNP
No. of MPs	36	34	1	16	41	3	11	22	44	3	2	21	41	5	3	2
Average age	54	55	42	43	50	46	39	45	47	51	50	44	49	40	44	54
Non-Scots	4	6	—	—	3	—	—	—	3	—	—	—	3	—	—	—
Educated outside Scotland	26	6	1	8	5	1	—	9	6	1	—	4	7	—	—	—
University education	21	10	1	7	16	3	10	15	23	3	1	17	23	5	3	1
Former councillor	2	9	—	5	23	—	3	8	24	—	1	8	21	—	—	1
Women	1	3	—	1	1	—	2	—	1	—	—	1	1	—	—	—
Occupation																
Land/farming	8	—	1	3	—	—	1	6	1	—	—	3	1	—	—	—
Business	16	6	1	8	5	2	3	10	5	2	1	6	4	1	—	1
Armed services	11	—	—	—	—	—	—	—	—	—	—	—	—	—	—	—
Professions	6	16	1	3	20	2	5	3	27	3	—	5	25	2	3	—
Scots lawyers	2	1	—	3	2	—	2	6	2	—	1	7	2	2	—	1
Unskilled/skilled	—	16	—	—	15	—	—	—	9	—	—	—	8	—	—	—

Note: Some MPs are entered twice under occupations, as when a barrister has strong business interests. If one extends the comparison back to 1910, one finds that there were then more non-Scots, more graduates, and more lawyers among the Scottish MPs. Dr C. J. Larner late of Glasgow University analysed the characteristics of Scottish MPs from 1910, and saw a sharp turn towards parochialism in the choice of MPs between 1910 and 1924, with a decline in the number attaining ministerial office thereafter (unpublished paper).

Labour's expansion has changed the characteristics of its MPs, especially since 1979. There are now more professional and middle-class Members, and over half have had a university education. This contrasts with the position before 1979, and especially before 1970, when Scottish Labour MPs were more rooted in the working or lower middle class than their counterparts in England. They are still, however, heavily drawn from the ranks of local government councillors and trade union officials. Only one or two are active in debates in British or foreign affairs, and most give their exclusive attention to Scottish or constituency matters.[3]

The Liberals, who numbered 5 in 1983, were all university-educated and middle class. The SNP's 11 MPs in October 1974 were largely professional, and university-educated. They were reduced to 2 after 1979. The SDP (3 MPs in 1983) were all university-educated.

One important deficiency in the House of Commons is that of Scots lawyers. There were only 3 in 1955 and 11 (2 Labour) in 1983 (lawyers trained in English law are excluded: there were 2 in 1955 and 1 in 1983). When it is considered that there must be two Scottish government law officers, and that much Scottish legislation has to deal with technical matters of Scots Law, it is clear that the House of Commons is starved of the appropriate legal expertise. (English Law is well served by the presence of around 100 MP lawyers.) From 1962 to 1970 the Lord Advocate was not in the House, and from 1960 to 1979 (with exception of the four months December 1963 to April 1964) the Solicitor-General for Scotland was not a Member.

The difficulty in obtaining candidates with Scottish legal qualifications comes from the fact that Scottish legal practice cannot be pursued in London. Many lawyers combine attendance in the House with some legal work, but the Scots cannot normally do this. For those who make the sacrifice, however, appointment as a government law officer is almost assured, followed possibly by elevation to the highest positions in the Scottish bench (see Ch. 2). There are thus rich rewards for the tiny group of Scottish legal-politicians. It is obvious that a legislative body in Edinburgh would attract far more lawyers as members than does the House of Commons, and would make the principal Scottish legal bodies more accessible during the passage of law reform Bills.[4]

What is the position of Scotland in the work of Parliament? In the session 1968–9, debates on purely Scottish Bills and topics occupied about 50 hours of the time of the House of Commons. This included major debates, lasting several hours, on the Education, Town and Country Planning, and Housing Bills. There was also about 10 hours of parliamentary questions to ministers on Scottish topics, with the Scottish Secretary or other Scottish Office ministers taking about two-thirds of the time. During the session, something like 1,300 written answers and 200 oral answers on Scottish topics were provided by government departments. Over and above this, Scottish MPs spoke about Scotland in general debates covering the whole of Britain.

Beyond the floor of the House itself, the Scottish Grand and Standing Committees of the House of Commons in fifty sittings spent 125 hours in debate. (See Table 14. A normal sitting lasts $2\frac{1}{2}$ hours.) The Select Committee on Scottish Affairs (1969–72; 1979–   ) takes up an equivalent time in its investigative and reporting activities. In Session 1981–2 it met 28 times to deliberate and take evidence.

These Scottish activities of the House of Commons represent the Scottish political system in its parliamentary aspect. The boundary of the system can be defined even in Westminster, for Scottish affairs interest mainly the Scottish MPs, and Scottish debates and question times have a character of their own. Needless to say, the Scots jealously preserve their right to an audience on the floor of the House for Scottish matters, while they have the added advantage of an exclusive 'club' of their own in the Scottish committees.

The Scottish Committees

These committees are now four in number, though two are not in continuous existence.

(1) The Scottish Grand Committee. Established in 1894, it consists of all 72 Scottish MPs. Up to 1981, 10–15 others were added to bring the Committee's party balance more into line with that in the House as a whole. Its functions fall into three categories: first, Bills. (a) Second reading debate stage. Such referral is dependent on the Speaker certifying that such Bills relate exclusively to Scotland, and the motion to refer them to the Scottish Grand Committee must be made by a government minister. Private Members' Bills are thus practically excluded. If 10 MPs object, the Bill must stay on the floor of the House. Such a veto has happened only twice, but there are cases where reference has been prevented by opposition being shown in advance of the Motion being put down (e.g. on the Scottish Development Agency Bill 1975).[5] (b) It reports to the House that it has

Table 12. *House of Commons procedure for Scottish Bills*

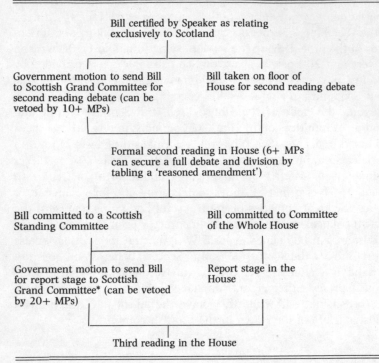

Bill certified by Speaker as relating
exclusively to Scotland

Government motion to send Bill
to Scottish Grand Committee for
second reading debate (can be
vetoed by 10+ MPs)

Bill taken on floor of
House for second reading debate

Formal second reading in House (6+ MPs
can secure a full debate and division by
tabling a 'reasoned amendment')

Bill committed to a Scottish
Standing Committee

Bill committed to Committee
of the Whole House

Government motion to send Bill
for report stage to Scottish
Grand Committee* (can be vetoed
by 20+ MPs)

Report stage in the
House

Third reading in the House

*This procedure is available only for Bills considered previously in the Scottish Grand
Committee.

considered such Bills, so that the formal second reading may take
place there (and not in the Committee). A vote in the Committee at
this point is extremely unusual, and of doubtful meaning. Only two
instances are recorded, in the last decade, and that on 11 November
1969 was allowed to give 'freedom of expression of opinion', not to
decide the second reading. If six or more MPs propose an amendment
at the formal second reading stage, there will be a second reading
debate on the Bill in the House. This happened in 1961, over the
Crofters Bill. (c) It can take the report stage of Scottish Bills which have
been considered by the Committee at second reading, and the Scottish
Standing Committee at committee stage. This is a recent innovation,
and so far it has not been used. However, it is now possible for a
Scottish Bill to go through all its stages, apart from formal second and
third readings, in the Scottish committees (see Table 12). It is also

86

possible for the Grand Committee to meet in Edinburgh. This it did for the first time on 15 February 1982, in the building intended for the Scottish Assembly. It debated youth unemployment and training, a subject which had been investigated by the Select Committee on Scottish Affairs shortly before. On 22 November 1982 it debated a Bill in Edinburgh for the first time (the Divorce Jurisdiction, Court Fees and Legal Aid Bill). This attracted considerable public interest, although only around half of the Scottish MPs were present. In fact, Edinburgh sittings are not popular with many MPs as they involve extra travel and accommodation problems.

Second, Scottish Estimates debates. Selected Scottish Estimates may be debated in the Committee, on up to six days each session. The Votes are grouped together into such categories as 'Crime' or 'Health', and are chosen by the Opposition.

Third, Matter day debates. Matters of concern to Scotland may be debated on up to six days each session. The topics are chosen by the government, but reference to the Committee can be blocked by 10 MPs (e.g. the proposed debate on technical education in July 1968), and there have been refusals to 'report back' (e.g. on 17 February 1977 and 9 December 1980, in debates on College of Education closures).

(2/3) The Scottish Standing Committees. There are now two, the first having been established in 1957, and the second in 1962. These committees take the clause-by-clause examination of Bills, and vote on such clauses and amendments to them (the 'committee' stage). Important Bills go to the first committee, and minor ones to the second. The composition of the committees is between 16 and 50 MPs, nominated by the Committee of Selection, of whom not less than 16 must represent Scottish constituencies.

In practice, major Scottish Bills are committed to a Scottish Standing Committee above the minimum size (e.g. the Housing (Financial Provisions) (Scotland) Bill 1971, was dealt with in a committee of 26). This meant that no Liberal or SNP MPs got a place, and forced the Parliamentary Under-Secretary for Health and Education at the Scottish Office to attend, in order to maintain the government majority, although he had no direct connection with the Bill.

In selecting the Scottish Committees, regard is paid to the qualifications of the members and the composition of the House. The second committee is not often used, and neither committee can sit when the Scottish Grand Committee is in session. Tuesdays and Thursdays, from 10.30 a.m to 1 p.m., are the usual hours for the Scottish committees, but they have met at all hours on some occasions (e.g. for the debates on the Education Bill 1970 and the Housing (Financial Provisions) Bill 1971). The procedure for Scottish Bills in the House of Commons is shown in Table 12.

The proportion of Scottish Bills going to the Scottish Committees has risen in recent years, especially since the establishment of the Scottish Standing Committees. From 1948 to 1959 less than a third of Scottish Bills went to the Grand Committee for second reading, and a little over two-thirds for the committee stage.[6] In the 1960s, however, the proportions were over half and three-quarters respectively. The record of two sessions in the parliament of 1966–70 (Table 13) shows how active the Scottish committees can be in legislation. In those sessions, 12/23 Scottish Bills were taken in the Scottish Grand Committee, and 17/23 in the Scottish Standing Committees. Many of the Scottish Bills taken on the floor of the House, or in the Committee of the Whole House, were minor Bills requiring little or no debate. *

(4) The Select Committee on Scottish Affairs. This is an investigatory committee, with power to examine witnesses and documents, and was first appointed in November 1969 to examine economic planning in Scotland. It reported in June 1970 (HC 267 (1969–70)). The Committee was re-established in May 1971, to examine land use in Scotland. It reported in October 1972 (HC 511 (1971–2)). Its membership was 16 in 1969–70 and 14 in 1971–2. Subcommittees were used, and the Committee held hearings in London and Scotland. In October 1979 the Committee was reconstituted, as part of the general scheme of Select Committees introduced in that year. Its remit is 'to examine the expenditure, administration and policy of the Scottish Office and associated public bodies', and it has conducted numerous investigations, into topics ranging from the White Fish Authority Levy to the Scottish Public Expenditure Programme. There are 13 members (the largest Select

---

*Using different criteria, G.E. Edwards in 'The Scottish Grand Committee, 1958 to 1970', *Parliamentary Affairs* XXV (1972), 307, 314, obtains a different result. He excludes Consolidation Bills, which make no substantive change in the law, and Private Members' Bills, which are outside the Grand Committee procedure. This gives 86.4% of Government Bills certificated as Scottish referred to the Scottish Grand Committee between 1958 and 1970. 81% of all Government Scottish Bills (including Consolidation Bills) were committed to a Scottish Standing Committee. Twenty out of twenty-three Scottish Private Members' Bills went there.

Table 13. *Scottish Bills in the House of Commons, Sessions 1966–7 and 1967–8*

Bill	SGC	SSC	HC	CWH
1966–7				
Law Reform (Miscellaneous Provisions) (Scotland)	×	×		
Local Government (Scotland)	×	×		
Housing (Financial Provisions) (Scotland)	×	×		
Water (Scotland)	×	×		
Remuneration of Teachers (Scotland)	×	×		
Countryside (Scotland)	×	×		
Police (Scotland)	×	×		
Licensing (Certificates in Suspense) (Scotland)		×	×	
Deer (Amendment) (Scotland)		×	×	
Legal Aid (Scotland)			×	×
Police (Scotland) (No.2)			×	×
Housing (Scotland)			×	×
1967–8				
Teachers Superannuation (Scotland)	×	×		
Erskine Bridge Tolls	×	×		
Sewerage (Scotland)	×	×		
Legitimation (Scotland)	×	×		
Law Reform (Miscellaneous Provisions) (Scotland)	×	×		
Sale of Venison (Scotland) (No. 2)		×	×	
Highlands and Islands Industry		×	×	
Social Work (Scotland)		×	×	
New Towns (Scotland)			×	×
Housing (Financial Provisions) (Scotland)			×	×
Prevention of Crime (Scotland)			×	

Key: SGC Second reading debate in Scottish Grand Committee
SSC Committee stage in a Scottish Standing Committee
HC Second reading debate on floor of House
CWH Committee stage in Committee of the Whole House

Committee of the departmental Select Committees), and the Chairman has been Labour, although the Conservatives have a majority on the Committee.

All committees of the House of Commons are supposed to reflect the balance of parties in the House as a whole, and this requirement has sometimes put a severe strain on the available resources with regard to the Scottish committees. The Scottish Grand Committee, for

Table 14. *Work of the Scottish committees, Session 1968–9*

Subject	Sittings	Members present (excluding chairman)
Scottish Grand Committee		
Electricity Bill	1	51
Agricultural Spring Traps Bill	1	45
Town and Country Planning Bill	2	48, 38
Housing Bill	2	38, 39
Age of Majority Bill	1	45
Estimates	6	44, 46, 42, 34, 44, 42
Matter: Arts and Amenities	1	39
First Scottish Standing Committee		
Agricultural Spring Traps Bill	2	24, 21
Education Bill	14	Between 16 and 29
Town and Country Planning Bill	11	Between 18 and 29
Housing Bill	6	Between 19 and 26
Second Scottish Standing Committee		
Electricity Bill	1	18
National Mod Bill	1	12
Age of Majority Bill	1	12

Source: Standing Committees. Return for Session 1968–9, HC 9 (1969–70).

example, until 1981 had between 10 and 15 other MPs added to produce this balance, but from 1962 to 1964, from 1970 to 1974, and from 1979 to 1981, the addition of 15 non-Scottish Conservatives could not produce a Conservative majority on the committee. This did not matter greatly politically, since no legislative vote takes place there. In 1922, when the committee did vote on the committee stage of Bills, the adverse majority for the Government at that time meant that all Scottish Bills had to be kept on the floor of the House.[7]

Today, the smaller Scottish Standing Committees take the committee stage. Until it was reduced in size in November 1971, the first committee gave the Conservative Government considerable problems as regards the maintenance of its majority there. The Conservatives in Scotland had only 23 MPs, and, under the old rules, 16 were required for a majority on the committee. Several Scottish MPs were members of the Government, and their continual presence on the committee could not be expected. Although the rules allowed for it, no English MPs were coopted on to the committee, and those that were coopted on to the Scottish Grand Committee were unwilling participants, and found their occasional remarks resented by the Scottish MPs.[8] After the election of 1983, the Scottish Conservative MPs numbered only 21, and the strain of manning the Scottish committees was considerable, even with the reduced Scottish Standing Committee.

The total work of the Scottish committees may be further illustrated by the record of a typical session (1968–9) (see Table 14). During that session the Scottish Grand Committee considered (a) 5 Bills in relation to their principle (i.e. second reading debate) at seven sittings; (b) 13 Estimates at six sittings; and (c) 1 Matter at one sitting. The First Scottish Standing Committee considered 4 Bills at thirty-three sittings, and the second Scottish Standing Committee 3 Bills at three sittings.

The Scottish committees are thus very active, and take up a great deal of the time of the Scottish MPs. The Scots are among the most hard-working MPs in terms of committee attendance, and they sit on other committees as well as the Scottish ones. In part, their zeal is due to the relative isolation they feel in London, making them habitués of the Commons. There they find both company and work of interest. The same might be said of MPs from the north of England.

Nevertheless, Scottish MPs are sometimes unable to find time to serve on both Scottish and UK committees, and the latter may be totally deprived of Scottish representation, even when Bills of some importance to Scotland are going through. Thus, the Education (Milk) Bill 1971, which aroused much opposition from Scottish local authorities, went through a committee which contained no Scottish MPs, and so did the Land Commission (Dissolution) Bill 1971. Scottish MPs may be members of two committees sitting simultaneously, and they develop a fine art of travelling swiftly between them to record their votes at divisions. Of course, many of these votes are placed in ignorance of the preceding debate.[9]

The content of Scottish committee work is not very momentous. No Bills are introduced in the Grand Committee which are controversial in a party sense, or have implications for England, and local government affairs dominate. Major Bills dealing with education, housing, local government finance, or industrial development are invariably taken on the floor of the House. Nevertheless, controversial Bills in a non-party sense may go to the Scottish Grand Committee, such as the divorce reform Bill in 1982.

Major party controversy does break out in the Standing Committees, however. Numerous sittings took place on the Social Work Bill 1968, and on the Education Bill 1970. The latter took three months and 75 hours of debate at the committee stage owing to a prolonged filibuster by the Labour group. This led to sittings during the night, and demonstrated the Conservative Government's inability or unwillingness to clamp down on debate by closure or guillotine. Such procedures would have required a vote of 100 MPs, more than the total for the Scottish seats.

This is the crux of the problem for the Scottish political system within Parliament. The Scottish committees give the Scottish MPs the right to discuss Scottish legislation and affairs, but not to overturn the wishes of the government. If the majority of Scottish MPs are of a different party from the government, the result is a sparring-match which can grind the parliamentary machinery almost to a halt. Yet neither party wishes to dismantle the system, and so does not go too far. Labour will not play into the hands of the Nationalists too much by asserting the right of Scotland to determine its own legislation, at least until devolution has been established. The Conservatives, now opposed to devolution, nevertheless feel that Scotland must be given some elements of parliamentary 'home rule' within the context of the overall supremacy of the House.

While some debates in the Scottish committees appear interminable, others might be considered brief. A British (or English/Welsh) Bill will be debated at second reading from 4 p.m. to 10 p.m. on one or more days. A Scottish Bill is lucky to receive two sessions of $2\frac{1}{2}$ hours each in the Grand Committee. Such debates are dominated by the front-bench speakers, who open and close them.

Similarly, Scottish Estimates debates are infrequent in comparison with those for the rest of the country, yet the range of functions covered is great. In all, Scottish Estimates debates do not have the time available to cover in depth the multifarious activities of the Scottish Office; Scottish Matter day debates have covered such subjects as the arts, tourism, gale damage, and Highland transport. Other debates have been on controversial subjects, such as education, housing, agriculture, and local government reform, but even these seem to lack the political impact that a debate in the whole House would achieve. The subjects are chosen by the Government, and are thus calculated to avoid embarrassment. Violent debates on the floor of the House, such as that on Upper Clyde Shipbuilders (2 August 1971), are unknown in the Scottish Grand Committee, which always seems one stage (at the least) removed from the centre of political power. This may be because it can never involve a vote of confidence in the government.

Another inadequacy is the time available for oral parliamentary questions. Each day, almost one hour is devoted in the House to question time, and departments are taken in rotation. Until October 1970, the Scottish Secretary, or other Scottish Office ministers, answered once in every six weeks. This meant that the opportunities for Scottish MPs to get oral answers on such matters as education, health, agriculture, law and order, transport, and local government were far fewer than for English MPs, who could get oral answers practically every day on one of these subjects.

The position of the Scottish Office time rota has been somewhat improved, so that it now comes up once in four weeks. In April 1971 the Government promised to allow Scottish ministers to answer supplementary questions on ministerial statements made by English ministers on matters covering Scotland as well as England and Wales. During that session, the Scottish Secretary had not been able to reply to questions on three occasions when his name had appeared on joint ministerial statements. Such statements are often made on matters such as the health services and agriculture, and yet give rise to different problems for Scotland.

It has become more evident in recent years that the machinery of Parliament has been inadequate to cope with the demands of Scottish legislation and the need to oversee the Scottish Office. The congestion in the committees, the strain on the MPs, and even the meetings in Edinburgh have not enhanced the stature of the Scottish parliamentary system. Scotland has to wait longer than England for some of its legislation, the most recent example being local government reform, which was introduced a year later for Scotland. Law reform has also been slow in Scotland, in part because of the parliamentary situation.[10] Scottish divorce law reform was delayed because the Divorce (Scotland) Bill 1971 was certified as relating exclusively to Scotland, and had to wait in a queue with UK Bills.[11] This is despite the fact that legislation had already been passed for England and Wales. Social reforms, such as those relating to homosexuality, Sunday entertainment, and family planning, are delayed in Scotland because of the difficulty of passing separate Scottish Bills, especially as many are Private Members' measures. It is fair to add, however, that many of the Scottish MPs themselves are not anxious to bring Scotland into line with England in these matters, and obstruct their passage. Moreover, ministerial time and concern may be as involved as parliamentary time.

The practice of inserting clauses relating to Scotland into what are essentially English Bills, instead of producing separate Scottish Bills, has been criticised by Scots lawyers. So too has the lumping together of law reforms in 'Law Reform (Miscellaneous Provisions) Bills' in preference to having separate measures with appropriate and clear titles. All these disadvantage the Scots lawyer, in comparison with the English, since the former must subject his reading of the statutes to elimination and amendment.[12]

The surveillance of government departments by MPs is not well performed by Parliament as a whole, and perhaps even less so by the Scottish members, even with the Select Committee on Scottish Affairs. Scottish questions are often extremely narrow or parochial, and rarely reach the springs of policy formulation. Where departments other than the Scottish Office are involved, the Scottish MPs are swamped by the questions of their colleagues in England and Wales. Even in debates on Bills affecting Scotland, such as the Transport Bill 1967, speeches by Scottish ministers are resented by English MPs, who seek to confine them to the Scottish Grand Committee.[13]

The Scottish committees have undoubtedly improved the position of the Scottish MPs. The Select Committee on Scottish Affairs has been able to get valuable evidence from civil servants on how policy is made in Scotland. But the MPs generally remain remote from St Andrew's House, and raise antagonisms there by the flood of written parliamentary answers which they demand, no doubt as compensation for their weakness in obtaining oral answers and in general debates.[14]

Since the Kilbrandon Commission reported in October 1973, legislative devolution has been firmly on the political agenda, and has been accepted Labour policy since 1974. It is also Liberal and Social Democratic policy, although no longer (at least from 1976 to 1983) Conservative policy. The Conservatives have taken up earlier schemes, originally proposed by Labour, to strengthen the Scottish Committees of the House of Commons, and, as we have seen, sittings in Edinburgh of the Scottish Grand Committee have been introduced, the additional non-Scottish members have been dropped, and extra 'Matter days' have been added. A new Select Committee on Scottish Affairs has been set up, on a more permanent basis than its predecessor.

These reforms represent an attempt to solve some of the problems raised by the demands for devolution within the context of the House of Commons. They of course do not amount to devolution itself, and have been criticised by devolutionists as being no substitute for a

Scottish Assembly, and for providing a smoke-screen for governmental control over the Scottish MPs.[15] However, in a sense these arrangements 'work', however strangely, and until devolution is established, they represent the only outlet for Scottish elected representation in the political system.

6

Political parties and electoral behaviour

The 'homogeneity' debate

The main features of the party system in Great Britain until 1974 were its simplicity and its homogeneity. Two major parties won nearly all the seats in the House of Commons, and captured around 90% of the votes. Moreover, regional differences within the country were not important, since the principal divisions in electoral terms were derived from socio-economic, not territorial, factors. These divisions reinforced the two-party system, which was based on a bipolarisation of society into the middle and working classes. Thus parties appealing to regional or nationalist sentiment did very badly.

As recently as the 1970 election these features seemed to hold good. The two major parties won nearly all the seats in Great Britain, leaving the Liberals with only 6 seats (7.5% of the UK vote) and others with 2 seats (6 if Northern Ireland is included). The only Nationalist success outside Northern Ireland was a single SNP member, for the Western Isles.

The picture altered considerably in 1974, when the two-party system and homogeneity received a powerful blow. Minor parties won 25% of the vote in both elections, and in Scotland they won 30.5% in February and 39% in October. In 1979, the two-party system recovered somewhat. Minor parties fell back to 19.2% of the vote in the country as a whole, and to 27.1% in Scotland. In 1983, the advent of the Liberal-SDP Alliance brought a new 'third-party' challenge to the party system. The Alliance took 25.4% of the UK vote, and 24.5% of the vote in Scotland. The total vote for parties other than Labour and Conservative in the UK was 30.0%, and 36.6% in Scotland.

Scottish political behaviour in the 1970s diverged increasingly from English political behaviour (Miller). This was not only because the SNP vote rose to a higher level than before, but also because the

96

gap between Labour and Conservative in Scotland grew progressively wider than the corresponding two-party difference in England. Thus in 1979, when the SNP vote fell back to 17.3% from 30.4% in 1974, Scotland diverged further from the English pattern of voting because the gap between the Conservative lead over Labour in England and Scotland rose to 21%, its highest yet (Miller, p. 261).* In 1983, this gap rose further to 25.8%.

In this context, it is easy to criticise the validity of the thesis of British homogeneity, which equates British politics with English politics. Books with titles such as *Politics in England* (Rose 1) and *English Party Politics*[1] appeared at a time when stronger regional variations in British politics, notably with regard to electoral behaviour and administration, were already becoming more apparent. Yet these works were not usually intended to distinguish 'English' politics from politics in other parts of Britain. Rather they perpetuated the use of 'England' in place of 'Britain' as a familiar, if inaccurate, substitute-word for the state properly called the United Kingdom of Great Britain and Northern Ireland. In a few instances there is an assumption that English political patterns are reproduced throughout Britain, and may in fact have been grafted on to areas such as Scotland and Wales as a result of political union. Thus Richard Rose, in *Politics in England* (1965 ed), wrote that 'politicians and representatives of Scotland, Wales and Northern Ireland must work within a political system dominated by Englishmen, and assimilate many of their attitudes in order to prosper. Because the central government rules over all four parts of the United Kingdom in varying degrees, it is still customary and correct to speak of British government in conjunction with English society' (p. 26).

Another writer, A. H. Birch, in *The British System of Government* (1st edn, 1967), maintained that 'the distinctions between the English, the Welsh and the Scots are cultural rather than ethnic and do not have many political consequences'.[2] Graeme Moodie, writing from Glasgow in 1961 (*The Government of Great Britain*), asserted that the British constitutional tradition is 'primarily English rather than British, as the Irish, Scottish and Welsh components of the United Kingdom have contributed little, constitutionally speaking, to the system of government'.[3]

These opinions were all expressed before the wave of Scottish

---

*This figure is obtained by adding the Labour lead over the Conservatives (10.2%) in Scotland to the Conservative lead over Labour in England (10.5%). In 1983, the Scottish Labour lead was 6.7% and the English Conservative lead was 19.1%.

97

nationalism in the later 1960s. Since that time students of government have been more conscious of the differences between the national units of the UK, and the renewed troubles in Northern Ireland have emphasised the 'foreignness' of politics in that 'province'. Rose, for example, in 1970, produced *The United Kingdom as a Multi-national State* (Rose 3), which rejected the homogeneity theory, and later produced a book on the politics of Northern Ireland (Rose 4). In 1982 he wrote *Understanding the United Kingdom* (Rose 6), which deals comprehensively with the political differences between Scotland, England, Wales, and Northern Ireland. So too does *The Territorial Dimension in United Kingdom Politics*, which he coedited in the same year (Madgwick and Rose).

It is now difficult to shrug off what happens in Northern Ireland, Scotland, and Wales as having no political consequences for the country as a whole. In the case of Ireland, indeed, the course of events has for centuries had a profound effect on the workings of the British constitution. In modern times, the obstruction of the Irish MPs led to a drastic revision of the procedure of the House of Commons (1882), and the Government of Ireland Act (1920) reintroduced quasi-federal elements into the British constitution. The existence of a separate legal system in Scotland, and a separate Established Church of Scotland, is also constitutionally significant, and, together with the other constitutional and parliamentary arrangements peculiar to Scotland discussed in earlier chapters, forms an essential part of the British constitution.

In a wider political context, the development of political parties in Britain owes something to Scots and to Scottish political thought. Nineteenth-century Liberalism was largely Scottish in origin, in part because of the 'non-conformist' education which Liberal leaders received at Edinburgh and Glasgow Universities.[4] Gladstone, Rosebery, and Campbell-Bannerman were Scottish Liberal Prime Ministers, and Asquith sat for a Scottish seat. The Labour Party may be said to have originated in Scotland, with the formation of Keir Hardie's Scottish Labour Party in 1888.[5] The first Labour Prime Minister was a Scot, Ramsay MacDonald. Although the Conservative Party has appeared more English on the whole, Lord Aberdeen, A. J. Balfour, Harold Macmillan, and Sir Alec Douglas-Home (now Lord Home) are examples of Scottish Conservative Prime Ministers.

The interaction of all the constituent parts of the UK is most clearly seen in the workings of the electoral system. A general election is won by the party which wins the largest number of seats throughout the

UK, not just in England. While this usually ensures that a party with a majority of English seats will also have a majority in the House of Commons, in 1910,1950, 1964, and February 1974 the Conservative Party won most of the seats in England, yet in each case the combined UK result produced a non-Conservative government. In the last resort, then, the English political system (as the Scottish and Welsh systems) is subservient to the British.

These are preliminary correctives to the idea of a self-contained 'English' politics. Yet it is remarkable that Great Britain, despite its 'multinational' diversity, has usually had a predominantly two-party system, in which minor parties or parties based on region, religion, or occupation present no serious challenge. Moreover, the two major parties are well-disciplined, so that their MPs generally obey the party whip in the House of Commons rather than divide into local or other groupings. Far from being a rival to the central party leadership, constituency parties usually support party discipline and reprimand party 'rebels', and these may not be readopted at the next election.

Since there is little scope for a back-bench MP to influence legislation or government policy, it is difficult for him to build up a strong constituency loyalty, which would support him if he 'resigned the whip'. He can rarely point to anything which he personally has been able to obtain for his constituency, a position unlike that in the USA, where congressmen and senators devote much of their time to promoting the economic interests of their districts or states. Their efforts count, since the loose party discipline in Congress means that they can trade their votes on an issue which does not directly concern their constituents for support on one which does. This 'log-rolling' does not exist in the British House of Commons, where nearly all votes are predetermined, and nearly all give the government a majority.

The reasons for the rigidity of the British party system have been well argued in the literature of political science.[6] The principal ones are the electoral system, which by shunning 'proportional representation' discourages minor parties; the responsibility of the Government to Parliament, which leads to the necessity of an assured majority party and a large 'opposition' party; and finally, the homogeneity of the country, which divides the people predominantly on lines of social class rather than by region, ethnic group, religion or urban/rural settlement. Such homogeneity prevents the rise of numerous parties, and has led to two major 'class' parties, supposedly representing the middle and working classes respectively.[7]

While each factor on its own would probably not produce the

British party system, the combination of all three seems to be irresistible. The two-party structure has a long history, despite periodic challenges to its stability. One such challenge came in the 1920s, when the Labour Party replaced the Liberal Party as the second largest party, and the latter slowly declined to its present minor position. Then from 1931 to 1945, Britain had coalition government, which made it difficult to talk of two-party competition for office.

Between 1880 and 1918 the Irish Nationalists posed a great threat to the British party system. Their aim was not to become a party of government at Westminster, but to disrupt the British parties in order to achieve Home Rule for Ireland. It is significant that their emergence related to the lack of homogeneity between Britain and Ireland, and their challenge was resolved by most of Ireland becoming independent.

This would seem to indicate that the key explanation for the British party system is the apparent homogeneity of British society. For the electoral system and the responsibility of government to Parliament could not counteract the political consequences of the social separation of Irish society from the rest of the British Isles. Even today, Northern Ireland has remained socially distinct from Great Britain, and possesses its own party system (it has also become painfully obvious that the Unionists in Northern Ireland are different from British Conservatives).

British homogeneity is not a simple matter, however. We have already seen that it cannot be taken as 'Englishness' spread throughout the land. England itself is intensely regional, with strong social contrasts between south and north, for example. Scotland and Wales add the complexities of national identity and separate political institutions to this diversity. Richard Rose (Rose 3) isolates four major social divisions in the UK which serve to separate its national components, England, Scotland, Wales, and Northern Ireland. These relate to (1) the division between the central and peripheral areas of the state; (2) religious cleavages; (3) urban/rural disagreement; and (4) class antagonism between manual and non-manual workers in industrial centres. In all these regards, Rose believes, the constituent nations of the UK are in conflict, and from this he rejects the 'thesis of the social homogeneity of Britain' (Rose 3, p. 19).[8] He goes on to reject the 'thesis of political homogeneity' as well, 'because of the historical importance of religious issues and national political differences within the several parts of the United Kingdom'. In a larger treatment of this theme (Rose 6), Rose concludes that 'The United Kingdom is unambiguously multinational' (p. 15).

The snag with this argument is that, although such national differences undoubtedly exist, there has been no serious challenge to the British political system from any geographic, religious, or nationalist force, other than Irish, for at least two hundred years (i.e. not since the Jacobites). And while the Irish question is by no means solved, it remains exceptional. The sharp rise in Scottish nationalism in 1974 was not such a fundamental or long-lasting threat to the unity of Britain as appeared at first. The SNP's vote is unstable, having risen and fallen twice during a decade. Moreover, only around one-fifth of the Scottish people supported total independence, according to opinion polls.

This seems to confirm the long-term (if not all the most recent) developments of British political history. Scotland and Wales have shown almost complete loyalty to the British state in times of supreme crisis, such as during the World Wars. It is well-known that Scottish regiments have played an important part in the British army since Napoleonic times. There was very little evidence of disaffection among the Scottish civilian population in the twentieth-century World Wars, although isolated pockets of revolt (e.g. the Clyde in the First World War and some Nationalists in Scotland) did exist. On the whole, Lloyd George and Churchill commanded the loyalty of Scotland, as they did of England.

The same is true of peace-time political leaders. The British party leaders are the best-known and most respected politicians in Scotland, and no Nationalist or other Scottish politician can rival them in this respect (Budge and Urwin, p. 129). While this is partly a result of the superior news coverage which the former command, it is principally the result of the sympathies felt by the vast majority of Scots for the 'image' or policies of the major parties and their leaders. Gladstone, for example, was idolised by Scots (he was a Scot himself, although a 'British' politician), and the current British leaders, with a somewhat different intensity, are the focus of loyalty of Scottish supporters.

The qualifications which must be made to this picture of electoral and party homogeneity come under three headings. First, Scotland (and Wales) differ from England in the electoral strength of the British parties, and in the amount, and sometimes even direction, of the 'swing' from one major party to another between general elections. Second, the British parties are organised separately in Scotland, and to some extent take on a character there which is

101

different from that of the parties as a whole. Third, Scottish nationalism is a direct challenge to British homogeneity, and now commands widespread electoral support.

In this chapter we shall examine the first two of these qualifications to the conventional analysis of British party politics. The third will be dealt with in Ch. 7, since it involves the whole phenomenon of nationalism as well as the specific fortunes of the Scottish National Party.

Electoral behaviour in Scotland

Voters in Scotland until 1974 overwhelmingly supported the British political parties, rather than purely Scottish ones. It can thus be said that political opinion in Scotland divided along lines similar to the divisions in England and Wales, rather than along lines which divide Scotland from the rest of the country. This was a result of the success of the British parties in integrating the political life of Scotland with that of England, or more accurately, in harmonising the special features of Scottish politics with the rest of British politics. Most political issues and political attitudes in Scotland are in fact the same as elsewhere in the country. A large part of social and economic policy-making, and nearly all foreign affairs, is 'British' in the sense that the constituent nations do not form themselves into coherent blocs of opinion which override the divisions between the parties.

There are very few examples in history of the Scottish politicians from different parties coming together to press a Scottish claim in direct challenge to their parties' authority. This is partly because the strength of party discipline inhibits such revolts, but it is also due to the flexibility of the British parties, which can anticipate such demands and accommodate them. Even in the 'nationalist' 1970s, the Scottish representatives of the Conservative, Labour, and Liberal Parties showed few signs of 'log-rolling' to the embarrassment of their parties. The Scottish MPs (with the exception of the SNP members) accepted that the British parties spoke for them.

There are, of course, issues peculiar to Scotland. Such are to be found, for example, in legal matters, education, the Highlands, and religion. Moreover, 'British' problems such as regional economic imbalance, housing, crime, and health may need special policies for Scotland. Scottish attitudes towards these are polarised within the main parties, and governmental action for Scotland follows. The British Parties, rather than separate Scottish Parties, have attempted to deal with such problems. Nevertheless, the unity of the British party system obscures the differences in the Parties' policies in the nations of the UK (further discussion of this point follows, pp. 114–19).

The voters in Scotland, then, are not necessarily expressing the same attitudes as those in England, even when they are voting for the same party. Miller (p. 89; and in Madgwick and Rose, p. 233) discusses the differences between Scottish and English electors in their attitudes to certain issues. While some of these reflect a North-South difference covering all of Britain, others are 'national' in character, marking Scots off from Englishmen, even those in the North of England. Not surprisingly, attitudes towards oil revenues and self-government are examples, but so too are attitudes towards social services, the redistribution of wealth, and comprehensive schools.

Labour voters in Scotland expect a much higher level of subsidy for council-house rents than do English Labour voters. Scottish parties are committed to the state denominational school system which operates in Scotland, but not in England. Opposition to British entry into the EEC was most marked in Scotland in August 1971, according to an ORC survey (62% were against entry, whereas all England except the north and west was in favour (*Glasgow Herald*, 27 August 1971)). (In the Referendum on 5 June 1975, 58% voted Yes, compared with 67% for the UK).

The parties in Scotland do not reproduce the strength of the parties which prevails in England. From 1832 to 1918, Scotland voted predominantly for the Liberal Party (the exception is the election of 1900). England in the same period was much more Conservative. Since the First World War, general elections in Scotland have tended to favour the Labour Party. The largest share of the vote has gone to that party at 12 out of 19 elections. England, on the other hand, has voted predominantly Labour at only 4 elections (see Table 15).

What is the explanation for the difference in voting behaviour in Scotland, as compared with England? In the period from 1832 to 1918, the predominance of the Liberal Party was bound up with the image which that party presented of sympathy with religious non-conformity in England, Presbyterianism in Scotland, parliamentary reform, and agrarian radicalism. The great strength of Presbyterianism in Scotland, the distaste felt for the 'managed' Scottish political system which existed before the 1832 Reform Act, and the rural distress and individualism of the Scottish countryside, all brought most Scots into the Liberal Party.

After Gladstone introduced Home Rule for Ireland in 1886, many

Table 15. *General election results, 1918–83*

Election	UK		Scotland		England	
	% of vote	MPs	% of vote	MPs	% of vote	MPs
1918						
Coalition	47.1	473	52.3	54	52.5	389
Con	6.1	50	2.0	2	3.7	20
Lib	13.0	36	15.0	8	14.7	25
Lab/Co-op	21.4	58	24.7	6	23.1	43
Others	12.4	90	6.0	1	6.0	8
1922						
Con	38.5	344	25.1	13	41.5	307
Lib	18.9	62	21.5	15	19.6	44
Nat Lib	9.4	53	17.7	12	7.3	31
Lab	29.7	142	32.2	29	28.8	95
Com	0.2	1	1.4	1	0.1	0
Others	3.3	13	2.1	1	2.7	8
1923						
Con	38.0	258	31.6	14	39.8	221
Lib	29.7	158	28.4	22	29.9	123
Lab	30.7	191	35.9	34	29.7	138
Com	0.2	0	2.4	0	—	—
Others	1.4	8	1.7	1	0.5	2
1924						
Con	46.8	412	40.8	36	47.6	347
Lib	17.8	40	16.5	8	17.6	19
Lab	33.3	151	41.1	26	32.9	109
Com	0.3	1	0.7	0	0.3	1
Others	1.8	11	0.9	1	1.6	9
1929						
Con	38.1	260	35.9	20	38.8	221
Lib	23.6	59	18.1	13	23.6	35
Lab	37.1	287	42.4	36	36.9	226
Com	0.2	0	1.1	0	0.1	0
SNP	0.01	0	0.1	0	—	—
Others	1.0	9	2.4	2	0.6	3
1931						
Coalition	67.2	554	63.9	64	69.1	455
Ind Lib	0.5	4	—	—	0.2	0
Lab	30.8	52	32.6	7	30.2	29
Com	0.3	0	1.5	0	0.1	0
SNP	0.1	0	1.0	0	—	—
Others	1.1	5	1.0	0	0.4	1

Table 15. (*contd*)

Election	UK % of vote	UK MPs	Scotland % of vote	Scotland MPs	England % of vote	England MPs
1935						
Coalition	53.3	429	49.8	43	54.5	357
Lib	6.8	21	6.7	3	6.3	11
Lab	38.1	154	36.8	20	38.5	116
Com	0.1	1	0.6	1	—	—
ILP	0.6	4	5.0	4	0.1	0
SNP	0.1	0	1.1	0	—	—
Others	1.0	6	—	—	0.6	1
1945						
Con	39.6	210	41.1	27	40.2	167
Lib	9.0	12	5.0	0	9.4	5
Lab	48.0	393	47.6	37	48.5	331
Com	0.4	2	1.4	1	0.3	1
ILP	0.2	3	1.8	3	0.03	0
SNP	0.1	0	1.2	0	—	—
Others	2.7	20	1.9	3	1.6	5
1950						
Con	43.5	298	44.8	31	43.8	253
Lib	9.1	9	6.6	2	9.4	2
Lab	46.1	315	46.2	37	46.2	251
Com	0.3	0	1.0	0	0.2	0
SNP	0.03	0	0.4	0	—	—
Others	1.0	3	1.0	1	0.4	0
1951						
Con	48.0	321	48.6	35	48.8	271
Lib	2.6	6	2.7	1	2.3	2
Lab	48.8	295	47.9	35	48.8	233
Com	0.1	0	0.4	0	0.03	0
SNP	0.02	0	0.3	0	—	—
Others	0.5	3	0.1	0	0.1	0
1955						
Con	49.7	345	50.1	36	50.4	293
Lib	2.7	6	1.9	1	2.6	2
Lab	46.4	277	46.7	34	46.8	216
Com	0.1	0	0.5	0	0.1	0
SNP	0.04	0	0.5	0	—	—
Others	1.1	2	0.3	0	0.1	0
1959						
Con	49.3	365	47.2	31	49.9	315
Lib	5.9	6	4.1	1	6.3	3

Table 15. (contd)

Election	UK		Scotland		England	
	% of vote	MPs	% of vote	MPs	% of vote	MPs
Lab	43.9	258	46.7	38	43.6	193
Com	0.1	0	0.5	0	0.1	0
SNP	0.1	0	0.8	0	—	—
Others	0.7	1	0.7	1	0.1	0
1964						
Con	43.4	304	40.6	24	44.1	262
Lib	11.2	9	7.6	4	12.1	3
Lab	44.1	317	48.7	43	43.5	246
Com	0.2	0	0.5	0	0.1	0
SNP	0.2	0	2.4	0	—	0
Others	0.9	0	0.2	0	0.2	0
1966						
Con	41.9	253	37.7	20	42.7	219
Lib	8.5	12	6.8	5	9.0	6
Lab	48.1	364	49.9	46	48.0	286
Com	0.2	0	0.6	0	0.1	0
SNP	0.5	0	5.0	0	—	—
Others	0.8	1	0.0	0	0.2	0
1970						
Con	46.4	330	38.0	23	48.3	292
Lib	7.5	6	5.5	3	7.9	2
Lab	43.1	288	44.5	44	43.4	217
Com	0.1	0	0.4	0	0.1	0
SNP	1.1	1	11.4	1	—	—
Others	1.9	5	0.2	0	0.3	0
1974 (February)						
Con	38.2	297	32.9	21	40.2	268
Lib	19.3	14	7.9	3	21.3	9
Lab	37.2	301	36.6	40	37.6	237
Com	0.1	0	0.5	0	0.0	0
SNP	2.0	7	21.9	7	—	—
Others	3.2	16	0.0	0	0.8	2
1974 (October)						
Con	35.8	276	24.7	16	38.9	252
Lib	18.3	13	8.3	3	20.2	8
Lab	39.3	319	36.3	41	40.1	255
Com	0.0	0	0.3	0	0.0	0
SNP	2.9	11	30.4	11	—	—
Others	3.6	16	0.0	0	0.8	0

Table 15.   *(contd)*

	UK		Scotland		England	
Election	% of vote	MPs	% of vote	MPs	% of vote	MPs
1979						
Con	43.9	339	31.4	22	47.2	306
Lib	13.8	11	9.0	3	14.9	7
Lab	36.9	269	41.6	44	36.7	203
Com	0.1	0	0.2	0	0.0	0
SNP	1.6	2	17.3	2	—	—
Others	3.7	14	0.5	0	1.2	0
1983						
Con	42.4	397	28.4	21	46.0	362
Lab	27.6	209	35.1	41	26.9	148
All	25.4	23	24.5	8	26.4	13
SNP/PC	1.5	4	11.8	2	—	—
Others	3.1	17	0.3	0	0.7	0

Key:

All	Liberal-SDP Alliance	ILP	Independent Labout Party
Con	Conservative	Ind Lib	Independent Liberal
Com	Communist	Nat Lib	National Liberal
Lib	Liberal	PC	Plaid Cymru (Welsh
Lab	Labour		Nationalists)
Lab/Co-op	Labour/Co-operative	SNP	Scottish National Party

Note: In elections from 1918 to 1945, the universities seats are excluded (3 were Scotland).

Sources: F.W.S. Craig, *British Electoral Facts, 1832–1980,* Parliamentary Research Services (Chichester, 1981); *The Times Guide to the House of Commons June 1983,* Times Books (London, 1983).

Scottish Liberals (and Liberals elsewhere) deserted him for Joseph Chamberlain's Liberal-Unionist Party. The defection was particularly severe in Scotland, owing to the ties with Ireland in trade and the immigrant population. The Conservative Party in Scotland (still 'Conservative and Unionist') has until recently derived its strength in the industrial west from the remnants of this Liberal-Unionist vote.[9] Liberal-Unionists, in the guise of National Liberals or Coalition Unionists, have been particularly strong in Scotland. In 1959, six were elected, but since 1964 none have stood. These were rural, rather than urban, Liberal-Unionists who had been Liberal before 1918.

The main feature of British electoral behaviour after 1918 was the development of class-based parties, with the majority of the working class voting Labour and of the middle class voting Conservative (Butler and Stokes, Chs. 4 and 5). This alignment of political opinion largely replaced that derived from religious affiliation, and so contributed towards the homogeneity of the country in electoral terms. For one of the basic differences between England, Scotland, and Wales is religion, and if this ceases to be reflected in politics, the nations will be drawn together.

At the same time, the development of communications, especially the popular press and broadcasting, broke down localism and focussed attention on the capital and British political issues. It tended to destroy social habits distinctive of the provinces and nations, and thereby consolidated the political trend towards uniformity. Finally, the great increase in government power over affairs previously considered local (e.g. education, health, social security, and industrial development) drew all the lines of political activity towards the ultimate point of decision, the centre.

If this is so, it is surprising that Scotland can still not be considered fully merged within the British 'norms' of electoral behaviour. The voting figures and opinion survey research indicate that Scotland is a strong 'political region' with its own patterns of voting, and that it has tended to diverge more from the British national average than other regions since 1955.

The strength of the Labour Party has already been mentioned. In recent elections this has been greatly exaggerated by the number of seats won, since the electoral system has not rewarded the SNP, the Liberals, or the Alliance in proportion to the votes they have won. Thus in 1970, the percentage voting Labour in Scotland (44.5%) was not very different from that in England (43.2%) and *less* than the Labour vote in Scotland in 1955 (46.7%) and 1959 (46.7%), when the Party was at a low ebb. But the percentage of Scottish seats which Labour won in 1970 (62%) was greatly inflated compared with the English figure (42%). The SNP won 11.4% of the votes, but only 1 seat; the Liberals 5.5% and 3 seats.

Part of the explanation for Labour's ability to win many Scottish seats is to be found in the social composition of the Scottish constituencies. There are proportionally more working-class seats in Scotland than in England. This is because Scotland is more working-class generally than England, but it is also because the way the constituencies have been drawn up gives an even greater bias to the

Labour Party.[10] Lastly, it has been shown that *within* each social class, Scots differ in their voting from the English. Many fewer Scots of all classes vote Conservative in Scotland than voters in England. In particular, a survey in 1979 showed that 50% of the working class in England supported the Conservatives while in Scotland only 24% did so (Rose 5, p. 42). At the same time, Scotland was not as Labour in the working class as two regions in England, the North and Yorkshire and Humberside (Rose 5, p. 40). In 1983, the Conservative vote in Scotland dropped further, with only 16% of the working class (social grades C2, DE) supporting the Party (see Table 18(c), p. 141). In the whole of Great Britain, on the other hand, the Conservatives were supported by 39% of social grade C2 (skilled manual) and 29% of social grade D (semi-skilled and unskilled manual) (*Guardian*, 13 June 1983).

This confirms surveys conducted between 1963 and 1966 by Butler and Stokes. Butler and Stokes applied the Disraelian usage of 'two nations' to the division between the South and Midlands of England on the one hand and Scotland, Wales, and the North of England on the other. These two 'nations' are based on economic rather than ethnic criteria, and mark the separation between the prosperous and backward parts of the British economy. Thus such forces as the level of unemployment, wage-rates, and social environment affect the proportion of the working class voting Labour.

One strong electoral force relates to religion. Budge and Urwin's study (1966) of electoral behaviour in Glasgow, and Bochel and Denver's article (1970)[11] on church and politics in Dundee have brought out the correlation between church affiliation and voting behaviour in these areas. Butler and Stokes (pp. 124–34) and Rose ((2) and (5)) also present evidence relating to the political opinions of those identifying with the Church of Scotland (the evidence for other churches does not isolate Scotland from the rest of Great Britain). Other recent work on religion and voting in Scotland is found in Miller (and Miller in Madgwick and Rose) and Brand (pp. 150–4).

While religion is in general much less political than it was before the 1920s, when the Irish Home Rule issue tended to make Protestants in some areas Unionist, and Catholics and other Home Rulers Labour or Liberal, there is still a legacy from the past in the party preferences of those who identify with the various churches. Around three-quarters to four-fifths of Catholics in Scotland regularly support Labour, while Church of Scotland members are biassed towards the Conservatives. Catholics are only a third to a half as likely to support the SNP as Scots as a whole. Rose concludes that the high Labour support in Scotland among the Scottish working class 'is almost entirely due to the substantial minority of Roman Catholics in its composition' (Rose 2, p. 13). Brand says that 'in areas where there is a large Catholic population, the Nationalist proportion of the vote is likely to be lower than elsewhere' (Brand, p. 153). Thus the Catholic voter contributes in no small measure to the continuity of Labour support in Scotland and to the weakness of the SNP.

Intensity of religious belief (as measured by church attendance) tends to increase the proportion of a church's members who adhere to the party favoured by the majority of the membership. In Scotland, the Roman Catholics are the best Church attenders and also the most devoted to the Labour Party. No doubt their attendance in England is comparable, but their Labour partisanship there is much less marked. Scottish Catholics are concentrated in working-class areas, and this amplifies their class voting. There is considerable acceptance of the view that religion or quasi-religion divides Scots in parts of Scotland along Catholic — Labour and Protestant — Conservative lines.

The presence in west central Scotland, and to a lesser extent in parts of east Scotland (e.g. in Edinburgh and Dundee) of a large Catholic population (rising to nearly half the total population in some areas)[12] has affected the political behaviour of working-class Protestants in these areas. In some cases, a militant Orangeism has developed, which has swelled the proportion of the working class voting Conservative. Although no survey work has yet been done, it is widely believed by observers that certain constituencies are strongly affected by Orange and Green conflicts, which distort 'normal' class voting behaviour.[13] Similar divisions have been found in England, notably in Liverpool.

In these constituencies too, the influence of events in Ireland itself is present. Contacts are maintained between Northern Ireland and Scotland, and occasionally candidates will take a stand on an Irish issue. The principal football rivalry in Glasgow and the west of Scotland is between a 'Catholic' team, Celtic (which sports the flag of Ireland at its ground), and a 'Protestant' team, Rangers (which flies the Union Jack). Such associations are part of the political culture of the industrial west of Scotland. Yet the disunity which such religious cleavages bring about should not be exaggerated. 'Orange' Conservatism is less prominent today than before 1955. Both Catholics and Protestants give massive electoral support to the Labour Party in Glasgow. Although over a third of the Labour vote comes from

Catholics, a greater part must come from Protestants and others.

The most obvious electoral 'deviation' in recent Scottish political history has been the weakness of the Conservative Party. While this was also evident in the period 1832–1918, its most modern manifestation dates from 1955. In that year the Conservative Party had a majority (50.1%) of the Scottish vote and 36 out of 71 seats. By 1966 it was down to 37.7% of the vote and 20 seats, and it reached its lowest since 1923 in October 1974 of 24.7%, with 16 seats. The Conservative Party's share rose somewhat, to 31.4% of the vote and 22 seats, in 1979, then fell back in 1983 to 28.4% and 21 seats.

This débâcle amounts to a huge loss in Conservative support in Scotland in under 20 years, and is unmatched in any other political region in Britain. Labour has been only a partial beneficiary of the flight from the Conservatives in Scotland, since it too declined from its high point of 49.9% of the vote and 46 seats in 1966 to 35.1% of the vote and 41 seats in 1983. Much of the decline in the Conservative vote came from the rise of the Liberals in the 1960s. This was soon overtaken by the rise of the SNP, which in 1974 captured 8 seats from the Conservatives. While the Liberals and SNP apparently took more votes from the Conservatives than they did from Labour at general elections from 1959 to 1970, Labour probably lost more to the SNP than to Conservative in February 1974. This was redressed in October 1974, when Conservative lost more to the SNP than Labour. In 1979, both major parties gained equally from the fall in the SNP vote, but in 1983 the Liberal-SDP Alliance took more heavily from Labour, which reached its lowest percentage of the vote since 1922. Scotland provided three of the SDP's 6 MPs, and five of the Liberals' 17 MPs. The Alliance recaptured areas which the Liberals had won in the 1960s, such as West Aberdeenshire (now Gordon), Ross and Cromarty (now Ross, Cromarty, and Skye), and Caithness and Sutherland. The 1983 election thus represented both a 'breaking of the mould' of the old party system in Scotland, and a reversion to the strong rural Liberalism of the 1960s.

The concept of a uniform swing has been one of the corner-stones of the theories of 'British homogeneity'. At each election, it was found, all parts of Britain produced roughly the same degree of swing between the parties. In 1970, for example, the swing from Labour to Conservative in the regions did not vary from the UK figure by more than 1.8%. In no region did the swing actually go in a direction opposite to that prevailing generally.

In 1974, Scotland seemed to demolish the notion of a meaningful

111

UK swing which is uniform throughout the country. In the February election, because Labour lost more to the SNP than to Conservative, there was a 'nominal' swing from Labour to Conservative of 1.2%. In the whole country there was a 'swing to Labour' of 1.2%. But the figures for swing showed only 'nominal' movements between the two major parties, since they really represented differential loss to third and fourth parties. Thus despite the 'swing' to Conservative in Scotland at the February 1974 election, that party's share of the vote had dropped 5.1% since 1970, and it lost 4 seats to the SNP. In the October election, Scotland showed a 3.9% 'swing' to Labour, compared with 2.3% in the UK. Yet Labour's Scottish total dropped by 0.3% from February, and the SNP's vote rose from 21.9% to 30.4%. In 1979 the swing to Conservative in Scotland was 0.7% (UK, 5.2%), but Labour rose from 36.3% to 41.6%, while Conservative rose from 24.7% to 31.4% (mainly because of differential gains from the SNP, which fell back from 30.4% to 17.3%). In 1983, the swing to Conservative in Scotland was 1.7% but the Conservative vote dropped by 3.0%, while the Labour vote dropped by 6.5%. In the whole of the UK the swing to Conservative was 3.9%, but the Conservative vote dropped by 1.5% and the Labour vote dropped by 11.3%. In this way, one of the pillars of the 'homogeneity' thesis practically collapsed after 1974. For not only did swing lose credibility generally when third and fourth parties were strong, but the Scottish results diverged markedly from those of the rest of the country. The SNP became the second party in terms of votes in 1974, and the disparity between the Conservative performance in Scotland and England grew even greater. The Liberals failed to make any breakthrough in Scotland in 1974 (unlike in England), and the SNP completely eclipsed them as carriers of 'third-party' voting. While it was possible to see the rise of Liberal voting in England as in some way related to similar 'third-party' voting for the SNP in Scotland, by October 1974 it was apparent that the SNP was forging well ahead of the comparable Liberal performance in England. The combined third and fourth party vote in Scotland in October 1974 was 38.7%, while in England the Liberals and other minor parties took only 21.0%. Thus Scotland massively rejected, in its votes, the 'two-party' system and British homogeneity. While the 'two-party' vote recovered somewhat in 1979, as we have seen, 'homogeneity' did not, as the gap between Labour and Conservative widened in Scotland compared with England.

After 1979, the Social Democratic Party, in Alliance with the Liberals, had notable successes in Scotland. Mr Roy Jenkins (who led the Party until 1983) won Glasgow Hillhead (from the Conservatives) in the by-election in March 1982, and retained the seat in the 1983 general election. Ross, Cromarty, and Skye was also gained from the Conservatives in 1983, and Caithness and Sutherland was gained from Labour. The total vote for the Alliance in Scotland was 24.5%, and the 'two-party' vote at 63.5% was almost the same as in October 1974 (61.0%). However, the major 'third party' was now the Alliance, not the SNP, and this clearly represented less of a threat to British homogeneity, since the Alliance was a British political force, and its vote in the UK as a whole (25.4%) was similar to that in Scotland.

Highland political behaviour is probably the least homogeneous with that in the rest of Great Britain (or even Scotland). This is treated in Ch. 13. In Scotland generally there is a separateness in the means of political communication, which gives politics its special 'Scottish' character. Scots learn about politics from their own television programmes, their own newspapers, and their own political conferences – as well as from British ones (see Ch. 11). Butler and Stokes have noted (p. 310) that people whose sources of political information are national (i.e. London-based) are more likely to follow the national swing from party to party at an election. Those whose information has been local (and here Scottish newspapers and television must be considered local) will tend to go against the national tide.

Only a part of the Scottish political behaviour can be explained by differences in political communication, of course. In some elections (e.g. 1950, 1951, and 1966) the Scottish swing was very close to the UK average, while the difference in political communication remained. This would suggest that other factors, especially the economic situation in Scotland, are as influential. Perhaps it is when economic problems of a regional nature become critical (as they did in Scotland generally in the 1960s and 1970s, and in a special form in the Highlands) that the Scottish (or Highland) means of communication become most important. For they focus on such problems, when the British media are dominated by news from the prosperous south of England. This combination of economic disparity and the publicity which it can get in Scotland may well account for many of the recent idiosyncrasies of Scottish political behaviour.

Apart from the SNP, the parties which operate in Scotland are British. In Scotland, however, each takes on a special identity. This identity affects the three cardinal areas of party activity – the making of policy, the choice of candidates, and the winning of elections. The Labour Party and the Conservative Party have, to varying degrees, decentralised their organisations so that each plays a part in the Scottish political system which is separate from its other activities. The Scottish Liberal Party is theoretically quite independent of the Liberal Party in England and Wales, although there is only one Parliamentary Liberal Party. The Communist Party is more unitary, but with a Scottish Committee. Although it is relatively stronger in Scotland than in England in terms of membership (around 5,000 out of the UK total of 19,000), votes, and seats won (there have been two Communist MPs from Scotland), its electoral impact is now negligible (0.1% of the vote in 1983).

The relationship between the parties in the country and the parties in Parliament adds another dimension to the problem of the distribution of political power within them. Constitutional theory demands that no party organisation outside Parliament should dictate to MPs what they must do.[14] In the last resort, then, policy decisions are made in Parliament, not in party conferences. But MPs are elected in constituencies, and would not reach the House of Commons at all were it not for their party affiliation and the efforts of party workers. In practice, there is great unity of purpose between local party workers, the Scottish and British party organisations, and the parliamentary party. Only rarely does one section seek to defy another, and the result is fundamental agreement tempered by occasional compromise or even mild dispute.

Scottish MPs are a separate group in the House of Commons, on account of the specialised nature of their work (Ch. 5). This means that they take the place of their parties as a whole, when, for example, they are debating Scottish legislation in the Scottish Grand Committee. To facilitate a common strategy in such matters, each party has its own Scottish Parliamentary Group organisation, and the Scottish Labour MPs elect their own executive committee, chairman, vice-chairman and secretary.[15] Regular monthly meetings are held to discuss Scottish problems, although these are rarely very influential, or well attended. The major parties, of course, have Scottish whips, who strive to maintain party unity. Scottish MPs, like the rest of their colleagues, must 'obey the whip', as there is no room at Westminster for an autonomous group of MPs within the major parties. Governments make Scottish as well as British policy, and oppositions unite to oppose. The wishes of the Scottish MPs on the government side will be closely heeded, as their support is especially needed in committee. The Scottish Labour MPs in opposition have proved a formidable squadron of minister-baiters and filibusterers. But they do not embarrass their own leaders: if anything, they work harder for their party than other Labour MPs, in terms of committee attendances and votes in divisions.

Away from Westminster, Scottish MPs are more conscious that they are part of a separate political system. This is seen most clearly in the development of Scottish party organisations, which have been established independently of the corresponding bodies in England and Wales.

The origins of modern party mass-organisations are to be found in the late nineteenth century. In England, the National Union of Conservative Associations was founded in 1867, and in 1877 Joseph Chamberlain founded the National Liberal Federation. Each body consisted of a conference of constituency delegates, and tried to assist the constituency associations in winning elections. Later, the conferences attempted to shape policy. but this was checked by the parliamentary leaders.

In 1893, the Independent Labour Party was founded, followed by the Labour Party (then 'Labour Representation Committee') in 1900. The Labour Party was an attempt to *create* a parliamentary party on the basis of a mass-organisation, whereas the Conservative and Liberal organisations came after parties had been established in Parliament.

In Scotland, the development of party organisations proceeded in parallel with that in England, but was significantly separate. The Scottish Liberal Association did not owe its formation to Joseph Chamberlain, and dates from 1882. The National Union of Scottish Conservative Associations was founded in the same year. (In 1912 it merged with the Liberal-Unionists to become the Scottish Unionist Association.[16] In 1965 it was renamed the Scottish Conservative and Unionist Association (SCUA).[17]) Keir Hardie founded the Scottish Labour Party in 1888, which merged with the Independent Labour Party in 1894. The Scottish Trades Union Congress in 1899 sponsored its own Labour Party, which until 1909 operated in competition with the (British) Labour Party.[18] Thereafter, the Scots joined the English and Welsh, and were given some autonomy in the form of the Scottish Council of the Labour Party (established 1915).

The establishment of separate party organisations in Scotland was intended to give the Scots their own conference, where they could discuss Scottish affairs. It was not meant to exclude them from the British conferences of the party, although clearly there would be little time in these for anything exclusively Scottish. In practice, only a few Scottish constituencies could afford to send delegates to England, and to this day Scottish party workers are scarce at the British conferences.

At the Labour Party annual conference usually only a minority of the constituency Labour Parties send delegates, and Scottish trade unionists are represented by British trade union delegates. The Conservative Party conference did not include Scottish constituency representatives until 1977. Only Scottish MPs, candidates, leading officials, some 28 representatives of the Scottish Conservative and Unionist Association who were on the Central Council of the National Union of Conservative and Unionist Associations, and 3 officials of the Scottish Branch of the National Society of Conservative Agents, attended. As a result of the adoption of a report by a committee under Russell Fairgrieve, MP, then chairman of the Party in Scotland, since 1977 constituency delegates from Scotland have been entitled to attend the British conference, with the same rights as other delegates.

The Scottish Liberal Party asserts that it is separate from the Liberal Party, and does not send delegates to the Liberal Party Assembly. Nevertheless, the Liberal Party Organisation Constitution makes provision for the attendance of Scottish delegates, and several Scottish MPs and candidates attend. As David Steel is Leader of the Liberal Party, and also a Scottish MP, the idea of a separate Scottish Liberal Party pertains to constituency and Scottish affairs, not to the Parliamentary Liberal Party. Nevertheless, the establishment of the Alliance with the SDP in 1981 had to be sanctioned by the Scottish Liberal Party conference as well as by the Liberal Party Assembly.

The Labour and Conservative Parties have each devised constitutions giving varying amounts of autonomy or independence to their Scottish conferences. (The Scottish Liberal Party conference has been entirely separate since 1946.) The Labour Party's is the most unitary, since it subjects the constitution and programme of the Scottish Council to the rule that these must be 'within the lines laid down from time to time by the British National Conference of the Party'.[19] In fact these lines are not stringent, for the British conference does not wish to sit upon the Scots. In 1968 the Scottish conference took it upon itself to effectively (though unofficially) abolish the rule that only Scottish affairs could be discussed at the conference.[20] This has allowed delegates freedom to cover British and foreign politics as well as purely Scottish matters, and resolutions on such topics have been sent from the Scottish conferences to the National Executive Committee.[21] Most resolutions at Scottish conferences are on Scottish subjects, however, and the British conference does not often express an opinion on these. The Scottish conference does not have any constitutional power to draw up the policy of the Party: it remains advisory to the British conference. This might have changed had devolution come about, since the Labour Party in Scotland would have fought the Assembly elections with a Scottish manifesto decided by the Scottish conference and Executive. In the absence of devolution, there was restlessness in some quarters of the party in Scotland about the powers to make policy for Scotland. In 1980 a Labour Party Commission of Enquiry looked at Party organisation, and the General and Municipal Workers' Union persuaded the Scottish Executive to press for greater independence for the Scottish Party to make policy and draw up its own manifesto, subject to endorsement by the National Conference or NEC.[22] This was carried at the 1981 Scottish Conference, but the NEC had not moved to change the Party rules by early 1984.

Only occasionally do important Scottish initiatives develop which prove influential: examples are the debates on a Highland Development Board before 1965, and on state Catholic schools in 1971. For many years the Labour Party in Scotland supported legislative devolution to Scotland, but after 1929 this was dropped from its programme. Widespread Labour support for devolution remained, however, but it did not get official approval until August 1974, when a special conference in Glasgow endorsed the setting up of a directly-elected Assembly with legislative powers. The circumstances surrounding this decision were unusual, in that it was the (British) National Executive Committee which had pressed for a Scottish conference on the subject, and which had already stated its support for devolution. This was contrary to a statement of the Scottish Executive rejecting an elected Assembly (*Scotsman*, 24 June 1974). Paradoxically, then, London virtually forced devolution on the Scottish Labour leadership, although the policy was subsequently given overwhelming approval by the mass membership and the principal trade unions (*Scotsman*, 19 August 1974, see also below, p. 146). By 1981, indeed, the Scottish Executive and Conference were

117

calling for much stronger devolved powers (including taxation, economic development, and universities),[23] which the NEC did not endorse until 1983, and which still caused unease among some English Labour activists.

The Scottish Conservative conference is also relatively unimportant in the counsels of the Party. In recent years, however, it has attracted the attendance of more leaders of the Party and has obtained more news coverage than any Conservative regional conference in England. This has encouraged a great increase in the number of resolutions submitted for debate. Some of these debates have been important for party policy in Scotland: the Conservative Leader Edward Heath's speech on Scottish devolution at the 1968 conference, and the substantial majority (3:1) for the Scottish Convention proposal at the 1970 conference, were crucial to the Party's policy on these matters. Thereafter, however, the Party vacillated. The 1973 conference seemed to reject devolution altogether, while the 1974 one accepted only an Assembly made up of local government councillors. Mr Heath's speech at the 1974 conference displayed many new aspects of Conservative Scottish policy (including a Scottish budget and Scottish development fund), and after the October election, the Scottish leadership supported a directly-elected Assembly. But when Mrs Thatcher succeeded Mr Heath as Conservative leader in 1975, she attacked Labour's devolution policy, and this was affirmed at the Scottish conference in 1976. At the 1977 Scottish conference, Francis Pym, the Conservatives' devolution spokesman, described the Party's commitment to an Assembly as 'inoperative' (Miller, p. 242). In this way, the Scottish conference played a subsidiary role to the decision of the party leaders (see also p. 156).

The Scottish Liberal Party's conference has also dealt with devolution and in 1968 the joint assembly with the Liberal Party Organisation revealed a split between the two Liberal 'Parties'. While the Scottish Liberals supported Home-Rule-all-Round, including an English Parliament, the English Liberals preferred to substitute English regional Parliaments. This difference of opinion hardened the rift between the Scottish and English Liberals, and emphasised the separation which had taken place in 1973 and 1976. By the late 1970s, the Scottish Liberals had come to accept that the English regions would be part of the proposed federal system, but they were not prepared to let Scottish self-government wait for the problems of these English proposals to be settled. When the Alliance between the Liberals and the Social Democratic Party (formed in 1981) was

118

established, the Scottish Liberals repeated their insistence that Scotland be treated as a 'nation' and not as a 'region'. The distinction between the Liberal 'federal' plan and the SDP 'devolution' plan was now subsumed under the original term 'Home Rule',[24] but the fact that the Liberals in Scotland consider themselves to be a 'Scottish' party, while the SDP is definitely 'British', is an important aspect of the Alliance in Scotland.

The Scottish party organisations have the function of helping constituencies to choose their candidates and win elections. This is primarily the task of the professional party workers at Scottish headquarters. Since around 1925, Scottish seats have been contested almost entirely by Scots. This has meant that the Scottish organis- ations have taken over from the British ones such influence as is possessed by the party 'apparatus' in the nomination of candidates. Constituency associations (or Area Parties in the case of the SDP, see Table 16) still jealously regard this as one of their main functions, and resent interference with their wishes. Nevertheless, the Scottish party organisations maintain a register of possible candidates and may press a name on a local party. It is significant that this register is distinct from the one maintained by the parties in England and Wales.

Endorsement of Conservative candidates as 'official' is in the hands of the chairman of the Party in Scotland, not the Standing Advisory Committee on Candidates of the National Union of Conservative and Unionist Associations.[25]

Labour candidates are all endorsed by the National Executive Com- mittee,[26] 'with due regard to the recommendation' of the Scottish Executive Committee, which assists in securing such candidates for all Scottish constituencies.[27] A very real power is possessed by the Scottish organiser of the Labour Party, both in influencing nomin- ations and in effecting endorsement.

The winning of votes is the third function of central party organisation. At their Scottish headquarters, the parties maintain a small permanent staff whose job is to gain publicity, raise finance, produce party literature, arrange for conferences and speakers, and improve organisation nationally and in the constituencies (see Table 16). Each party responds differently to this task.

The Labour and Conservative Parties are the most dependent on support from London. The Scottish Council of the Labour Party has a small income (£50,000 in 1982) which is derived largely from affiliated trade unions and constituency parties. These pay fees to both Glasgow and London (just as trade unions pay twice in Scotland if

Table 16. *The Scottish organisation of the Conservative, Social Democratic, and Labour Parties, and the organisation of the Scottish Liberal Party, 1983*

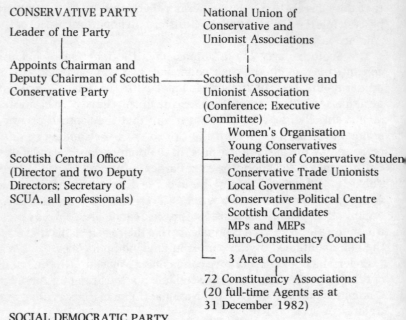

CONSERVATIVE PARTY

Leader of the Party

Appoints Chairman and Deputy Chairman of Scottish Conservative Party

Scottish Central Office (Director and two Deputy Directors; Secretary of SCUA, all professionals)

National Union of Conservative and Unionist Associations

Scottish Conservative and Unionist Association (Conference; Executive Committee)
　　Women's Organisation
　　Young Conservatives
　　Federation of Conservative Students
　　Conservative Trade Unionists
　　Local Government
　　Conservative Political Centre
　　Scottish Candidates
　　MPs and MEPs
　　Euro-Constituency Council

　　3 Area Councils

72 Constituency Associations (20 full-time Agents as at 31 December 1982)

SOCIAL DEMOCRATIC PARTY

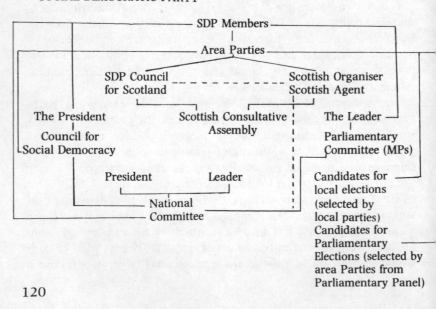

SDP Members

Area Parties

SDP Council for Scotland — — — — — — Scottish Organiser Scottish Agent

The President
Council for Social Democracy

Scottish Consultative Assembly

The Leader
Parliamentary Committee (MPs)

President　　Leader

National Committee

Candidates for local elections (selected by local parties)

Candidates for Parliamentary Elections (selected by area Parties from Parliamentary Panel)

120

Table 16. (*contd*)

LABOUR PARTY

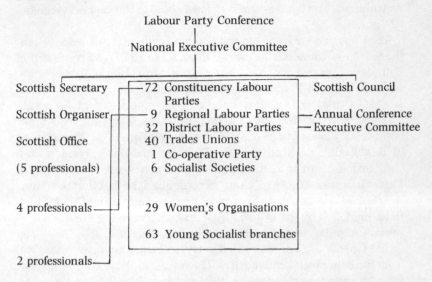

Note: Constituency Labour Parties and Trades Unions in Scotland are also affiliated directly with the (British) Labour Party, to which they pay separate affiliation fees.

SCOTTISH LIBERAL PARTY

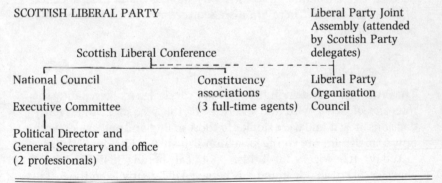

Note: This table is based on information kindly provided by the chief officials of the parties.

121

they affiliate to both the TUC and the STUC). This income does not cover the total expenditure of the Labour Party in Scotland, for the salaries of the Scottish Party officials are paid by the National Executive Committee. During elections, aid is given to selected constituencies by London and is at least equal to the support given by Glasgow.

The Conservative Party organisation in Scotland is divided between the SCUA and the Scottish Central Office. Since 1977, as a result of the Fairgrieve Report, there has been a close integration of these bodies with the London Party organisations. Scottish party income (over £500,000 in 1977) is now handled by London, except for small amounts such as the 'Quota Scheme' in which targets are set for constituency associations (£30,000 was raised in 1978). The salaries of the officials in the Scottish Central Office are paid for by London, and their appointment is in the name of the Party Leader and Scottish Party chairman. The 1977 changes recognised the fact that the Party in Scotland was unable to finance its own operations, and that it had to be supported by the British Party organisation if it were to have a hope of winning back the seats it had lost since 1955.

The Liberals are a decentralised party, and constituencies get no aid from the Edinburgh headquarters. However, some are comparatively wealthy, especially those with sitting members. The SDP, on the other hand, is a more centralised party, and constituencies are given aid from national sources. All the parties produce constituency and Scottish election manifestos, with varying degrees of independence and sophistication. There are also Scottish as well as British party political broadcasts (see Ch. 11).

Conclusion

The British party system until the 1970s succeeded in aggregating the interests of Scots with the interests of the rest of Britain. Party divisions in Scotland were similar to those in England and Wales, with only a small minority voting for a 'non-British' (i.e. Nationalist) party.

Today, the theory of British political homogeneity is under considerable strain. Scotland has behaved differently from the rest of the country at recent elections, most notably of course in its strong support for the SNP, but also in its differential support for the major parties. This calls into question much of the conventional wisdom regarding British politics.

Scottish electoral behaviour has always revealed special features, notably relating to religion, the comparative strength of the parties, the Highlands, and 'swing'. There are also distinctive party organisations, promoting their own conferences and policy resolutions. But all this is within the context of a strong political unity with other parts of the country. The Scottish Conservative and Labour Party organisations, for example, are closely tied up with their UK counterparts. Moreover, politics in Scotland is concerned largely with 'British' issues, and never departs radically from the British political culture, as does that of Northern Ireland. In Scotland, for example, Catholics and Protestants mix easily within the parties, especially the Labour Party.

Nationalism has changed Scottish politics, whether permanently or not it is impossible to say at this stage. Its meaning and strength must now be considered, for it is obvious that no account of Scottish parties and voting behaviour is complete without a full discussion of the SNP, and of Scottish nationalism in all its varieties.

7

Nationalism

In one sense, most Scots are nationalists. They are conscious of their nationality, prefer to think of themselves as Scots, and can attribute characteristics to Scots in general which are different from those of other nations (for example, England).

Surveys in recent years have attempted to quantify these dimensions of national consciousness. In some cases (e.g. Budge and Urwin, p. 113) the form of the question asked excluded the possibility that respondents might say they were British rather than (or as well as) Scottish, English, Welsh, or Irish. Given this qualification, 76% in Govanhill (Glasgow) and 93% in Craigton (Glasgow) thought of themselves as Scots. In 1970, the *Glasgow Herald* reported surveys in which the option of 'British' was offered. In Glasgow, 18% opted for this ('Scottish' 78%), and in other large towns in central Scotland the totals varied from 16% to 24% 'British', and from 75% to 78% 'Scottish' (*Glasgow Herald* 11, 13, 16, 18 March 1970). Further evidence is found in the Kilbrandon Commission's *Attitudes Survey* (Kilbrandon 7, p. 47). 94% of those questioned in Scotland accepted as correct for them the designation 'A Scot'. In the North of England, 92% accepted 'A Northerner'.

In 1979, however, the Scottish Election Survey gave different results. Only 52% of people in Scotland identified themselves as 'Scots', 35% as 'British', 2% as 'English', 1% as 'Irish', and 10% as 'other, mixed, don't know' (Rose 6, pp. 14–15). The change was probably the result of the politicisation of national identity in the devolution campaign (see Ch. 8). Anti-devolutionists wanted to stress that 'Scotland is British', and even pro-devolutionists outside the SNP were conscious of the 'slippery-slope' argument that devolution would lead to independence for Scotland. They too might prefer a British identity to stress that they did not seek independence for Scotland. However, this interpretation does not seem to apply to Wales or England, for despite the 'Britishness' (in the sense of anti-

124

devolution opinion) in these nations, they showed a stronger national identification than Scotland in 1979 (Wales, 57% 'Welsh', 33% 'British'; England, 57% 'English', 38% 'British') (Rose 6, *loc. cit.*).

The 1971 Census shows that 91% of the population of Scotland had been born there, the same figure as for the inhabitants of England (Wales had 81% of its population born there.) Despite the politicisation of national identification during the devolution campaign, which reduced the numbers identifying as Scottish, it is still true that the numbers identifying as Scottish in some way is close to the number of Scots-born. This is because most of the 'British' identifiers wish to combine this identification with a Scottish identification. One indication that this is the case is the near-unanimous support among the Scottish population for 'Scotland' in international sport (see below, p. 129). Another is the easy attribution by Scots of different national characteristics to themselves and to the English (Budge and Urwin, p. 123). Glasgow school-children show a strong awareness of Scotland and things Scottish, though as they grow older they increasingly fit these into a British framework.[1]

Such subjective awareness of nationality has practical results. It colours the relationships of Scots with other national groups, and even in England and other countries most Scots still identify in some way with Scotland. Perhaps as importantly they are identified outside Scotland as Scots if they retain a Scottish accent, or if their origins become known in some other way (e.g. when applying for a job).

In Britain, national consciousness is as deep-seated in England as in the more publicised forms in Scotland, Wales, and Ireland[2], and the reception (occasionally) which the 'lesser' nationalities have throughout history faced in England (cf. Hanham 3, pp. 79–80) has fed their feeling of separateness, and at the same time demonstrated the advantages of assimilation to the majority. Similar feelings are felt by members of any minority group of 'outsiders' (e.g. by those from the north of England living in the south, and by 'lowlanders' living in the Highlands), but these groups do not share the emotional loyalty to a separate nation, which a Scottish education and upbringing have imparted.

Yet on the whole, the assimilation of Scots with English has been relatively easy. From the Union of 1707, the Scottish nobility moved the focus of their activities to London, and began to send their children to English 'public' schools. By the late nineteenth century, some of the Scottish upper-middle class were likewise being educated in such schools, or in near-copies in Scotland.

125

The more general migration of population to England and abroad in the twentieth century has not provided any notable social problems for the receiving countries. As far as England is concerned, Scots have entered the business and professional worlds of London and elsewhere with conspicuous success, and a few have become leading politicians and civil servants. Despite their remaining national identity, they have settled in England in total harmony with the indigenous population, and soon become almost 'as English as the English'.

In Scotland itself national consciousness has far more pronounced results. The whole fabric of Scottish society is now geared to stressing Scottish nationality and the separateness of Scotland from the rest of the United Kingdom. The educational system is one of the strongest influences to this end. Historically derived from the Scottish Reformation, the Scottish parish schools were, until 1872, under the management of the presbyteries of the Church of Scotland. Even today, there is a discernible Church influence in the non-denominational state schools (and a much stronger Roman Catholic influence in the sector of the state system provided for Catholics).

The teaching of Scottish history, social problems, and literature was neglected in the Scottish schools until the 1930s and 1940s. The 'Presbyterian' and early twentieth-century schools were barely concerned with these subjects, except in a semi-legendary form. Nevertheless, national heroes such as William Wallace, Robert the Bruce, and John Knox were familiar to every Scottish school-child, as were the Battles of Bannockburn, Flodden, and Culloden. In this 'history', Scotland faced its enemy England, and was alternately victor and vanquished. Eventually, it merged with England as a partner and became prosperous (very few Scottish historians have attacked the Union and its consequences).

While much of this teaching of history stressed the conflicts between Scotland and England, the period after 1707 (perhaps 1745) was treated as 'non-Scottish'. Anglo-Scottish conflict then became resolved, and Scotland ceased to be different from England. Practically no histories covering modern Scottish developments were used in Scottish schools at this time, and secondary school teaching of history was concerned with 'British' (English in fact), or 'European' history. Similarly, 'English literature' meant what it said. Apart from Robert Burns[3] and a little Scott, there was practically no time for Scottish writers.

What is the explanation for this neglect of national studies (so different from the practice in other nations in the nineteenth

126

century)? In essence it was the desire to assert 'Britishness'. Scots, if they were to succeed (i.e. if they were to prosper in and out of Scotland), must be educated in such a way as to compete with the English on their own ground. They must be conversant at all levels with educated Englishmen, and be eligible for the highest employment in England. To this end, Scotland should be considered as merely 'North Britain'. Even the capital, Edinburgh, should be addressed as 'Edinburgh, NB . In such a climate, there was little room for militant Scottishness in the educational system.

The change to the national consciousness of today is a complex process whose subtleties are beyond the scope of this book (see Hanham 3, Webb, and Brand). Even as 'North Britain' was assimilating to England, nationalists were asserting Scotland's 'claims'. In 1853 a group of literary, clerical, and romantic notables led a short-lived movement to promote Home Rule and the revival of Scottish history, literature, and heraldry. More important was the nationalist movement of the 1880s which drew inspiration from the Irish Home Rule movement. It found a home in the Liberal Party, which from 1894 became committed to 'Home-Rule-all-Round' (i.e. for Scotland, Ireland, Wales, and England).

By this time, most of the radical 'Left' were in favour of devolution. The new Scottish Labour Party and the Crofters Party, in addition to the Liberals, supported it. Not many in the traditional Scottish institutions did so, however. The Church of Scotland, threatened by the Liberal policy of disestablishment, was neutral, and most lawyers (always a Conservative group) stood aside. The nobility, with a few exceptions, were thoroughly North British. Business saw no advantages in Home Rule, nor indeed did the trade unions, since at this time the Scottish economy was healthy, and seemed to be prospering as a result of Imperial and English trading connections. (The trade unions, however, organised themselves into a Scottish Trades Union Congress in 1897.)

There was thus an insufficient groundswell of popular demand for devolution before the First World War, although Private Members' Bills promoting a Scottish Parliament did pass their second reading in the House of Commons in 1908, 1911, 1912, and 1913. The Liberal Government did not give them much support, however (Hanham 3, pp. 97–103; Coupland, pp. 303–6). After the First World War, the Speaker's Conference of 1920 produced respectable Home Rule schemes for the nations of the UK. The Irish sabotaged part of that package, and the Liberal Party was no longer there in strength to

127

carry out the rest. The Scots showed few signs of regret at losing their 'Council' (the name given to the legislature in the 1920 schemes), and were soon plunged into industrial unrest and economic depression, which polarised politics along class lines.

Some of the 'Left' still retained their desire for Scottish self-government, and the Scottish Labour Party remained committed to this until 1929. (The STUC dropped its devolutionary policy in 1931 (Hanham 2, p. 116).) The Labour Governments of 1924 and 1929–31 gave Home Rule Bills no time, however, and most nationalists decided that nothing could be expected from the 'British' parties. (For a full account of Labour and Scottish Nationalism see Keating and Bleiman; also Jones and Keating in Madgwick and Rose.) In 1928, the National Party of Scotland was formed, followed in 1932 by the Scottish Party. These merged in 1934 to become the Scottish National Party (SNP).

The SNP at its foundation was more in the tradition of the 1853 Scottish romantics than of the only-too-close Irish nationalists of the 1920s. There was a strong literary core from the 'Scottish Renaissance', an eccentric nobleman (the Duke of Montrose), and some lawyers (e.g. Professor Andrew Dewar Gibb, and the solicitor J. M. MacCormick). But once more there were few businessmen, trade unionists, churchmen, or 'ordinary people'.

With the advent of the SNP, Scottish nationalism takes on a double aspect. On the one hand, there is the electoral history of the SNP, and the demand for political devolution, while on the other there is the continuing development of Scottish national consciousness in all its forms. The former is a chronicle of 'waves' of support, followed by troughs of decline; the latter is a steady growth to the position today in which national consciousness is to be found throughout Scottish society.

The fortunes of the SNP have of course affected the intensity of national consciousness, but such consciousness is greater than the number of votes won by that party at elections. It is not necessarily concerned, as is the SNP, with 'national self-determination', or with political devolution. It is rather an assertion of Scottishness on the part of an amorphous group of interests and individuals, whose identity is caught up with that of Scotland.

In the first place, there are the historic 'vested interests' of the Union. These comprise the Church of Scotland, the legal profession, and the educationists (universities and colleges as well as schools). Following close behind are the local authorities, the Scottish Office, and the Scottish MPs. These groups are all intrinsically bound up with the position of Scotland, and each in its different way is threatened with pressures of assimilation with England which would render them or their special functions unnecessary. Numerous other organisations with a lesser pedigree of nationality have adopted a Scottish form. These desire to resist assimilation with English organisations, whether for reasons of convenience or from an actual division of interest (see Ch. 12).

The independent position of Scottish football is central to working-class Scottish consciousness (as it is to the teams themselves). The formation of a separate Scottish Football Association in 1873, in contradistinction to the Football Association (1863), indicated the strong separatist feeling among the Scots. They disliked having to travel to England to play the game, and they feared that in that country they would be little fish in a big pond. Today the intense nationalism of Scots at Scotland v. England internationals preserves a semblance of football Scottish ethnicity which otherwise splits into Irish-Catholic and Scottish-Protestant factions behind Celtic and Rangers respectively. The smaller Scottish teams have a vested interest in maintaining separate Scottish League Divisions, since many would otherwise probably disappear altogether from League structure. As it is, they survive intact within the Scottish League, big fish in a small pond, and Scottish teams find a regular place in international matches. Scottish international representation would be difficult to obtain through membership of the English League.

Cultural nationalists make a small but vociferous contribution to Scottish nationalism. They encourage the use of a Scottish means of expression in literature, and cultivate Scottishness in the other arts. A few support the SNP, or political devolution, but most are uninterested in politics, preferring to change Scottish society through education and cultural activities. The SNP, for its part, takes little interest in cultural matters. This is not surprising, since, when asked to choose between 'preserving the traditions and culture of Scotland' or 'improving the standard of living for the people in Scotland', 6% of Scots chose the former, and 91% the latter (ORC survey, quoted in *Scotsman*, 13 May 1974).

Some of the efforts of the cultural nationalists have borne fruit in the radical changes in the content of Scottish education and of the mass media over the last forty years. Scottish history and literature have now become more acceptable to the Scottish Education Department as examinable subjects, and their coverage at schools and universities has accordingly increased. There is now considerable emphasis on modern Scottish history and social problems in Scottish education, from primary schools to research at universities. The press and broadcasting media have become more strongly differentiated from the media in England, and have complemented the educational development (e.g. in the schools broadcasts on Scottish subjects).

The common reference point for most individuals and organisations today is Scottish society, and they defend their interests in terms of the defence of Scotland itself. Thus the Church, law, education, trade unions, and even industry use a species of nationalist argument in their public pronouncements. For example, the workers of Upper Clyde Shipbuilders in 1971 frequently stated that 'Scotland' demanded the maintenance of full employment on the Clyde.

But this kind of nationalism does not necessarily give political benefit to the SNP. Most Scottish interests find the existing political structure adequate as a channel of communication, and do not combine to press for a change in the system. This is partly because it is able to deal with a wide range of Scottish demands without reference to the British system. And where reference must be made to that system (as in economic policy), Scottish opinion is able to find sympathy from non-Scottish quarters. Thus in the Upper Clyde Shipbuilders' affair, the whole Labour movement expressed support for the Scottish workers. (That this solidarity may be breaking down can be seen in the competing interests between Scotland, Wales, and England in shipbuilding and steel cutbacks in the early 1980s, when Scottish workers were not generally supported by workers in Wales or England.)

Even in areas where 'Anglicisation' is the issue, there is rarely an overt attack on Scottish institutions from England. Instead, there is a Scottish and an English division of opinion among the Scots themselves. Examples are the disputes over educational curricula,[4] bishops in the Church of Scotland,[5] and assimilation of Scots Law to English Law.[6]

The affairs of these 'arenas' of Scottish life hardly bear on the fortunes of the SNP at all. Instead, the state of the SNP depends mainly on the performance of the Scottish economy (actual or potential) in relation to that of England, and to the 'credibility' of using an SNP vote as a pressure on government to improve economic conditions in Scotland. It is also related to the SNP's credibility as the vehicle for achieving devolution or self-government.[7]

The waves of nationalism since the founding of the SNP bear out these conditions. The first, in the early 1930s, came at a time of severe depression in Scotland and when the Labour vote had collapsed as a result of the formation of the National (Coalition) Government. A vote for the SNP in this confused political situation was as politically effective as a vote for a major party (though not many in fact decided to follow that course in the few seats which the Party contested – see Table 15, pp. 104–5).

A similar suspension of normal party politics occurred at the end of the Second World War, when Dr Robert McIntyre won Motherwell at a by-election (April 1945). The SNP's success was largely due to the wartime party 'truce', which meant that the Conservatives did not contest the seat.

In the late 1940s there was a second nationalist wave, although this time the SNP played a minor role. The principal nationalist body was the extra-parliamentary organisation, the Scottish Convention, which organised a mass petition (the Scottish Covenant) in 1949, to demand a parliament for Scotland 'within the framework of the United Kingdom'. Two million people are reputed to have signed this document.

Once more, the nationalist mood was brought about by economic stringency, in the form of the 'austerity' measures of Sir Stafford Cripps, the Labour Chancellor of the Exchequer. But the two-party system was not weakened as in the 1930s, and the voters in Scotland swung to the Conservatives in the 1950 election, in much the same fashion as those in England (2.6% compared with 3.0%). As for the SNP, all three candidates lost their deposits (so did six other Home Rule candidates). The Conservative Government in 1952 responded to the wider evidence of the Scottish Covenant that something was amiss by establishing the Balfour Commission on Scottish Affairs (1952–4) and minor administrative changes followed its report.

Economic conditions in Scotland in the early 1950s were apparently no worse than in England, nor was the party system so out of joint that an SNP revival could be expected. But the Covenant had shown that nationalism was a powerful sentiment, and could be used successfully for political ends. This, however, took attention away from the SNP as the vehicle for constitutional change. Pressure was still being put on the major parties, and it was more credible to sign a Covenant to achieve Home Rule than to vote for the SNP.

The late 1950s were the start of the third nationalist phase. The economic and party-political conditions now came together to help the SNP. Scottish unemployment rose to a level well above that in

131

England, and emigration increased. Wages rose relatively slowly, and the decline of the older, heavier industries was more pronounced than in most parts of England. New industry could not compensate for the loss of jobs which this entailed (McCrone 1, 2). The environment in Scottish cities seemed poor in comparison with that in English cities, especially in housing, school-building, and amenities.

Comparisons between the situation in Scotland and that in England were made as a result of the Conservative campaign in the 1959 general election, which stressed the new affluence of British society. The spread of television, particularly commercial television with its advertising appeals to this affluent society, no doubt emphasised the contrast. Scots knew that much of the new affluence had passed them by. In the election, they swung from Conservative to Labour, against the overall trend.

Then in two by-elections in the early 1960s (Glasgow, Bridgeton in 1961, and West Lothian in 1962), the SNP achieved 18.7% and 23.3% of the vote respectively. The party's candidate at Bridgeton, Ian Macdonald, was so encouraged by the result that he decided to offer his services as full-time organiser of the SNP. From that time, a third factor was added to the economic and political preconditions for Nationalist electoral success – organisation. Macdonald built up the grass-roots organisation of the SNP by aiding the formation of branches, raising finance, and maintaining an efficient central office. Soon membership was rising fast, and the new activists seemed more practical, and less romantic, than those in the Party in former years. One of them, William Wolfe, a local businessman, contested West Lothian in 1962. In 1969, he became chairman of the Party.

While later by-elections in this period (1959–64) were by no means equal to this showing (partly because the Liberal revival stole the Nationalists' thunder), in the general election of 1964 there were 15 SNP candidates, a three-fold increase compared to 1959. Wolfe greatly increased his vote in West Lothian, coming second in the poll, but there was as yet no evidence that the SNP was a political force in the industrial heartland of Scotland.

In the 1966 election, in the four major cities the SNP lost all its deposits, and elsewhere achieved second place in only 3 seats (Kinross and West Perthshire, West Stirlingshire, and West Lothian). The average SNP vote in the 23 seats it contested was 14.5%, amounting to 5% of the Scottish total.

The years from 1966 to 1979 are now legendary in Scottish political history. A substantial literature[8] has been written which describes

132

and analyses the fortunes of the SNP. Much of this literature has been of a polemical nature, written in the heat of battle by protagonists. Other contributions, by political analysts, are often marked by conclusions and predictions which events have since proved false. Perhaps it is even now unsafe to be too certain about the meaning of Scottish politics during that period.

The chronicle of events is clear enough. The first by-election after 1966, at Glasgow, Pollok, in March 1967, showed an SNP vote of 28%. This had been a marginally held Labour seat, and it now fell to the Conservatives. In May 1967, the municipal elections were contested by a large number of SNP candidates, who won 16% of the votes and gained 23 seats. The climax came at the Hamilton parliamentary by-election in November 1967, when the SNP actually won the seat, with 46% of the vote. In this 'safe' Labour seat, the Labour vote fell from 71.2% to 41.5%. The Conservative vote dropped from 28.8% to 12.5%. Interest in the election was obviously high, for the turn-out (73.7%) was slightly above that at the general election.

The shock this result created in Scottish politics was renewed at the municipal elections in May 1968, when the SNP won 30% of the vote, gaining 100 seats. In Glasgow, the Party held the balance of power between the Progressive/Conservative ruling group and the Labour Party.

There then came a decline. No further by-elections took place until October 1969 (Glasgow, Gorbals), when the SNP vote fell to 25%. The local elections in May 1969 had already shown that the tide was turning, with the SNP vote at only 22%, and 20 gains. At the last by-election before the 1970 general election (South Ayrshire) the party polled 20%, and the vote at local elections in May 1970 (12.6%) was similar to that at the general election the following month (11.4%). In that election the SNP lost Hamilton, but gained the Western Isles. Although it lost 43 deposits (a deposit is lost when a candidate gains less than 12.5% of the vote), it came second in 9 seats.

The period immediately after 1970 showed that while the Party had dropped down from its 1968 peak, it was not entering a sharp decline, and was able to make a massive recovery in 1973 and 1974. At the Stirling and Falkirk by-election in 1971 it came second to Labour with 35%, and at the Dundee East by-election in March 1973 was within 1,141 votes of winning that 'safe' Labour seat. Victory finally came at the Govan (also safe Labour) by-election in November 1973, which was won by a majority of 571. The Party's performance in local elections after 1970 was not generally impressive, however, and all the SNP councillors in Glasgow had lost their seats by 1972. At the regional and district elections in May 1974 there were few SNP candidates, and outside the Central Region the Party did badly (5/103 councillors in Strathclyde; 0/53 in Grampian, despite having 3 MPs there; 9/34 in Central).

Meanwhile, there had been a big advance at the general election of February 1974. Building on the confidence gained at the 1973 by-elections, and on its strength in seats where it came second in 1970, the SNP was able to mount a campaign in 70 of the 71 seats (the exception being Jo Grimond's Orkney and Shetland). Six seats were gained (Aberdeenshire East, Argyll, Banffshire, Clackmannan and East Stirlingshire, Dundee East, and Moray and Nairn) and one (Govan) lost. The Western Isles was held with a greatly increased majority. Four of the gains were from Conservative and two from Labour. Then in October 1974 another four seats were gained from the Conservatives (Angus South, Dunbartonshire East, Galloway, and Perth and East Perthshire), making a total of 11 MPs. The Party's share of the Scottish vote rose to 30.4% (it had been 21.9% in February), and it was now the second largest party in Scotland. No deposits were lost, and second place was secured in 42 of the 71 Scottish seats. It was easily the biggest nationalist advance in recent British electoral history.

After 1974, and until 1978, the Party continued to do well (25–35%) in local elections and in opinion polls. There was no parliamentary by-election in Scotland until April 1978, by which time the Labour Government had introduced its devolution legislation in Parliament. Thus the credibility of using an SNP vote to achieve devolution was diminished when Labour was the party in office which was attempting, albeit with great difficulty in the House of Commons, to deliver a Scottish Assembly. Nevertheless, commentators and politicians had expected that the SNP would continue to grow (see, for example, Webb, p. 109, and Brand, p. 147), and its failure to win the by-elections in Garscadden and Hamilton in 1978 marked a distinct turning-point in its fortunes. The Party's decline was confirmed when its vote in the general election of 1979 dropped to 17.3% from the 30.4% it had won in October 1974. Opinion polls from 1979 to 1983 put the Party at below the 1979 level, although at by-elections after 1979 the Party secured a higher share of the vote than it had gained in these seats in 1979 (see Table 17). In the general election of 1983 it sank back to its 1970 level, with 11.8% of the vote. It kept its two seats (Western Isles and Dundee East) occupied by the Party leaders Donald

Table 17(a). *Change in the SNP vote at general elections, 1955–83*

	No. of votes	No. of candidates	% of Scottish poll
1955	12,112	2	0.5
1959	21,738	5	0.8
1964	64,044	15	2.4
1966	128.474	23	5.0
1970	306,802	65	11.4
1974 (Feb.)	633,180	70	21.9
1974 (Oct.)	839,628	71	30.4
1979	504,259	71	17.3
1983	331,975	72	11.8

Table 17(b). *The SNP vote at Parliamentary elections, 1966–82*

		% of votes cast
1966	General election	5.0
1967	Glasgow, Pollok by-election	28.2
	Hamilton by-election	46.0
1969	Glasgow, Gorbals by-election	25.0
1970	South Ayrshire by-election	20.3
	General election	11.4
1971	Stirling, Falkirk and Grangemouth by-election	34.6
1973	Dundee East by-election	30.2
	Glasgow, Govan by-election	41.9
	Edinburgh North by-election	18.9
1974	February general election	21.9
	October general election	30.4
1978	Glasgow, Garscadden by-election	32.9
	Hamilton by-election	33.4
	Berwick and East Lothian by-election	8.8
1979	General election	17.3
1980	Glasgow, Central by-election	26.3
1982	Glasgow, Hillhead by-election	11.3
	Glasgow, Queen's Park by-election	20.0

Stewart and Gordon Wilson, but it lost 53 deposits, and came second in only seven seats.

Obviously, an analysis of the SNP 'phenomenon' is essential to an understanding of the Scottish political system and the nature of Scottish nationalism. The task is, however, not an easy one, not only because the SNP 'rose and fell' twice in the period 1960–79, in differing circumstances, but also because of the wide range of

135

academic (and other) interpretations which have been put on these events.⁹ There are many theories relating to the subject, and there is a large body of survey evidence and narrative history which cannot be reproduced here. For this, reference should be made to the works cited. Moreover, the subject of nationalism merges at times with the subject of devolution, although most devolutionists outside the SNP try to keep them apart. In this edition, a separate chapter (Ch. 8) is devoted to devolution, although it is recognised that the links between devolution and nationalism are close.

Most explanations of Scottish nationalism are really explanations of the votes cast for the SNP. This is of course a narrower definition of Scottish nationalism than the one adopted earlier in this chapter, which included such things as national identity and national consciousness in non-political matters such as education and sport. Measuring the votes for the SNP is a much easier task than measuring Scottish nationalism generally, yet most people assume that the two things are much the same. When the SNP vote rises, it is considered that Scottish nationalism rises, and when the SNP vote falls, Scottish nationalism is said to fall too. There is some evidence, mentioned before, that Scottish national identification did apparently fall with the fall in the SNP vote, and with the 'politicisation' of devolution, but it is not clear that other kinds of Scottish nationalism did so too. For example, the amount of support for devolution and independence is not a simple reflection of the ups and downs of the vote for the SNP, although it is connected (see Miller).

If one concentrates on the SNP vote alone, there are broadly two approaches which can be used, a 'structural' one, and a 'behavioural/rational choice' one. In the 'structural' approach, voting for the SNP reflects the changing structure of Scottish (and British) society. In the 'behavioural/rational choice' approach, Scots vote for the SNP because they wish to achieve some end, whether it be independence for Scotland, devolution, more attention for Scotland, or just to 'protest' against the choices offered by the other parties. Some explanations combine both of these approaches, and seek to relate the behaviour of voters to the structure of society. Others assert that structure and behaviour cannot readily be linked together.

Those books and articles which were written when the SNP vote was at its height (1967–9, 1974–8) stress the 'strength' of Scottish nationalism; those which were written when the SNP vote had fallen (1970–3, after 1979) see its 'weakness' or are ambiguous about the SNP's future prospects. This should make us wary of jumping to conclusions, and should help to distinguish short-term effects from long-term ones. In the short term, SNP voting has changed in strength rapidly; in the long term it appears to come in waves which are rising higher with each successive wave. For example, the wave in 1974–8 was greater than that in 1967–9.

Relating the votes to the structure of society is difficult, since structural changes, unlike changes in votes, do not take place rapidly. Nevertheless, many theorists try to establish such a relationship. Tom Nairn uses a Marxist approach to explain the development of Scottish nationalism in terms of the interplay of economic and cultural forces in the British state, which he claims has reached a point of 'break-up'. His book first came out in 1977, when the SNP was at its height. He revised it in 1980, when the SNP had declined.[10] His focus is on nationalism in general terms, and he does not discuss SNP voting in detail, although he assumed in 1977 that such voting was an indication of how Scottish nationalism would lead to the 'break-up of Britain'. By 1980, Nairn no longer considered the SNP to be the vehicle of such a break-up, yet he continued to stress the strength of Scottish nationalism, and to explain it with reference to uneven capitalist development in Britain and the exploitation of Scotland in the British state. A somewhat similar approach by Michael Hechter explains Scottish nationalism in terms of 'internal colonialism'.[11] In this analysis, Scotland and other 'Celtic' areas are seen to be colonies within Britain, and nationalism arises as a reaction to this exploitation.

Many writers relate the rise of the SNP to the state of the Scottish economy, and especially to its run-down character compared to the prosperous parts of England. The SNP does well, according to this argument, when Scotland is seen to be doing badly relative to the rest of Britain. This is a mixture of a 'structural' and a 'behavioural' explanation, and it brings into play the sense of 'relative deprivation'. The link between 'actual' deprivation (e.g. high unemployment) and 'relative' deprivation (feeling deprived compared with others) is complex, and the link between both forms of deprivation and SNP voting is even more obscure. In the first wave of SNP voting, Scotland appeared to be an area in decline. In the second wave of SNP support, the discoveries of North Sea oil gave the promise (and some actuality) of Scottish prosperity relative to the rest of the country. Scots were pessimistic in the first period, and optimistic in the second. The SNP did better in the optimistic period, although it could be said that a sense of 'relative deprivation' was present in both cases, since even in their 'optimism' Scots feared that they would not reap the benefits of the new-found wealth around their own shores.[12]* For example, in an ORC survey (*Scotsman*, 4 October 1974), 68% in Scotland thought that Scotland would probably get very little from the North Sea oil discoveries, since it would all go to the oil companies and the British Government. The same percentage believed that 'the oil in the North Sea should be used to benefit all of Britain and not just Scotland alone', but 58% supported the view that 'the oil in the North Sea belongs to Scotland, and the tax revenue from it should be used for the benefit of the Scottish people'. Despite the new-found oil wealth, only 39% thought that Scotland would soon be strong enough economically to be independent of the rest of Britain, and 49% disagreed. Nevertheless, 57% thought that Scotland had much better economic prospects than other parts of Britain.

Many commentators have linked the discovery of North Sea oil with the rise in the vote for the SNP in 1973–4. Certainly, they came together, and the SNP campaigned in 1974 on the slogan 'It's Scotland's Oil'. But Miller has suggested that SNP growth was not *caused* by the impact of North Sea oil. Rather, it was only one factor which removed the constraints on voting SNP among people already supportive of 'self-government' ('Oil and, by extension, the feeling that Scotland could "go it alone economically" cannot be seen as more than a constraint breaking influence that reduced the perceived costs of an already desirable objective'[13]).

This connects with the 'protest vote' explanation of SNP voting, which Miller also rejects. A 'protest voter' is assumed to be so discontented with his own party (but not attracted to the other major party) that he votes for a third party (in this case the SNP) in order to shock his own party into changing its ways. This vote is typically cast at by-elections, and the voter returns to his own party at a general election. The protest voter does not support the policies of his adopted party, nor does he identify with it.

At first sight, this explanation of SNP voting seems to fits the facts.

---

*But see Roger Brooks, 'Scottish nationalism: Relative deprivation and Social mobility', unpublished PhD thesis, Michigan State Univeristy, 1973. Brooks argues that SNP supporters are not conscious of personal relative deprivation, and many see themselves as upwardly mobile. Yet they share a feeling that Scotland *collectively* is deprived. This fits the hypothesis that the SNP does best in areas of fast social change (New Towns, oil-boom areas), where incomes are higher and class divisions less important, and least well in more static communities (e.g. large towns in central Scotland). Support for the SNP in 1974 was particularly strong in social class C1 (skilled non-manual), and most of the activists are middle class.

By-election victories in 1967 in Hamilton and in 1973 at Glasgow, Govan were overturned at the subsequent general elections. Surveys showed that only a minority of SNP voters favoured the Party's policy of independence for Scotland, or identified with the Party, or cast their votes for it consistently at successive general elections.

Miller argues, however, that there is a strong correlation between the desire for self-government and support for the SNP. Very few supporters of the constitutional status quo support the SNP; nearly all SNP supporters want devolution or independence. They are thus voting positively, not negatively, for a party which corresponds with their desires. In other words, they are choosing 'rationally'. (Another type of 'rational' voting is 'tactical voting', whereby supporters of a major party lying a poor second in a constituency switch to a third party if it has a good chance of ousting the incumbent. This fits SNP voting in several Scottish constituencies in 1974, for example by Labour supporters in Moray and Nairn and Conservative supporters in Dundee East.)

These theories do not, however, explain the decline in the SNP vote. Why did the SNP vote fall from its peak in 1974–6 to almost half that level in 1979, and continue to fall afterwards? Does this show that it had been a protest vote all along? The answer must be that it does not. The connection between support for the SNP and support for self-government remained as valid in 1979 and after as it did in 1974, but what Miller calls the 'natural' support for the SNP (those who identify as Scots and who desire Scottish self-government, however defined) is now shared between the SNP and Labour and the Liberal-SDP Alliance. These other parties are as 'credible' a vehicle for self-government (meaning devolution) as is the SNP, and so those who desire devolution can rationally cast their votes for them. As long as they can appear to be able to deliver devolution, then, they can expect to be supported by Scottish devolutionists. If they cannot, then the SNP should recover, Miller argues, and some Scots might turn to political violence (Miller, p. 263). A permanent Conservative Government in Britain faced with a Labour Scotland demanding devolution would encourage such extremism, in Miller's view.

This prospect seemed to be verified by the 1983 election result, and a group of Scottish Labour MPs then threatened to use obstructive tactics in Parliament because they believed that Scotland had not given a 'mandate' to the Conservatives to govern Scotland. These strong devolutionists did not, however, have the support of their Scottish colleagues generally for such tactics, and the legitimacy of a

British election result is accepted by the Labour Party as a whole. Any idea of a separate 'mandate' for parts of the UK is not part of Labour philosophy, but there is a growing tendency within the Labour Party in Scotland to talk in such terms, and this has made Labour in Scotland much more of a 'nationalist' party since 1979. The SNP, meanwhile, has become a mere spectator of this new nationalism, and has been unable to regain the initiative.

A profile of the electoral support for the SNP can be obtained from surveys. In May 1974, when the SNP was reaching the top of its second 'wave', the Party was particularly strong among young

Table 18(a). *Voting intention by class, age, and sex, May 1974*

	Total %	Class				Age			Sex	
		AB %	C1 %	C2 %	DE %	18–34 %	35–54 %	55+ %	Male %	Female %
Con	29	57	41	21	19	19	31	36	21	35
Lab	38	13	21	43	49	35	36	43	42	35
Lib	8	10	8	10	6	8	10	5	8	8
SNP	26	20	28	25	27	37	24	15	28	24
Others	1	—	1	1	1	2	—	1	2	—

Table 18(b). *Voting intention by class, age, and sex, March/April 1979*

	Total %	Class				Age			Sex	
		AB %	C1 %	C2 %	DE %	18–34 %	35–54 %	55+ %	Male %	Female %
Con	29	61	44	24	22	25	27	38	28	32
Lab	45	15	29	49	54	39	45	48	45	43
Scottish Lab	2	*	2	2	1	3	2	*	3	1
Lib	6	11	5	4	7	5	7	6	6	5
SNP	19	13	20	21	16	28	19	9	18	19
Others	—	—	—	—	—	—	—	—	—	—

(* = less than 1%)
Note: The figures above excluded those who were undecided, refused to answer, or would not vote. These were 18% of the total sample in May 1974, and 19% of the total sample in March/April 1979.
Source: System Three Scotland.

Table 18(c). *Voting intention by class, June 1983. (Note: Figures for age and sex were not available)*

| | Total % | Class | | | |
		AB %	C1 %	C2 %	DE %
Con	26	50	41	16	16
Lab	40	11	24	49	55
SDP-Liberal Alliance	23	31	26	24	15
SNP	11	8	10	10	14
Other	*	—	—	*	—

(* = less than 1%)
Note: The figures above exclude 15% of the sample, comprising 9% undecided, 3% refused to answer, and 3% will not vote.
Source: System Three Scotland.
For the actual voting figures in the general elections of 1974, 1979, and 1983, refer to Table 15.

voters, and its support was spread fairly evenly across the social classes (Table 18(a)). In 1979 and 1983, the SNP lost much of its vote, but the spread across the social classes remained (see Table 18 (b),(c); also Rose 5, p.42). At all times it seems to have attracted defectors equally from the major parties, although this varies from constituency to constituency. Up to 1974 it seems to have appealed to first-time voters or previous abstainers. Its declining support after 1978 was particularly marked among young voters and New Town voters, many of whom had consistently supported the party since the late 1960s. The reasons for the decline in the SNP's support have already been touched on. They relate to the credibility of using an SNP vote to achieve devolution, and to the changing party system in Britain. With regard to the latter factor, the polarisation of the major parties into Left and Right, and the emergence of a new 'third party', the SDP, removed some of the attraction of the SNP. SNP voters are distinguished by their 'balanced trust' or 'balanced distrust' of the major parties (see Miller, pp. 159–60). By 1979, and even more so by 1983, the two major parties were becoming very different from one another, and this 'balanced trust' was less common. In addition, the SNP's own political image became more extreme after 1979. It decided to abandon its support for devolution as a 'half-way house' towards independence, and to go for independence direct. It flirted with civil disobedience, and it came under pressure from socialists within its ranks (including the ex-Scottish Labour Party leader, Jim Sillars) to adopt a socialist policy. The socialist '79 Group' was expelled from the Party in 1982, but the damage was done. The Party was now seen as more militant, divided, and unpopular with moderate or right-wing voters, and the new Liberal-SDP Alliance was attractive to such people. In 1983, the SNP did badly in constituencies where the Alliance did well.

Nevertheless, the SNP is still a strong political party with an

Table 19(a). *The organisation of the Scottish National Party, 1983*

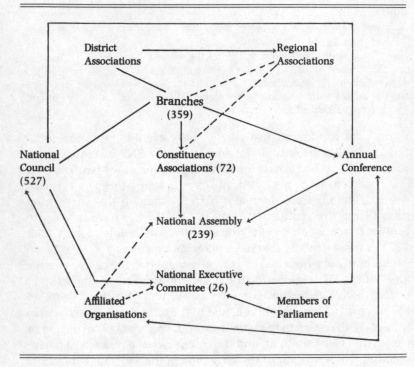

Table 19(b). *Membership of the Scottish National Party, 1962–83*

1962	2,000	1966	42,000
1963	4,000	1967	80,000
1964	8,000	1968	120,000
1965	16,000 (June)	1971	70,000
1965	20,000 (November)	1974	85,000
		1983	c.20,000

efficient organisation. Its former successes owed a great deal to the style of its campaigning, with catchy slogans, posters, and 'personalities' such as Winnie Ewing, Margo MacDonald, George Reid, and Jim Sillars. By 1983, however, nearly all of these had either left the Party or had taken jobs in the media which required them to be politically neutral. Only Winnie Ewing remained of the former 'populist' leaders, but as a Euro-MP, not a Member of the British Parliament. Her attempt to get back into Parliament in 1983 for Orkney and Shetland ended in failure when she came third after the Liberal-Alliance candidate (who won comfortably) and the Conservative. At the grass-roots, in its heyday, the SNP had more members than other parties, although the figures quoted in Table 19 (b) are at times exaggerated. Even so, well-attended rallies, motorcades, and social functions were a feature of SNP constituency politics, and other parties had to follow suit to retain public and media attention.

The SNP has been described as a decentralised party, and its strength is in its local branches (not constituency associations). By 1967, such branches had been formed throughout Scotland, although many had small memberships. While it is true that policy tends to be less tightly controlled by the party managers of the SNP than it seems to be in other parties, organisational decisions have been quite centralised.[14] The party's financial income has varied with the number of its members, but there have also been some large gifts and legacies, one of which (administered by the Neil Trust) amounts to £250,000, to be used for election purposes.

The effect of the SNP and Scottish nationalism generally on political opinion is seen in the stance taken on devolution by other parties. Whilst this is directly related to the electoral threat posed by the SNP, it also derives from a more general 'conversion' of opinion in Scotland to devolution, and to a generally heightened national consciousness in Scotland since the 1960s. The subject of devolution is treated in the next chapter.

8

Devolution

Devolution, or 'Home Rule', is a very old issue in Scottish politics. As we saw in the last chapter, it dates back to at least the middle of the nineteenth century, and was adopted as a policy by the Liberal Party in Scotland in 1888.

In its most recent phase (from the 1960s), as well as being the policy of the Liberal Party, devolution has been successively espoused by the Conservative Party, the Labour Party, the short-lived Scottish Labour Party, and the new Social Democratic Party. The SNP supports independence but also campaigned for devolution in the 1970s. However, since many of these parties have at one time supported, and at another opposed, devolution, the history of devolution is complex and baffling (accounts can be found in Bochel *et al.*; Bogdanor; Drucker and Brown; Keating and Bleiman; Miller; and Rose 6, pp. 187–203). So too is the story of the shifts of opinion on the subject among the electorate and among the principal organised groups in Scotland. It is no wonder that political scientists and others have often been misled in their interpretations of this period in Scottish politics.

Very few politicians or writers on politics paid any attention to Scottish devolution until the mid-1960s. This is despite its long history, and the support which existed for a Scottish Parliament in the Scottish population, in the Liberal and Labour Parties, and in some organisations such as the Church of Scotland and the Scottish Trades Union Congress (STUC). There has always been ambiguity about the importance of the issue for the Scottish people. Budge and Urwin, in their Glasgow, Craigton survey in 1965, found that 44% wanted to see a 'Scottish Parliament, Government, Council' established, and a further 28% thought Scotland should have 'More say in running its own affairs'. When asked specifically if they thought Scotland should have its own Parliament, 65% replied that it should (Budge and Urwin, p. 128). But how important this issue was for them is not clear, nor was it asked what they would do politically to achieve their aim.

Similarly, bodies such as the Church of Scotland, the STUC, and the Labour Party have not consistently supported devolution. What they have wanted has varied considerably over the years. The Church's idea of devolution in the early 1950s was for an 'advisory body, the membership of which would include Scottish MPs of all parties and representatives of Local Authorities', and in 1962 it supported only 'such developments as would allow Scotsmen to deal with their own affairs, social, economic and legislative' (Kilbrandon 4, p. 49). The STUC and the Labour Party have debated devolution off and on since the First World War. To begin with, they were clear that a Scottish Parliament was what they wanted, and in the 1945 election many Scottish Labour candidates included that in their platform (Keating and Bleiman, p. 134). By 1958, however, the Labour Party had withdrawn from 'legislative devolution' (an elected Scottish Parliament) and, although stressing its 'belief in the principle of the maximum possible self-government for Scotland', said that this had to be 'consistent with the right to remain in the United Kingdom Parliament and continue full representation there'. Many read this as 'no devolution'[1] (Keating and Bleiman, pp. 146–7). The STUC after 1931 looked for economic and administrative reforms rather than political ones, and it was not until 1970 that it tentatively suggested to the Royal Commission on the Constitution that 'the advantages might lie in providing for Scotland a legislative assembly' with 'carefully defined powers over strictly domestic matters, including presumably some responsibility for financing them' (Kilbrandon 5, p. 115). In its oral evidence, however, the STUC backtracked from the idea of a 'legislative' Assembly, and went instead for a 'deliberative' body (*ibid.*, p. 122). All these organisations of course rejected complete independence for Scotland, which only the SNP supported.

It was the electoral successes of the SNP, however, which definitely changed the political climate on devolution. The response of the two major parties to the SNP 'wave' of 1967–8 was to institute enquiries into the devolution question. The Conservative Party in Scotland set up a study group in 1967, which reported in favour of a Scottish Assembly at their conference in 1968. Edward Heath, the party leader, endorsed this at the conference, and set up a 'Constitutional Committee', with Sir Alec Douglas-Home as Chairman, to provide definite and detailed proposals. The result was the Report on Scottish Government (March 1970), which recommended a 'Convention',

145

directly elected, to take on the work of the Scottish committees of the House of Commons. This was accepted by the Scottish conference in May 1970, by a three-to-one majority, and became official Conservative policy. It did not, however, pay any obvious electoral dividend, and when the SNP showed signs of decline the Party conference reneged on the proposal (May 1973). At the following conference, however (May 1974), an Assembly indirectly elected from local councillors was accepted. After the October 1974 election, the Conservative leadership in Scotland came out in support of the Labour Government's proposal for a directly-elected Assembly (*Scotsman*, 16 October 1974).

While this was the position taken by Labour after August 1974, it was in marked contrast to the Party's earlier pronouncements. The response to the SNP's earlier challenge was the announcement of the setting-up of a Commission on the Constitution in December 1968 (the 'Crowther', later 'Kilbrandon', Commission). At the same time, the Labour Scottish Secretary, William Ross, denounced nationalism and devolution as 'shabby' and 'irrelevant', and proposed no major alteration to the government of Scotland other than that Edinburgh sittings of the Scottish Grand Committee 'could be tried' (*The Government of Scotland*. Evidence of the Labour Party in Scotland to the Commission on the Constitution, Glasgow, March 1970, p. 19).

Meanwhile, some Labour MPs and activists renewed Labour's traditional 'Home Rule' policy. In the 1960s, John Mackintosh was the most prominent of these (see Mackintosh), but by 1974 a 'ginger-group' of MPs led by Jim Sillars (MP for South Ayrshire) was demanding 'substantial' devolution (*Scottish Labour and Devolution, A Discussion Paper*, 1974). The crucial voice in the Labour Party, however, was that of the trade unions, and Alex Kitson of the Transport and General Workers' Union (TGWU) (formerly leader of a Scottish trade union), who was also a member of the Labour Party's National Executive Committee, persuaded that Committee to support devolution. The Executive of the Scottish Council of the Labour Party was not in favour, but at a special conference in Glasgow on 17 August 1974, the Party in Scotland overwhelmingly adopted the devolution stance. Powerful unions such as the TGWU, the Amalgamated Union of Engineering Workers, and the National Union of Mineworkers were all in favour, as were about half the constituency parties. This led on to the Labour Government's formal support for an elected Scottish Assembly (*Democracy and Devolution: Proposals for Scotland and Wales* (HMSO, Cmnd 5732, September 1974)).

146

All this has to be seen against the background of the changing climate of opinion in Scotland regarding devolution and nationalism, and the widespread support for an Assembly which had been seen in the evidence to the Commission on the Constitution. The Report of that Commission (Kilbrandon 6), published at the end of October 1973, may also have been influential in shaping opinion. Eight of the 11 Commissioners who signed the majority Report favoured a form of legislative devolution for Scotland in which 'transferred' matters would come under a Scottish Assembly. These matters would be basically those pertaining to existing Scottish legislation and Scottish Office functions. The UK Parliament would retain the ultimate right to legislate on all matters, but by convention it would seek the consent of the Scottish Government if it entered the 'Scottish' sphere (Kilbrandon 6, p. 337). It was this scheme which appealed most to the Scottish organisations who were canvassed during 1974 for their reactions, and which was basically adopted by the Government. Other schemes supported were a 'deliberative and advisory' Assembly with limited legislative powers (one Commissioner) and 'executive devolution' in which a Scottish Assembly would 'execute policies within a framework set by UK legislation' (Kilbrandon 6, p. 252) (two Commissioners). The minority Report, signed by two Commissioners, objected to 'transferred' powers, and wanted decentralisation of all central government funtions to the regions (Kilbrandon 7). It is important to note that all 13 Commissioners supported an elected assembly of one kind or another for Scotland.

The Kilbrandon Report by itself would probably not have inspired the Government to move quickly on devolution, and indeed the Report was not given a debate in the House of Commons (devolution was not debated until 3–4 February 1975). Although civil servants did start to study the implications of devolution before the February 1974 election, it was that election, with its SNP successes, which brought the matter forcibly on to the agenda. The increased size of SNP representation in the House of Commons during 1974 (11 MPs after October) and the swelling of the SNP vote to 22% in February, followed by 30% in October, made it seem that Scotland was now on a collision course with the rest of the United Kingdom.

That view depended, however, on an interpretation of the meaning of the SNP vote, and how it related to opinions on Home Rule, something which, as we have seen, was a difficult matter for politicians and academic commentators alike. It also depended on what Scots in general wanted by way of constitutional change. These

Table 20. *Attitudes towards constitutional change in Scotland*
Table 20(a). *Kilbrandon Survey (1970) and ORC Survey (October 1974)*

	Kilbrandon Survey (1970)	ORC Survey (October 1974)
	%	%
Leave things as they are at present	6	21
Keep things much the same as they are now but make sure that the needs of Scotland are better understood by the Government	19	14
Keep the present system but allow more decisions to be made in Scotland	26	17
Have a new system of governing Scotland so that as many decisions as possible are made in the area	24	24
Let Scotland take over complete responsibility for running things in Scotland	23	20
Don't know	1	4

Table 20(b). *System Three Scotland Survey (October 1974)*

	October 1974	Con	Lab	Lib	SNP
	%	%	%	%	%
A completely independent Scotland	14	2	3	2	32
More say in our own affairs but within the UK framework	76	82	87	91	65
Keeping the present system	5	12	5	6	0
Don't know	5	4	5	1	3

Source: System Three Scotland, Glasgow Herald, 8 October 1974.

148

Table 20(c). *ORC surveys (October 1974 to April 1979)*

	Oct. 74	Party				Dec. 75	Oct. 76	Feb. 79	April 79	Party			
	Oct. %	Con %	Lab %	Lib %	SNP %	%	%	%	April 79 %	Con %	Lab %	Lib %	SNP %
Keep the present system	21	37	28	11	3	14	23	32	35	52	35	32	6
Have a Scottish Assembly, not directly elected, but made up of the representatives of the new regional councils, which would handle some Scottish affairs and would be responsible to Parliament at Westminster	14	19	18	11	6	14	8	13	8	11	6	13	5
Have a directly elected Scottish Assembly which would handle some Scottish affairs and would be responsible to Parliament at Westminster	17	20	18	24	7	19	20	16	13	10	16	17	9
Have a Scottish Parliament which would handle most Scottish affairs, including many economic affairs, leaving the Westminster Parliament responsible for defence, foreign affairs and international economic policy	24	18	25	44	21	28	27	20	28	18	30	32	41
Make Scotland completely independent of the rest of Britain, with a Scottish Parliament which would handle all Scottish affairs	20	2	7	3	63	21	18	14	12	5	9	4	38
Don't know	4	4	4	4	—	5	4	5	4	4	4	2	1

Source: ORC, *Scotsman,* 4 October 1974 and 26 April 1979.

Table 20(d).   *MORI surveys (March 1979 to March 1983)*

	March 1979	Nov. 1981	March 1983
	%	%	%
A completely independent Scottish Assembly separate from England	14	22	23
A Scottish Assembly as part of Britain but with substantial powers	42	47	48
No change from the present system	35	26	26
Don't know	9	5	2

Source: MORI, *Scotsman*, 11 March 1983.

opinions could be gleaned from surveys, but the results differed according to the types of question asked, and the number of alternatives available. The Kilbrandon Commission set the pattern for these surveys in its Attitudes Survey of 1970 (Kilbrandon 8), and these options were taken up by the ORC in the *Scotsman* in 1974 (see Table 20(a)). System Three Scotland in the *Glasgow Herald* in 1974 reduced the number of options to three, which gave different results (Table 20(b)). Then the ORC changed the Kilbrandon options to accord more with what the parties were proposing in 1974. These options were used until after the Referendum on devolution in 1979. The results showed a rise in support for the status quo (except in December 1975) and a fall in support for independence after December 1975 (Table 20(c)).

The attitudes of party supporters to the constitutional options changed between 1974 and 1979. Conservatives moved to a strong 'status quo' position by 1979, in line with party policy. Labour supporters were badly split. Despite the introduction of the Labour Government's devolution Bills, Labour supporters in 1979 were more in favour of the status quo than in 1974, and their preferred form of devolution (the third and strongest type) did not correspond with the Scotland Act, which resembled more the second, weaker variety. SNP supporters, on the other hand, showed more support for devolution in 1979 than in 1974, and less for independence. Such opinions were contrary to SNP policy. Finally, Liberals moved strongly to the status quo and away from strong devolution, although their party was the party of a federal solution to British government.

150

Since 1979, MORI in the *Scotsman* has polled along the lines of three simple options (Table 20(d)). This shows a rise in support for independence, and a fall in support for the present system.

The difficulty in interpreting these polls is that they are based on different options which do not necessarily relate to any particular form of devolution on offer. 'Devolution' in general might attract the support of well over half of the Scottish electorate, but Labour's 1978 Scotland Act was not as popular, as the Referendum in 1979 showed. Moreover, supporters of independence may not have voted for devolution in the Referendum.

The political result of all this confusing survey data was two-fold. It misled the politicians into thinking that Scotland was presenting a united demand for Home Rule when in fact opinion was divided among many options, none of which had majority support. And second, the devolution option presented by Labour was not the most popular of the devolution options, even among Labour supporters (of whom over a third preferred the status quo), yet it was persisted with. The parties were generally unable to keep their supporters in line with official policy on devolution (or independence in the case of the SNP). The Conservatives fared better in this, so the splits benefited the status quo, since in the vote in the Referendum only one-third of the electorate turned out to vote for the Scotland Act, and under two-thirds of Labour voters intended to vote 'Yes' (Bochel *et al.*, p. 144) (see Table 22(b), below). After the Referendum the puzzle remained (Table 20(d)). Support for independence rose again, as did that for 'substantial' devolution, while support for the status quo fell. But it was still unlikely that any one option would be favoured by a good majority of the Scottish electorate. The only chance seemed to lie with the strongest form of devolution, but whether that would ever be offered by the British Parliament was uncertain.

This account of electoral opinion anticipates the story of how the 'élites' in politics dealt with devolution after 1974. There is both an 'official' or open record of what happened and an 'unofficial' or inside account from some participants. Both throw light on the nature of constitution-making in Britain.

We have seen that the Labour Government elected in February 1974 had adopted devolution officially by August 1974, and campaigned on the setting up of Scottish and Welsh Assemblies in the October 1974 election. According to Tam Dalyell,[2] after the results of the February 1974 election, which showed an SNP vote of 22%, the Prime Minister Harold Wilson single-handedly committed his Government to introducing a White Paper and a Bill on devolution, although such a commitment was not in the Queen's Speech, nor had it been endorsed in the Cabinet. Wilson was particularly impressed by evidence from MORI that among Labour voters 83% were in favour of some kind of Scottish Parliament.

Although the Labour Party conference had not included devolution in its programme in 1974 (it did not do so until September 1976, when the block votes of the unions overwhelmed the opposition of many English constituency Parties), Labour had devolution in its October 1974 manifesto, and in Scottish Labour Party campaigning the Assembly was to have 'economic teeth' and control over the Scottish Development Agency (Drucker, pp. 30–1). In the event, the devolution White Paper of November 1975 contained no such powers, which led to the defection in December 1975 of Labour MPs Jim Sillars and John Robertson to the new 'Scottish Labour Party', which soon became committed to virtual independence for Scotland (it disappeared from Scottish politics in 1980 after Sillars joined the SNP; Robertson returned to the Labour Party).

This split in the Labour ranks was only the first to emerge as the legislative process got under way. Not only were there dissenting strong devolutionists in Scotland, but there were even more anti-devolutionists, especially in England, and more crucially, in Scotland as well. Despite this, the Government proceeded to introduce a Scotland and Wales Bill in December 1976 (for a full account see Bogdanor; also Drucker and Brown, and Bochel et al.). Although it passed its Second Reading comfortably (there was some cross-voting: 10 Labour MPs voted against and 30 abstained; a few Conservatives voted for), there was much hidden opposition in Labour's ranks, and the Government was forced into promising that a Referendum would be held on the Act in Scotland and Wales. This was intended to 'buy off' opposition to a Guillotine Motion which would be necessary to stop unending debate on amendments. The strategy did not work, for the Guillotine Motion was lost on 22 February 1977. Twenty-two Labour MPs voted against, and 23 abstained. The Conservatives were solidly against, even those who had voted for the Second Reading.

It seemed that devolution was lost because of the power of Parliament, but it was Parliament that brought it back on to the legislative agenda. Because the Government had no overall majority it needed the support of minor parties to continue in office. It could not rely on the SNP, and the Liberals agreed to make a 'Pact' if (among other things) devolution were re-introduced. This 'Lib-Lab

Pact' led to the introduction of the Scotland Bill and the Wales Bill (they were now separated from each other) in November 1977. The Guillotine Motion was soon passed, but the rebels were not finished yet. Mr George Cunningham, a Scot, and Labour MP for a London seat, introduced an amendment which made it necessary for 40% of the electorates in Scotland and Wales to vote for the Acts in Referendums if the Acts were to be brought into operation. This was passed against the wishes of the Government by Conservatives and Labour rebels. This final revolt proved to be the death-knell for the Scotland Act, for the 40% threshold was not reached in the Referendum in March 1979. The Bills, however, had passed through Parliament by July 1978.

Clearly the progress and content of the legislation depended to an unusual extent on what back-benchers in the House of Commons were prepared to support. Devolution to them, if not to many other people, was an important issue,* although most resented the time taken up by it to the exclusion of other Bills. The fact that the Government had no overall majority, and that its own discipline was so weak on the issue, partly accounted for the troubles experienced. But there was more to it than that. The Government's heart was not in the cause of devolution, any more than was the heart of the Labour Party in Parliament or in the country (even in Scotland). To many English MPs, it was giving in to 'the Scots' (not just the SNP). To many Labour and Conservative Scots, it was giving in to the 'Nats' (SNP). The alliance of anti-devolution MPs in England and Scotland made it difficult for the Government to work up enthusiasm for the Bill or to present it as the demand of the Scottish people. Within the Labour Cabinet there were very mixed feelings on the subject. According to Barbara Castle in her Diaries,[3] in July 1974 'Willie' Ross, the Secretary of State for Scotland, said 'we ought not to have gone so far... but having started the whole enquiry, we had aroused expectations we could not resist'. Most Cabinet Ministers appeared to be opposed, and even Harold Wilson, on completing the draft of the devolution White Paper of September 1974, remarked to Cabinet colleagues, 'And God help all who sail in her'.[4] Later Labour Ministers were no more keen on devolution, on the whole.

* Surveys consistently showed that no more than 10% of Scots thought that devolution or self-government was 'one of the most important problems the Government should do something about' (*Scotsman*, 27 April 1979). Miller, however, reports that in the Scottish Election Survey in October 1974, 61% said that devolution was important in deciding their vote (Miller, p. 87).

Officials were also opposed, especially in Whitehall. The Scottish and Welsh Offices were put into a subordinate position to the Cabinet Office in the drafting of the Bills, whose content revealed that very little power was to be handed down from central government. When the Minister of State in charge of devolution in the Wilson Government, Lord Crowther-Hunt (who had helped to produce the minority Report for the Constitutional Commission), tried to get a stronger scheme of devolution adopted to cover England as well as Scotland and Wales, he found it blocked by civil servants, although Ministers generally put up no fight for it.[5] Blocked too was a scheme for tax powers for the Scottish Assembly, although the civil servant in charge of the Constitution Unit at the Cabinet Office, Sir John Garlick, later revealed that local and sales taxes could easily have been introduced.[6] This was also the opinion of some academics,[7] and tax powers are now part of the Labour Party's proposals for a Scottish Assembly.

The resulting devolution legislation (the Scotland Act) was a complex piece of constitutional engineering – a gothic structure which very few understood or liked. The division of powers between Edinburgh and London seemed to resemble that between central and local government more than that between Washington and the States in the USA. America has, of course, a 'federal' system of government, and devolution was distinguished from federalism by the politicians, especially as under devolution Parliament was to retain its 'sovereignty' over the Scottish Assembly, while in a federal system the states and the federal government each have theoretical sovereignty within their spheres of government, the whole of which is regulated by a Constitution and Supreme Court.

Detailed analysis of the Scotland Act is not attempted here (see Donald I. MacKay (Ed.), *Scotland: The Framework for Change*, Paul Harris (Edinburgh, 1979); Bogdanor; Rose 6). It is now a matter of history, but the key issues in devolution remain to be resolved when the next attempt at legislation is made (Table 21).

By the time the Scotland Act had gone through Parliament, and was ready for presentation to the Scottish people in a Referendum, various changes had taken place in the views of parties and organisations in Scotland on the subject. As we have seen, the Labour Party was now in favour of legislative devolution, and the STUC followed suit. The Church of Scotland became more devolutionist in the 1970s, and its Church and Nation Committee asked all ministers to support a 'Yes' vote in the Referendum (many refused). The Conservative Party, on the other hand, moved away from supporting

Table 21. *Key issues in devolution*

1. *Type of division of powers*. Will powers be 'transferred' to a Scottish legislature, or 'delegated'? Will Westminster have a 'veto' over Scottish legislation, or will it have a positive power to legislate itself in areas within the Scottish sphere? (The Scotland Act was ambiguous here. While Parliament retained sovereignty, in effect devolved matters would not come before it. But the Secretary of State could refer 'Assembly legislation' which he thought impinged on 'reserved' (non-devolved) matters to Parliament, where it might be over-ruled (the 'policy override'). He could also refer proposed Assembly legislation which he considered *ultra vires* to the Judicial Committee of the Privy Council for 'judicial review', where it might be ruled unconstitutional. Even after Assembly Bills had been passed, they could be taken to court by anyone on grounds of *ultra vires*.)

2. *Legislative spheres*. What subjects will be within the competence of the Scottish legislature? Will it have 'all' of education, health, etc., or merely 'part' of these functions (e.g. omitting the school-leaving age, teachers' pay, and the universities from education)? What about industry, energy, transport, and employment? (The Scotland Act divided nearly every function of government between the Assembly, the Scottish Secretary, and Whitehall. For example, it kept the universities (but not schools and colleges) and most economic functions (but not rates) on a British basis; the police and judges came under the Scottish Secretary (but not law reform or the courts). Some bodies were split between the Assembly and the Scottish Office (e.g. the Scottish Development Agency (SDA) and Highlands Board)).

3. *Secretary of State for Scotland*. Will this office be retained, and if so, will the Scottish Secretary exercise functions (e.g. over the SDA) for which he will be responsible to Westminster, not Edinburgh? (The Scotland Act retained the Secretary of State for Scotland, as a minister responsible to Westminster, but of course with much-reduced functions. In return, he became something of a 'Governor-General' – see 1. above).

4. *Finance*. Will there be an 'expenditure'-based system (i.e. block grant from the Treasury, to be spent by the Scottish government), or a 'revenue'-based system (i.e. taxes raised in Scotland)? Or a mix of the two? Will there be any revenue from North Sea Oil? (The Scotland Act provided the Assembly with a Block Fund, to be decided by negotiation between the Treasury and the Scottish Executive , according to a formula covering all devolved services, and lasting for four years at a time. No other revenues were to be available, although local rates were a source of indirect income.)

5. *Scottish–UK relationship*. Will Scotland be represented in the UK Cabinet (see Secretary of State for Scotland, above)? Will all Scottish MPs be retained in the House of Commons? Will they be allowed to vote on

155

Table 21.   *(contd)*

English, Welsh, or Northern Irish matters, when English, etc., MPs are not allowed to vote on devolved Scottish matters? ('The West Lothian question'.) (The Scotland Act retained the office of Secretary of State for Scotland, but whether he would remain in the Cabinet would be up to the Prime Minister of the day. Since the office had considerably reduced powers, that might be doubtful. All Scottish MPs were retained, with full voting powers.)

6. *Type of Scottish Government.* Will the executive be a Cabinet-type, with Prime Minister, or a local-authority-type with a fused executive–legislative committee structure? Will there be proportional representation, and fixed legislative terms? Will Westminster and Edinburgh elections be held on the same dates? Could the UK Government dissolve the Scottish legislature? Is it to be a 'Parliament' or an 'Assembly'? (The Scotland Act was sensitive to matters of constitutional status. The only 'Ministers of the Crown' were to be those serving the UK Government, not those responsible to the Assembly. There was to be no 'Prime Minister' or 'Cabinet' in Scotland, only a 'First Secretary' and a 'Scottish Executive'. The latter was to be a Cabinet-type body, with 'Secretaries' rather than 'Secretaries of State' or 'Ministers'. There was to be no Proportional Representation. Legislative terms were fixed at four years, but the Assembly could be dissolved on the proposal of at least two-thirds of the total membership. The Secretary of State for Scotland could call an election two months before or two months after the fixed date. It was of course to be an 'Assembly', not a 'Parliament'.)

7. *The EEC.* Should a Scottish government be directly represented in the EEC? (The Scotland Act gave no such representation, but some EEC decisions would have to be carried out through Assembly legislation or Executive action. For these, informal links would take place between Edinburgh and Brussels and a sort of 'representation' established for the Scottish Executive.)

devolution when Mr Heath was replaced as Leader in 1975 by Mrs Thatcher. While at first she supported a Scottish Assembly (Miller, p. 241), by the time the Labour Bill was presented to Parliament she had moved to opposing devolution (at least in the form offered by Labour). In this she was no doubt strongly influenced by the imperatives of 'adversary politics', and it is significant that the major parties changed positions on devolution as they changed from government to opposition and vice versa. A few Conservatives who had backed Heath on devolution rebelled against Mrs Thatcher and resigned their front-bench opposition positions, including the Shadow Scottish Secretary, Mr Alick Buchanan-Smith. But by 1977 no

Conservative MP was supporting the Guillotine Motions on the devolution Bills. Finally, the erstwhile devolutionist Lord Home (Sir Alec Douglas-Home) told television viewers two days before the Referendum vote to vote 'No' to the Scotland Act, as it did not go far enough (e.g. in tax powers).

Along with the Conservatives, nearly all businesses and business organisations (e.g. the CBI) came out against devolution. Some companies even threatened to remove themselves from Scotland if devolution came about. Other critics of devolution included the universities, the judges, and many professional people. In part, the Conservatives were just following Mrs Thatcher's cue, but many were profoundly uneasy that Scotland would be run by a group of Labour-dominated (Glasgow-dominated?) politicians whose respect for the 'Scottish Establishment' was limited. Even worse, the SNP might gain control, and lead Scotland to independence. It is thus not true to say (as many Marxists have) that the 'bourgeoisie' or Scottish Capitalists were behind the Home Rule movement. Rather the reverse.

The Referendum campaign was marked by intra- as well as inter-party squabbling. There were no 'umbrella' Yes and No campaign organisations as in the EEC Referendum in 1975, for although there was a 'Yes for Scotland' and a 'Scotland says No' group, these were not recognised or financially aided by the Government. The former was dominated by the SNP, and the latter by the Conservatives. Labour ran its own Labour Movement Yes Campaign, but there was an unofficial Labour Vote No Campaign, alongside the Conservative No Campaign. There was a tiny Conservative Yes Campaign, and SNP Yes Campaign (although the SNP allowed its branches to work for the Yes for Scotland Campaign), and a small Alliance for an Assembly, which included individual devolutionists from different parties (Bochel et al., Ch. 2).

Party political broadcasts were banned by the Court of Session on the grounds that these would give a 3:1 advantage to the 'Yes' side (this was the result of a Labour anti-devolutionist's legal action!). By 1979 some of the Scottish press had turned hostile to devolution, where in the past it had been most favourable (the *Scottish Daily Express* is the most obvious example. The principal pro-devolution papers were the *Daily Record*, *Sunday Mail*, and *Scotsman*). All in all, the near-consensus in favour of devolution which had prevailed in Scotland in 1974 had disappeared by 1979.

It is perhaps not surprising that in this confusion the electorate did not give a clear mandate in the Referendum held on 1 March 1979.

Table 22. *The Referendum on the Scotland Act, 1 March 1979*
Table 22(a). *The result*

Turnout	Yes		No		Abstention
% of electorate (official estimate)	% of votes	% of electorate (official estimate)	% of votes	% of electorate (official estimate)	% of electorate (official estimate)
63.6	51.6	32.8	48.4	30.8	36.4

Table 22(b). *Voting intention by party*

	Yes %	No %	Don't know %
Total			
(excluding 17% Don't know)	52	48	—
Con	19	71	10
Lab	56	29	15
SNP	84	8	8
(Other parties not given)			

Source: System Three poll of 24–5 February 1979, *Glasgow Herald*, 27 February 1979.

The result of that vote is given in Table 22(a) and a breakdown of voting intention by party in Table 22(b).

The meaning of this vote has been the subject of some debate. As a measure of the votes cast, it gave a small majority to the 'Yes' side. As a percentage of the electorate, the 'Yes' vote apparently fell well short of the 40% threshold set by Parliament. However, this shortfall was arbitrarily calculated by the Secretary of State for Scotland, since the total electorate was estimated by him. Starting with an electorate estimated to be 3,787,312 on 1 March 1979, he deducted 40,200 to take account of changes since the Register had been drawn up in October 1978 and of students and nurses likely to be registered at more than one address. But he could have deducted a much larger figure, according to some commentators. Bogdanor, for example, thinks that 623,552 should have been taken off, and this would have meant that the 'Yes' vote was only 54,485 votes short of the 40% threshold[8] (38.9%).

As Abstention was tantamount to voting 'No' under this system, the significance of those who did not vote was greater than in a parliamentary election. Given the confusion in the minds of many voters because of the contradictory advice coming from pro- and anti-devolution factions in all the parties, the largest number (36.4%) did in fact stay away from the poll. This led some to comment 'The Don't Knows Won!'.

When people in Scotland and in Parliament came to consider the result further, and what should be done about it, the ambiguities remained. An ORC survey published in the *Scotsman* on 26 April 1979 showed that only 26% thought that the 'Yes' side had won, and that the Assembly should be set up. A further 33% thought the 'Yes' side had won, but had not won a big enough majority to justify setting up the Assembly. Thirty per cent thought the 'No' side had won, and that the Assembly plan should be scrapped. However, 60% of the respondents wanted the Government to come up with new plans for an Assembly, and only 51% of those who had voted 'No' wanted to 'leave the Government of Scotland as it is now'!

The Government could not make up its mind what to do, and MPs were as much impressed by the narrow majority for the Scotland Act as by its failure to reach the 40% threshold. The Prime Minister, Mr Callaghan, promised 'all-party talks', but this infuriated the SNP Members, who could now tilt the balance against the Government in Parliament, since the Lib-Lab Pact had ended. At the end of March 1979, the SNP proposed a Vote of No Confidence in the Government, and the Conservatives carried this on 28 March 1979 by one vote. They went on to win the general election in May 1979, although the results in Scotland gave a large Labour majority. Devolution did not seem to be much of an issue in that election, but the 'parties of devolution' won 49 of the 71 seats in Scotland. However, the Conservative Government proceeded to repeal the Scotland and Wales Acts in July 1979. The only concession to Scottish devolution was the inauguration of 'all-party talks' to improve the position of Scotland in Parliament (these led to changes relating to the Scottish Grand Committee, see Ch. 5, p. 94). Another phase in the devolution story was over.

The latest phase is concerned with picking up the pieces and starting again. We have seen that the Labour Party in Scotland has committed itself to an even stronger form of devolution than that contained in the Scotland Act. In particular, tax and economic powers are to be included. A Campaign for a Scottish Assembly was

159

established in 1980 on an all-party basis, and it holds periodic rallies, etc. The new Social Democratic Party is committed to devolution, as is of course the Liberal Party. But the SNP, curiously, is now in favour of 'Independence, nothing less'. It is clear, however, that many in the SNP would support a Devolution Bill if another were to be produced.

The harsh lessons from the 1979 Referendum are still felt, however, by devolutionists. How could a strong pro-devolution majority, consistently expressed in polls throughout the years, be turned into a hair-breadth majority, with a Yes vote from well under half of the electorate? Blame can be attached to Westminster, to the procedures and conduct of the Referendum, and to the divisions within the pro-devolution parties, etc. Perhaps the Labour Party never really wanted devolution, and was thus delighted with the result. This, however, does not square up with the feelings among most Scottish Labour MPs today, and some are threatening to obstruct Parliamentary business if another Conservative Government refuses to grant Scotland devolution. At the same time, Labour is unwilling to cooperate with other parties to achieve devolution. In 1983 a 'Labour Campaign for a Scottish Assembly' took its place beside the 'all-party' Campaign for a Scottish Assembly, just as in the Referendum Campaign, the Labour Party had its own 'Yes' campaign. This fragmentation of effort, and the very strong reluctance which the Labour Party has of cooperating with other parties, is a continuing weakness of the campaign to bring about Scottish Home Rule.

To avoid the problems which arose in Parliament over the passing of the Scotland Bill and the ambiguities of the Referendum, it has been suggested (e.g. by Gordon Wilson, Chairman of the SNP, and by Richard Rose (Rose 6, p. 223)) that a Constitutional Convention be held in Scotland to decide on the form of devolution which Scots would support. This would then give a devolution Bill legitimacy, and avoid the uncertainties of prolonged policy-making on the subject in Whitehall and Westminster. It would also do away with the need for a Referendum. There is logic in this, but the Northern Ireland Constitutional Convention of 1975–6 is not a happy precedent, since it displayed divisions rather than consensus, and it is most unlikely that London would give up its role in deciding the fate of Scottish government. But a 'handed-down' devolution is always likely to be viewed with suspicion in Scotland, and it is no wonder that Scots do not heartily endorse what they have not participated in proposing.

The 'Achilles heel' of devolution to many people, in Scotland as well as in England, is the 'slippery-slope' argument. This states that devolution is linked with 'separatist' nationalism, and once an Assembly is set up in Edinburgh it will lead on inevitably to independence for Scotland. There is no way of proving this argument false, except by reference to the relatively low support for independence in opinion polls, and the long history of untroubled Union between Scotland and England since 1707. The low salience of devolution as a political issue among Scottish voters is another indicator of stability. Indeed, it seems that the reaction of many London politicians and media figures to Scottish nationalism is one of 'scare-mongering' resulting from their lack of knowledge of Scotland.

A more fundamental objection to devolution is that much of the nationalism of recent years has been an expression of protest unrelated to support for devolution. The mobilisation of Scottish opinion in favour of a separate Parliament, Convention or Assembly has been part of a 'band-wagon' based on the SNP's electoral successes, which were themselves largely based on a 'protest vote'. Had such a demand been deeply felt, it would have been voiced continually, not just from the late 1960s.

In reply, historians of Scottish nationalism are able to trace political demands for national self-determination or devolution back over 100 years, in which the same arguments have been used repeatedly (Hanham 3). As recently as the early 1950s, the evidence to the Balfour Commission on Scottish Affairs anticipated in most respects that to the Commission on the Constitution.

These developments, repeated in cycles, have made Scottish nationalism a most unreliable political force. While it is ever-present in Scottish society, in the form of national awareness and a multitude of Scottish organisations, the very security and fulfilment of such nationalism which these organisations represent has made political nationalism less relevant. Scottish interests can be preserved without national self-determination.

Nevertheless, nationalism is of first-order importance to the Scottish political system. It sustains the Scottish Office and the other institutions of the system, which could hardly exist without it. It colours the speeches of Scottish MPs in the House of Commons, and permeates the demands of interest groups. It makes Scotland a framework of reference for the mass media, education, and research.

It is too much to expect that the nation should speak with one voice. Scotland is a nation subdivided into the interests of locality, region, class, religion, and political party. If it were united, and consistent, this would no doubt suit some of the politicians and most of the civil servants. It would certainly clarify the situation for many in England who want to learn what would keep Scotland quiet.

There is now a wide consensus that Scotland lacks a legislative branch of government which can balance its executive and judicial branches (represented by the Secretary of State for Scotland, and the courts). Over 10,000 civil servants operate a purely Scottish administrative structure, and a large contingent of lawyers the Scottish legal system. With them, Scottish local authorities, interest groups, and other organisations have an ongoing relationship.

But this is not enough for democratic government. Scotland has its own law, is separately administered, and is a separate community. Its political system can only be made complete with the establishment of a separate legislature, directly elected by the Scottish people, to make laws for Scotland and control Scottish administration.

9

Local Government

Scotland has its own system of local government. The present system dates from 1975, and was established by the Local Government (Scotland) Act, 1973 (see Table 23 for its structure). From the very beginnings of local government, Scotland has had its own local authorities, and these can be contrasted with the local authorities in England, Wales, and Northern Ireland. Here the comparisons will be with the English system, which is the model followed in Wales and Northern Ireland (the latter has, however, a very reduced system today).

The establishment of the present local government systems in Britain involved a process of enquiry and legislation. Two Royal Commissions on Local Government were set up in the 1960s: Redcliffe–Maud for England (*Report*, Cmnd 4040),[1] and Wheatley for Scotland (*Report*, Cmnd 4150). The new structures were established by Acts of Parliament, that for Scotland being the Local Government (Scotland) Act, 1973. Scotland was one year behind England in changing over to the new system, and the first elections took place in May 1974. The transfer was completed in May 1975, when the system became fully operational.

It is pertinent to ask why Scotland and England should have different systems of local government. In part, the reason is historic. Each country developed its own self-governing local communities from medieval times, and in Scotland these were the Royal Burghs. They were typically small towns or villages, and represented isolated pockets of trade and civilisation in a somewhat barbarous environment. Only after 1889 were County Councils established, and the pre-reform structure dated from 1929.

While a belief in the virtues of local government has undoubtedly been part of Scottish political culture, there has also been an equal emphasis on the efficient performance of functions. Where the structure of authorities stands in the way of efficiency, Scots have

163

Table 23.   *The Scottish system of local government*

	Population (1981)
Regions (9)	
Highland	191,966
Grampian	483,000
Tayside	391,529
Central	273,012
Fife	340,182
Lothian	735,892
Borders	100,470
Strathclyde	2,400,000
Dumfries/Galloway	144,218
Island areas (3)	
Shetland	25,812
Orkney	18,862
Western Isles	30,691
Districts (53) including	
Glasgow	763,162
Edinburgh	446,361
Dundee	179,674
Aberdeen	212,542

Community Councils: these are not 'local authorities' but are elected bodies established by District
Councils to allow for the expression of community opinion.

Functions and Services

Regions and Island Areas (elected every four years):
   Major planning and related services, including strategic
planning, industrial development, transportation, roads,
water, sewerage.
   Education; social work; regional housing; police; fire;
community centres;* registration of births, deaths and
marriages; registration of electors. In the island areas,
police, fire, and aspects of education and social work are
administered jointly with other authorities.

Districts (elected every four years):
   Local planning and associated services, including
urban development and countryside;† building control;†
housing; community centres, parks and recreation,
museums and art galleries; libraries;† environmental
health, including cleansing, refuse, Shops Act, burials;

164

regulation and licensing, including cinemas and theatres, betting and taxis; tourism.

*Exercised concurrently by Regional and District authorities.
†Except in Highland, Dumfries/ Galloway and Borders regions, where the function is Regional.

Note: Local government election results since 1974 are recorded in the series by J. M. Bochel and D. T. Denver, including *The Scottish Local Government Election Results 1974*, Scottish Academic Press (Edinburgh and London, 1975); *The Scottish District Elections 1977*, Department of Political Science, University of Dundee (Dundee 1977); and subsequent issues. Also articles by these authors in *The Scottish Government Yearbooks* of 1978, 1979, 1981, 1983.

been ready to change it, and there does not seem to be the almost mystical belief in local democracy which has dominated English thought (derived in part from John Stuart Mill, a Scot whose ideas on this subject are based on English experience).[2]

In Scotland, the 'intermediary' tier of government, the Scottish Office, has taken over some of the area occupied by local government in England, and has played a stronger directing rôle than have the local government ministries in England. In education, for example, local authorities have been subject to much more detailed controls in Scotland, and the Scottish Education Department soon after its inception in 1872 produced a uniform system covering curricula, examinations, training of teachers and school buildings. Most of these controls remain today.

The physical characteristics of Scotland also contribute to a different approach to local government. Scotland has only five million people – the population of two large English counties. It must nevertheless support numerous local authorities, since its territorial area is so large, and its communities scattered and distinct. While 80% of the people live in the central belt, the remaining 20% are spread over two-thirds of the land. In the Highlands and Islands (seven old counties), a distinct region composed of many self-contained communities, around 300,000 people live in an area stretching the length of Scotland, from Shetland to Kintyre.

There is thus no possibility of producing a scheme of evenly matched local authorities, equal in size and area. This can be attempted in England, where the distribution of the population is less

165

askew. In Scotland, there are few large cities which can act as the focal point of a regional authority. Only four (Glasgow, Edinburgh, Dundee, and Aberdeen) are over 150,000, and three of these are in the central belt. The great majority of towns in Scotland are small, and compared with England, there are relatively few of over 50,000 people.

There is one large exception to the pattern of small towns. Glasgow has three-quarters of a million people, and its surrounding country forms a conurbation (the 'Central Clydeside Conurbation') of almost one and three-quarter millions.

The main problem for Scottish local government can thus be simply stated: how to produce a structure which provides equably for both Clydeside and the Highlands.

The pre-reformed structure will be described only briefly here, as a preliminary to a discussion of the Wheatley Report and the new system. In it, there were four Counties of Cities, Glasgow, Edinburgh, Dundee, and Aberdeen (all-purpose authorities); 21 Large Burghs (exercising all powers but education and valuation); and 176 Small Burghs (with functions of housing, sanitation, streets, licensing of public houses, and amenities). These were the urban authorities. In addition there were 33 County Councils and Joint County Councils, whose authority was shared with the Burghs. The Counties provided only education and valuation within the Large Burghs, and all the functions within the Small Burghs except those mentioned under 'Small Burghs' above. In the non-urban 'landward areas' the Counties exercised all functions, although some minor ones were delegated to District Councils, of which there were 196.

Apart from this basic structure there were various bodies, made up of delegates of several local authorities, which were appointed to perform specific functions. There were 13 water boards, 11 fire authorities, and 20 police forces. This process of functional co-operation in local government had gone further in Scotland than in England, and was an indication of the difficulty of matching the function to be performed with the authority to perform it. The Scottish Office has been a powerful force in promoting the setting up of such bodies.

The Scottish Office, indeed, has been the master-mind behind the whole local government reform movement. When economic planning began to dominate its thought, in the early 1960s, it became acutely aware of the shortcomings of the local government structure. The attraction of industry to Scotland required the provision of a suitable 'infrastructure', such as housing, roads, water supply, and schools. Factories could not be built without these, yet local authorities were not anxious, or always able, to incur the necessary expense. Nor were they very willing to coordinate their activities.

One way round such difficulties was to set up New Towns. These could provide the resources for industry without the problems facing local authorities. By 1971 there were five New Towns in Scotland, East Kilbride, Glenrothes, Cumbernauld, Livingston, and Irvine. East Kilbride had local authority status as a Large Burgh, and Cumbernauld and Irvine were Small Burghs. (East Kilbride and Cumbernauld are now District Councils.)

There are other institutions which are peculiar to Scotland. The Scottish Special Housing Association is a government-financed body which builds houses at low rents where industry is being developed, or where a local authority is proving inadequate. The Scottish Development Agency (1975–) is engaged in projects of urban renewal (e.g. the Glasgow Eastern Area Renewal (GEAR) project), and industrial development. In the Highlands, the Highlands and Islands Development Board (1965–) acts as a complement to local government in planning and the attraction of industry. However, these bodies cannot take the place of local government, and the Royal Commission on Local Government in Scotland (Wheatley Commission) reported in 1969 in favour of a radical reform of the system, in which the imperatives of planning for economic development appeared uppermost.

The Wheatley proposals were that Scotland should have a two-tier system of local government. The top tier ('Regions') would consist of 7 authorities, and the lower tier ('Districts') of 37. Nearly all important functions would go to the top tier, but minor aspects of local planning and of housing and amenities, as well as of libraries, licensing, and administration of justice would go to the lower tier. Voluntary community councils, outside the structure of local government, could be set up. Each authority would be independently elected and levy its own rates. The Commission, however, did not have the power to consider any reshaping of local government finance, and this was to be decided by the central government itself.

The reasoning behind these proposals was squarely in the Scottish tradition of attempting to provide for the efficient local administration of functions. 'It is when local government operates at the scale which its services demand that true local democracy emerges' (Wheatley 1, p. 50). The services demanded one Highland regional authority (7 counties) and one West of Scotland authority ($2\frac{1}{2}$ million people). The old conundrum of the shape of Scotland and the distribution of its communities was thus forcibly resolved in the Wheatley Report in favour of centralisation.

Even more important was the effect on local government of proposals for devolution to Scotland. If Scotland were to have a Parliament or Assembly, and an Executive, what effect would this have on the structure of local government? Would large regional authorities still be necessary, given that much of their power would be shared by the Scottish Parliament? Because local government reform came first, and devolution second, the Regions were a *fait accompli*, and devolution had to be grafted on to it. Yet the two reforms were not necessarily consistent with one another.

The original Wheatley Commission recommendations were not accepted in detail by the Conservative Government or by Parliament, although the principles were. Strong pressures were immediately mobilised in Scotland to resist certain aspects of the Report, some of which were party-political, some communal, and some related to various 'vested interests' of councils and officials. In the islands, the Borders, and in Fife, vigorous campaigns were mounted to preserve, or achieve, independent status as local authorities. By February 1971, the Government conceded the cases of Orkney and Shetland to be separate 'island authorities', and by December 1971, the Western Isles was recognised for the first time as having a claim to its own local government (previously, the Western Isles had been split between Ross and Cromarty and Inverness-shire). Thus the large Highland Region of Wheatley was dismembered. Nevertheless, it remained a huge authority in terms of area.

The Borders and Fife also put up a great fight for recognition. The Borders won in 1971, but Fife was resolutely resisted until pressure within Parliament itself during the passage of the Local Government Bill resulted in the restoration of its identity. At the same time, suburban areas around Glasgow (Bearsden, Milngavie, Clydebank and Bishopbriggs), which had been included in the Glasgow District, were removed by the House of Lords to form three new Districts, and the Commons did not overturn the decision. Meanwhile, some other departures from the Wheatley Report had been made in the distribution of functions between the Regions and Districts. Housing became primarily a District function, a change which gave the Districts a much-needed political and administrative boost.

Thus some important alterations were made, not only to the

Wheatley scheme, but to that of the Government in its draft legislation. The final Act did not satisfy everyone. The Labour Opposition, led by William Ross, campaigned during the passage of the Bill for the abolition of the Strathclyde Region, on the grounds that it was too large. They preferred to split it into four Regions, with an overall metropolitan authority for strategic planning and some other functions. But some Labour MPs seemed quite happy with the reforms, and divisions did not take a strictly party line. Indeed, it was because of cross-party pressures that so many changes were made during the passage of the legislation.

Certain aspects of local government were left over to be dealt with later. Community councils were to be established by the Districts and Islands by May 1976. A community council would express community viewpoints and 'take such action in the interests of that community as appears to it to be expedient and practicable' (1973 Act, s. 51 (2)). Financial arrangements for the new authorities, although dealt with in outline in the Act, had to be worked out further in practice. No new sources of revenue were given, and the only substantial innovation was the establishment of a Commission for Local Authority Accounts in Scotland. No salaries for councillors were introduced. A local government 'Ombudsman' was a matter for the future. More important innovations were to come in the management of the new authorities, as the result of a report by an advisory group under the chairmanship of I. V. Paterson, the County Clerk of Lanarkshire (*The New Scottish Local Authoritis: Organisation and Management Structures*, HMSO (Edinburgh 1973)). In line with the corresponding 'Bains Report' in England, the Paterson Report recommended 'corporate management' arrangements in both the elected-councillor and official sides of the authority. In the former, a Policy and Resources Committee would head the committee structure of the council, and would lay down overall policies for other committees. On the official side, a Chief Executive would be appointed to oversee the administration and lead a team of Directors of functional departments. By 1975, most authorities had adopted the 'Paterson' structures. In Strathclyde Region, for example, a Policy and Resources Committee, consisting entirely of Labour councillors, was formed. This type of one-party committee is new in local government, for committees under the old system were multi-party. While coordination of policies throughout the authority is achieved, the contribution of the minority parties to the top level of policy-making is lost. In the case of Strathclyde, the huge predominance of

169

the Labour Party makes the danger of 'one-party' rule more severe. On the official side, the restructuring has involved the creation of many new posts and office-buildings, with consequent public complaint at the expense involved for ratepayers. Conservatism in appointments of chief executives and in political and administrative practices has moderated the degree of innovation implied in the new structure.[3]

Similarly, the new councillors are drawn largely from the ranks of the old, despite hopes that the reforms would attract a 'new breed of men'. While many of the latter came forward to the parties for adoption as candidates, those chosen to run were usually established party stalwarts. Local elections have posed some new political problems. The city Districts of Aberdeen, Dundee, and Edinburgh have often had different party profiles from their surrounding Regions (Grampian, Tayside, and Lothian respectively), with opposing parties leading at the different levels. This has been a recipe for conflict. (For sources of these results see Note to Table 23.) There has also been a danger of indecision, since many authorities have lacked overall control by any one party. While some parts of Scotland have been converted to party politics, others have retained the old 'non-partisan' approach (e.g. Highland, Borders, Dumfries–Galloway, and Islands). The SNP has been very poorly represented, despite its importance at Parliamentary elections from 1974. Labour has been overwhelming in Strathclyde and Glasgow. In a variety of ways, then, the new system has represented a mixture of old and new, with many unsolved problems for the future.

The work of the councillor has changed to some extent. Officials took on more administration as the old time-consuming committee system was altered. Clearly, the greater distance between home and council reduces the amount of time a councillor (at least of a regional authority) can spend in the chamber. Conversely, his contacts with his constituents have to be catered for in improved 'consulting-rooms' at the grass-roots level. Decentralisation of administration by officials is also necessary.[4]

The wider aspects of the changes are perhaps lost in these details. The avowed aim of the Wheatley Commission, and of the government in the White Paper of 1971 (*Reform of Local Government in Scotland*, Feb. 1971, Cmnd 4583), was to strengthen local government by transferring some authority to it from central government. There would, for example, be fewer calls on the professional skills and technical advice of central departments since the staff of the new local authorities would be so much better. The numerous controls exercised by St Andrew's House over local decisions would be relaxed. In finance, the authorities would be more 'viable', and would therefore escape some of the financial bondage to central government.

The record of the new local government system since its inauguration in 1975 is the subject of some controversy. This has been especially true of local finance, about which there has been considerable discontent, not only among local government practitioners but also among those in central government and in the public at large.

The complexity of the subject, and the frequent changes in the system of local finance, make it difficult to summarise the issues involved. (For a detailed discussion see Keating and Midwinter, Chs. 7, 10.) At the root of the problem is the fact that local government income is based largely on two apparently unsatisfactory sources, rates and central government grants (especially the Rate Support Grant). Rates are unpopular, partly because they are a tax on property and not on income, but also because they are paid only by certain sections of the community, not by the total electorate. Householders provide about two-fifths of the income from rates, while the rest is paid by commerce, industry, and other property-owners. The income from rates and grants which each local authority receives varies according to the type of authority. Strathclyde Region (the largest authority in Scotland) expected to receive 56% of its income from government grants, 33% from rates, and 11% from other income in 1983–4. Glasgow District (the largest District authority, with important housing responsibilities) expected to receive 34% of its income in rates, 31% in grants, and 35% in rents and charges. In some Highland authorities, the proportion of income from central grants has risen in recent years to as high as 80%. Overall Scottish local authorities grants are about 50% of current revenue income, rates about a quarter, and the remainder comes from fees, charges, etc. (Capital income is financed mainly by borrowing, and the interest is charged to the current account.)[5]

The finance of local government was not dealt with in the Wheatley Report, but was investigated by a *Committee of Inquiry into Local Government Finance* (the Layfield Committee), which covered the whole of Britain. This body reported in 1976 (HMSO, Cmnd 6453) somewhat inconclusively that either central government should take on more responsibility for local income, or local government should be given extra finance-raising powers, especially an income tax. While favouring the latter on balance, the Layfield Committee recommendations were not strong enough to encourage change, and the same rating system has remained despite promises (especially from the Conservative Party) to reform (or even abolish) it.

What has changed considerably since 1980 has been the power of central government to control local expenditure and to intervene in the setting of the level of rates. This direct intervention into local budgeting has led many to complain that local government has lost its independence and has become the mere agent of central government.

Although the Conservative Government of 1979–83 is blamed for this development, its roots lie with the Labour Government of 1974–9. In order to achieve cuts in public expenditure across both central and local government, the Scottish Office issued 'cash limits' and expenditure 'guidelines' to each local authority in Scotland. It was made clear that the level of Rate Support Grant for the whole of Scotland would be tailored to these guidelines, although individual authorities could not legally be penalised for overshooting them.

The Conservative Government elected in 1979 decided to change the law so that a stricter control could be exercised over local spending and taxing. This was accomplished by the Local Government (Miscellaneous Provisions) (Scotland) Act 1981, and the Local Government and Planning (Scotland) Act 1982. The former allowed the Secretary of State for Scotland to cut the Rate Support Grant of authorities he considered were planning 'excessive and unreasonable' expenditure (i.e. in excess of his guidelines). The latter gave him the additional power to order a reduction in the level of rates of such authorities, forcing them to cut back their projected expenditure and return any 'excess' rates already paid back to the ratepayers.

In 1982 and 1983 several authorities were put on a so-called 'hit-list' by the Government, and were penalised. Most of these were Labour authorities, and the Government was accused of acting in a partisan way by singling out its opponents for attack. The Convention of Scottish Local Authorities, which represents all Scottish local authorities and is Labour-dominated, issued strong protests, including a pamphlet entitled *A time to listen – a time to speak out: central–local government relations* (Edinburgh,1982).

Undoubtedly the central government was taking new powers which hit at local autonomy. It was also shifting the burden of local finance towards the local authorities, since it cut the level of Rate Support Grant overall from 68.5% of relevant expenditure in 1978–9 to 61.7% in 1983–4. In addition, controls over capital expenditure and Housing Revenue were introduced.

172

It can be argued, however, that the central government has a legitimate right to do these things. It is responsible for the economy in general, and local spending and taxation is a large part of public finance (a little over half of the expenditure within the Secretary of State for Scotland's programme is accounted for by local government spending). A system of central grants to local government which merely underwrites local budgets cannot be acceptable, especially if the Government's financial philosophy is against expanding public spending. But there is no doubt that local government practitioners (if not the general public) are alarmed at these controls. Even Conservative councillors have voiced their concern, although Conservative authorities have been let off lightly, even when 'overspending'.

In general, there has been some criticism of the entire local government system. The old 'Counties of Cities' (Glasgow, Edinburgh, Aberdeen, and Dundee) have resented their loss of 'all-purpose' status, and their relative weakness compared with 'Metropolitan Districts' in England (the principal difference is that the English city authorities have control over education and social work, while in Scotland this was given to the Regions). The division of functions between the Regions and Districts is not clear-cut, and there is confusion in certain areas, especially social work, housing, education, planning, industrial development, leisure and recreation, and tourism. A *Committee of Inquiry into Local Government in Scotland* (the Stodart Committee) was set up to look into these problems, and reported in 1981 (HMSO, Cmnd 8115). It rejected the request by several District Councils to become all-purpose authorities, mainly because that would undermine the identity of the surrounding Regions. It did, however, recommend a clearer division of functions between the two tiers of local government. The Local Government and Planning (Scotland) Act 1982 gave effect to these proposals, at least in part. The 'big' functions of social work, housing, and education were unchanged. Leisure and recreation became a District function almost entirely, and tourism a District function, along with 'area tourist organisations' under the Scottish Tourist Board. Industrial development went to the Regions although the Districts retained promotional rights and the provision of sites and factories. All in all, this seemed to be no clear resolution of the overlapping functions of the two tiers.

Local government is a large part of the political activity of the Scottish political system. As mentioned above, it accounts for over half of Scottish Office spending, and the Scottish Secretary and his

173

department are closely concerned with all the Scottish local authorities. The relationship is more personal than that between Whitehall and English local government, but of late it has not been more friendly. In general, the system of Scottish local government, despite the smaller size of Scotland, does not seem to be closer to the people than the system of local government in the rest of Great Britain. It may even be more remote and authoritarian in practice, and the large Regions contrast with the proliferation of strong District Councils in England. The development of Community Councils and School Councils since 1975 has marked a new citizen participation, but this is probably less strong than in England. In particular, School Councils have less power in Scotland than School Boards of Governors in England. The whole spectrum of local government in Scotland, including central–local relations, is an arena of politics which divides Scotland off from England. But the development of Scotland requires an overall strategy which covers the whole country, and which brings central and local government together in a harmonious whole. Elected local authorities face an appointed Scottish Office, often of an opposite political persuasion. Only devolution can provide the political authority of an elected Scottish body to work alongside the elected Scottish local authorities.

10

Organisations and interest groups

The process of representation in Britain includes the activities of organised groups as well as those of MPs and political parties. Parliamentary representation serves to reflect the shared opinions and interests of people over a wide range of policies, for these are channelled through the medium of the parties. It also has the function of ensuring that the wishes of the 'governed' are taken into account by the 'governors', since in Britain governments require the support of a majority of MPs in the House of Commons. Finally, it gives an element of geographic representation, in that MPs must look after the general interests of their constituencies, and of the individual constituents within them. Scottish constituencies have a special status within Parliament (see Ch. 5), and in many of them local sentiment is strong.

Organised groups represent specific economic or occupational interests, or shared attitudes on some particular aspect of policy. Some are formed specifically to put pressure on government (e.g. trade unions whose members are employed by government departments or public bodies), while others exist primarily for other purposes, but turn to political pressure on occasion (e.g. churches). They are not involved in the general function of governing, nor do they usually seek to provide a comprehensive programme of political action in areas which do not directly concern them. (The exceptions to this are churches and trade unions, which tend to take a broad view of their rôle in representing their members' interests.)

A Glaswegian, who is also a railwayman and a Roman Catholic, is represented in at least three different ways. As an elector in a parliamentary constituency, he can look to his MP to safeguard his interests at Westminster. As an employee of British Rail, he may join a trade union, which will negotiate on his behalf with the management and the government. As a Catholic, he is under the care of his

175

priest, and ultimately the Hierarchy of the Church, who speak for him in religious and educational matters.

It would be difficult to say which of these three channels of representation is the most important for him, or whether each is in harmony with the other. The example indicates that, even at the level of an individual person, there are difficulties in producing a simple, consistent picture of interests and demands.

It is even more difficult for the entity called Scotland. The parliamentary representation of Scotland has already been discussed, and here it must be re-emphasised that the Scottish MPs themselves do not on their own constitute a legislative body. They are essentially part of the House of Commons, with no legislative powers of their own. Nevertheless demands are channelled to government from Scotland via the Scottish MPs, who play a distinctive rôle in 'representing Scotland'. For example, on 29 October 1971, the front-page headline in a Scottish newspaper read 'Scotland says "No" 36 times', above a report of the vote in the House of Commons on British entry to the EEC. In that vote, 36 Scottish MPs had voted against entry and 32 for. The paper concluded that 'Scotland as a nation' was in opposition to entry ((Glasgow) *Evening Citizen*, 29 October 1971).

The other channels of representation are the interest and attitude groups,[1] the government and public bodies in Scotland (which 'speak for Scotland' within the machinery of government itself), and an amorphous Scottish 'public opinion' expressed in the media and in opinion polls.

Since policy-making for Scotland is formulated and executed at two centres of power, Edinburgh and London, the representative process of the Scottish political system is concerned with two 'access' points, while the English political system must concern itself with only one. Table 24 shows in diagrammatic form the various channels and their principal directions.

The arrows show the main 'flow' only. All the points are interconnected to some extent, and in the case of the channels 3 and 4 it depends on the subject-matter whether the Scottish Office will become involved. For example, trade unions concerned about industrial closures will exert most pressure on the Department of Trade and Industry in London, and not on the Scottish Office, since the latter has no powers of decision (though it may have influence) in that field.

The diagram is also oversimplified in that it assumes that all flows are in one direction – to the government. In fact, the flows are circular, with the government providing impetus or 'feedback' to the

Table 24. *Channels of representation of the Scottish political system*

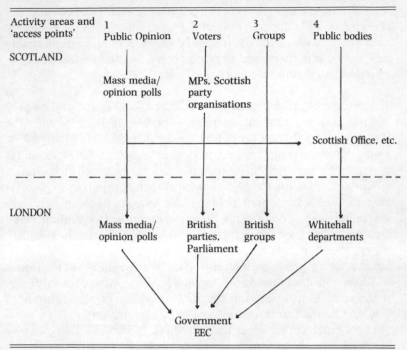

Activity areas and 'access points'	1 Public Opinion	2 Voters	3 Groups	4 Public bodies
SCOTLAND	Mass media/ opinion polls	MPs, Scottish party organisations		Scottish Office, etc.
LONDON	Mass media/ opinion polls	British parties, Parliament	British groups	Whitehall departments
		Government EEC		

entire system. Thus governments inspire the formation of consultative groups, so that they may learn what different interests think about policy. A large number of such groups have been set up on a Scottish basis, and these communicate the wishes of government to their constituent members, as well as vice versa.[2]

Much of the flow of information may not deeply involve the government at all, except as 'arbiter'. In certain areas of public life, for example, law, education, medicine, and other professions, the principal organisations carry on a discourse among themselves which is as important as the discourse between them and government. The Government often allows these professions virtual autonomy over their own affairs, ratifying decisions reached by their official representatives.

In the Scottish context, such practices take on a special form of their own. For it is common to allow Scots to settle their own disputes without reference to London. The plethora of Scottish organisations representing Scottish interests is an indication of this, for if decisions had to be taken in England, there would be a need for British organisation on the grounds of realism and convenience, and the pressure of assimilation of Scotland to England would inevitably increase. As it is, outside the industrial arena, Scotland is remarkably self-contained in its range of organised groups, and by inference, its own decision-making network.

The 'historic' Scottish institutions of Church, law, and education play a 'quasi-governmental' rôle in that they perform tasks on behalf of the state. For example, the Church of Scotland runs 'List D schools' for young offenders, is represented on local education committees, and is part of the Constitution through its position as the Established Church of Scotland. The Church of Scotland, unlike the Church of England, is virtually free from formal political influence. It is completely self-governing, and there are no Crown appointments. While a small amount of revenue comes from unextinguished teinds (English: tithes), the Church is almost totally supported by voluntary contributions. Lacking bishops, it has no official representation in the House of Lords and its ministers are ineligible to be MPs. The Crown is represented at the annual General Assembly of the Church of Scotland by the Queen or the Lord High Commissioner.

The Church of Scotland likes to think of itself as the 'voice of Scotland', and its General Assembly has some claim to be the nearest thing in Scotland to a representative body. Yet the membership of Church is only 919,000 (1982), out of a population of 5 million (adults *c.* $3\frac{1}{2}$ million), and the procedure used to choose delegates to the General Assembly bears little resemblance to a democratic election by all Church members.[3] It is arguable whether Assembly deliberations represent accurately the opinions of the Church members, and no 'general elections' take place on the issues discussed, which range over a wide conspectus of political as well as religious matters.

Despite these qualifications, the Church of Scotland has sometimes had great political influence. Its views on Africa were listened to by governments in the late 1950s, when its liberalism (derived largely from the large contingent of missionaries) led to the support of such causes as self-government for Nyasaland. Assembly debates have been attended by government leaders, such as Iain Macleod in 1959, and Harold Wilson in 1969.

Some Scottish Government members have been active churchmen, notably William Ross (Secretary of State for Scotland, 1964–70 and

1974–76). Ross reflected the conservative wing of the Church in such matters as liquor licensing, Sunday observance, homosexuality, family planning, and divorce. In all these, the Church as a whole tends to conservatism, and parliamentary legislation on the above subjects was either not forthcoming or seriously modified in its application to Scotland. It is likely that such variations between Scots and English Law owe much to the influence of powerful voices in the Church of Scotland, and their political allies. There is evidence, however, that this pressure was weakening by the 1970s, and the Church failed to prevent the passing of the Licensing (Scotland) Act 1976. Moreover, the lobbying of MPs by the Kirk on divorce and homosexual law reform was very low key.[4]

In the late 1960s, resolutions calling for a Scottish legislative body were accepted by the General Assembly, and the Church and Nation Committee gave evidence to the Commission on the Constitution to this effect. Other notable policy stands were: opposition to the Sunday Entertainment Bill (1967); acceptance of homosexual law reform (1968), which had been opposed in 1967; proposals for divorce law reform (1969); and support for providing unmarried women with contraceptive pills (1970). The Church opposed entry to the EEC in October 1970 and May 1971, but supported entry in October 1971. In 1981 unilateral nuclear disarmament was rejected, but virtually accepted in 1982. The inconsistencies sometimes revealed owe much to the rotating membership of the Assemblies and Commissions of Assembly.

The position of the Roman Catholic Church on many of these questions reinforces the pressure exerted by conservative Presbyterians. The failure of the Divorce (Scotland) Bill 1970 and the restrictions on free family planning in the late 1960s gave as much satisfaction to the strong Roman Catholic faction within the Scottish Labour Party as it did to the Presbyterians. But the Catholic interest in licensing restrictions and Sunday observance is much less marked than that of the Church of Scotland. It is, however, intensely concerned with abortion law reform, and has been active in campaigning against such reforms, either directly (as in statements by the clergy) or indirectly through organisations such as the Society for the Protection of Unborn Children. Some of this activity has been prominent in elections, such as the Garscadden by-election (1978). In 1979, Labour candidates were asked to state their views on abortion by organisations such as the Scottish Lay Apostolate Council.[5]

The Roman Catholic Church is a quasi-governmental body as a

result of its position in the state education system. Under the Education (Scotland) Act 1918, Roman Catholic schools were transferred to the state, which maintains them as an integral part of the public provision of education. This is unlike the position in England and Wales, where the Roman Catholic Church is still in charge of buildings, appointments, and curricula, although it is in receipt of government grants covering nearly all running expenses. The merger of Catholic schools with the state system in Scotland was the result of the relative poverty of Catholics in Scotland, who could not afford the finance necessary to pay for their own schools.[6] The bargain then struck gives the Catholic community 100% financial support for their schools, which are officially controlled by the education committees of local authorities. Appointments of teachers are made in accordance with the wishes of Church representatives, and a Catholic content is retained in the curriculum.

Today, the position of such denominational schools is under attack from a section of the Labour Party in Scotland. This group wishes to abolish the separate Catholic schools, as a corollary of the comprehensivisation of education. Such a change is strongly resisted by Catholic sopkesmen and their allies in the Party who point to the potential loss of the Catholic vote in such areas as Glasgow.

Both Labour and Conservative governments tend to stand aside from this issue, and await a settlement of differences between the relevant interests. While the Catholic leadership is reluctant to agree to change, there is some evidence that the laity is not strongly in favour of separate schools,[7] and with declining school rolls, some Catholic schools have had to be closed, leading to long journeys to school for Catholic children.

Public opinion is moving against 'segregation' in education, whether religious, racial, or meritocratic, and the Labour Party's policy of favouring comprehensive schools has had special repercussions in Scotland on account of the religious division of the state system. The Labour Party in Scotland has accepted that total integration is desirable in the long run, but it is in no hurry to precipitate a clash with the strong Catholic element in the party.[8]

The strong links between the churches and education should be borne in mind when considering the organised groups concerned specifically with the teaching profession. Nevertheless, these groups help to break down religious distinctions, since they recruit their members from both the non-denominational and Catholic schools. However, the issue of denominational schools spilled over into the

180

Educational Institute of Scotland (EIS), the largest teachers' organisation, in 1979, when a motion calling for integration was passed.[9] This brought a threat of mass resignation from the Catholic members, which was only averted by the promise (similar to that given by the Labour Party) that integration would not be imposed on an unwilling Catholic community. The EIS has seven places specifically for Catholics on its Council, and most Catholic teachers are EIS members, although there is a small Association of Catholic Teachers.

The EIS is the principal teachers' association, with 46,000 members. These account for three-fifths of all Scottish teachers, and the Institute is the principal spokesman body in consultations with the Government. Its organ, *The Scottish Educational Journal*, appears weekly, and is read by a large number of teachers. *The Times Educational Supplement* started a Scottish edition in 1965, with about a quarter of its content separate from the London edition.

Other important teachers' organisations are the Scottish Secondary Teachers Association (SSTA) (7,500 members) and the National Association of Schoolmasters/Union of Women Teachers (NAS/UWT) (2,500 members).* The latter was a purely Scottish union (the Scottish Schoolmasters Association) until it merged with the mainly English NAS/UWT in 1975. It is the main British schoolteachers' union operating in Scotland. (Another is the small Professional Association of Teachers.) Proposals to link the EIS formally with the National Union of Teachers, the largest teachers' union in England, were defeated in 1980. This was despite the fact that the EIS's Salaries Convener was in favour. His argument that it was futile to negotiate pay settlements for Scottish teachers separately from those in England did not convince the members, who feared that the Scottish union would be swallowed up by the English union.[10]

Not only are there fears of lack of identity as between Scotland and England, but there are also 'demarcation disputes' within Scotland. The Scottish Further Education Association (SFEA) (1,600 members) competes with the Further Education section of the EIS (3,800 members).* The SSTA and NAS/UWT compete with the EIS, and claim that the latter does not adequately represent the views of certain types of teacher, since it is dominated by primary school women teachers. The Professional Association of Teachers (PAT; 2,500 members)* is pledged not to strike; the Scottish Honours Graduate Teachers' Association seeks to protect Honours graduates, and so on.

*Membership figures of organisations are for 1983.

The Government and local authorities negotiate pay and conditions of service with teachers and lecturers through two Committees, one for schools and one for further education. The Secretary of State decides which bodies are to be represented, and by how many votes. The negotiations are then carried out between these bodies and the 'employers', the local authorities, in the form of the Education Committee of the Convention of Scottish Local Authorities (COSLA). The Secretary of State has two delegates on each committee, but his power is much greater than his number of votes. He can effectively veto a pay settlement by refusing to finance it through the Rate Support Grant. Arbitration may then be resorted to, and ultimately a vote in Parliament, if the Secretary of State does not accept the arbitration award.

In 1983 the composition of the two committees was:

Scottish Joint Negotiating Committee for Teaching Staff in School Education:

Management side	— 15 COSLA
	2 Secretary of State for Scotland
Staff side	— 13 EIS
	3 SSTA
	1 NAS/UWT
	1 PAT

Scottish Joint Negotiating Committee for Teaching Staff in Further Education:

Management side	— 12 COSLA
	3 Governing Bodies of Collages of Education
	4 Governing Bodies of Central Institutions
	2 Secretary of State for Scotland
Staff side	— 8 EIS
	4 SFEA
	3 Association of Lecturers in Colleges of Education in Scotland
	2 Association of Lecturers in Scottish Central Institutions
	2 Association of Scientific, Technical and Managerial Staff

The process of pay negotiations is separate from that in England and Wales, but Government pay policies in the public sector have produced almost identical awards in all parts of Great Britain.

However, the separate machinery allows for a different distribution of increases in Scotland from that elsewhere. Thus, separate salary scales operate in Scotland, and these tend to reward Honours graduates and penalise primary school teachers. Since the 'Houghton' pay enquiry of 1974, which covered all of Great Britain, the differences between Scotland and England have been diminished, but they still exist.

The whole sphere of Scottish education is an autonomous 'arena', with the Government represented by the Scottish Education Department. The autonomy of the arena was strengthened in 1965 by the establishment of the General Teaching Council for Scotland, a body which has no counterpart as yet in England, and which is intended to provide the teaching profession with a measure of self-government.

The General Teaching Council (GTC) registers qualified teachers in Scotland (their qualifications are different from those of English teachers), advises the Secretary of State for Scotland on the conditions for registration, and exercises professional discipline. It consists of 49 members, of whom 25 must be teachers and elected by registered teachers in Scotland. Fifteen are appointed by local authorities; 4 elected by the principals of colleges of education; 4 nominated by the Secretary of State; and 1 elected by college of education teachers. In 1982, the EIS secured 20 of the 25 teacher seats, and the SSTA secured 4 seats.

The relationship between the Scottish and English education 'arenas' is spasmodic and at times tinged with suspicion. Scottish teachers consider their professional qualifications superior to those of English teachers, largely because until the 1970s graduates in England could become qualified teachers there without possessing a professional certificate from a college or institute of education. This led to the exclusion of English teachers without professional qualifications from Scottish schools. As a result, there has been little coming and going between the staffs of schools in England and Scotland. In 1982 the English and Welsh Education Ministers announced that from 1984 all new teachers in England and Wales had to be graduates with an O-level pass in Mathematics. These conditions penalised Scottish teachers, since not all are graduates or have the Mathematics pass. The Scottish Secretary came under pressure from the EIS to introduce a four-year degree course for primary school teachers, since without it such teachers would not be able to gain employment in England. In 1983 he announced that such a course would be introduced in 1984, thereby bringing Scotland into line with England

183

and Wales. This illustrated the typical duality of the Scottish political system: an assertion of independence, coupled with a demand for equality with England.

The Scottish universities stand somewhat on one side of this arena. About 70% of their students are from Scottish schools, and their entrance requirements and courses derive from Scottish traditions. But they come principally under the University Grants Committee and the Department of Education and Science, not the Scottish Education Department. In 1971, most of the Scottish universities and colleges withdrew from the Scottish Union of Students to join the (UK) National Union of Students. The SUS was then wound up, and by 1975 all Scottish universities except Glasgow were affiliated to the NUS. The NUS maintains a separate Scottish organisation and holds a Scottish conference. This is paralleled by the Association of University Teachers (Scotland) on the staff side.

The legal profession in Scotland is more interested in maintaining its independence from the English legal profession than in ensuring comparability. It is more exclusive than the teaching profession, for all practising lawyers in Scotland must be qualified in Scots Law. This means that part of their education must have been spent in Scotland.

Law and politics have always been closely intertwined in Scotland, and after 1707 the Court of Session and the Scottish Bar took over Parliament House in Edinburgh. While the Church of Scotland General Assembly makes claims to be the 'voice of Scotland' in the absence of a Scottish parliament, the Scottish bar and judiciary can reasonably claim that it was for nearly two centuries the effective government of Scotland. As we have seen, until 1885, when the office of Secretary for Scotland was established, the Lord Advocate looked after the affairs of Scotland in the Government, and even to this day the influence of lawyers in Scottish public life remains great.

The importance of Scots Law in the Scottish political system has already been stressed (see Ch. 2). The Act of Union, as far as the position of the law is concerned, has continued undiluted to the present time. So too has the part played by Scottish judges, advocates, and solicitors in quasi-governmental activities. For example, numerous public bodies include one or more judges, and such official organs as the Council on Tribunals have Scottish committees, appointed in this case by the Secretary of State for Scotland.

The principal professional organisations are the Faculty of Advocates, representing the Scottish Bar, and the Law Society of Scotland,

184

representing the solicitor branch. The latter has its own *Journal*, and there are several other periodical publications concerned with Scottish legal matters (the most well-known being the *Scots Law Times*). The scales for legal aid are determined by the Law Society, and it also regulates solicitors' fees.

Although few Scots lawyers are MPs or peers, their influence in legislation is considerable. The drafting of law relating exclusively to Scotland requires parliamentary draftsmen qualified in Scots Law, and law reform is largely inspired by the Scottish Law Commission, chaired by a judge. It issues periodic reports on aspects of law in need of change. On occasion, joint reports with the English Law Commission are produced, one indication that much modern law is common in principle to both Scotland and England.

On the whole, the relationships between the legal profession and the other sections of community, and between it and government, are harmonious and somewhat detached. The historic clash of Law and Kirk in the 1830s, leading to the Disruption of the Church of Scotland in 1843, is now forgotten, as is the subsequent Free Church case in 1904 (for an account of these see Kellas, *Modern Scotland*, 2nd edn, George Allen and Unwin (London, 1980), Ch. 4). The self-government of the legal profession, which is probably greater than that of the medical profession, and much greater than that of the teachers, means that it rarely has to negotiate with the Government about pay or conditions of service. At the same time, the structure and staffing of the courts and the other sources of politico-legal patronage loom large in the horizons of many lawyers, and for them the relationship with government must be close and profitable.

The three historic Scottish institutions of Church, education, and law are to a large extent the basis of the national identity of Scotland. Their separateness ensures the survival of the Scottish nation. Yet there are numerous other organisations which are Scottish in form, and contribute to the Scottishness of organised group activity.

The old Scottish local government system gave rise to bodies such as the Convention of Royal Burghs and the Association of County Councils. In 1975, a Convention of Scottish Local Authorities was formed, to represent both the new Regions and the new Districts. The authorities themselves are important influences in the shaping of policy, and it is significant that Scottish local authorities are almost entirely confined, in their dealings with government, to putting pressure on the Scottish Office, as the department concerned with local government. This makes their appearances on the English political scene minimal. In recent years, however, concern about industrial development and rail closures has brought them into contact with Whitehall ministries, and they have always had dealings with the Scottish officials of the Department of Industry on the siting of factories.

Next in importance in terms of Scottish identity are the 'omnibus' associations, comprising a number of organisations which have combined to form a Scottish spokesman body. The Scottish Trades Union Congress (STUC) dates from 1897, and includes trade unions and trades councils (the latter are excluded from the British TUC). It has over 815,000 affiliated members from around 70 unions.

Although few trade unions are purely Scottish today,[11] in contrast to the situation when the STUC was founded, the Scottish members of British trade unions often face employers whose associations are Scottish, or who maintain that Scottish conditions are different from those elsewhere. This necessitates separate negotiations in Scotland. For example, local government officers, electricity workers, and newspapermen are members of British unions, but their employers are the Scottish local authorities, the Scottish electricity boards, and the Scottish Daily Newspaper Society respectively. This has led to specifically Scottish industrial disputes, and some insulation from English disputes. When London newspapers are on strike, their counterparts in Scotland often continue publication (the same is of course true in reverse, when the Scottish papers are on strike).

In its evidence to the Royal Commission on Trade Unions and Employers' Associations (1966–8) the STUC described itself as 'spokesman for Scotland' on the industrial, economic, and social scene 'and not only within the trade union movement'. As such, it is another attempt to fill the gap left by the absence of a Scottish legislature. It claims that it has

> provided a service to organised labour in Scotland which it is doubtful if the Trades Union Congress could have performed so effectively. The texture of Scottish life with its separate traditions in Law, Church, Education and Government is such as would have compelled the establishment of a separate Congress...
>
> As the most representative organ of Scottish opinion it has assumed a growing role at a time when the tendency towards regionalism may well continue to develop.[12]

This rôle can be seen in the large number of Scottish public bodies and advisory committees which include one or more members nominated by the STUC (see appendix to this chapter, pp. 194–6). And its position as a leader of Scottish opinion was given expression on 14 February 1972, when it organised a 'Scottish Assembly' in Edinburgh to discuss Scottish unemployment and industrial development. Over a thousand delegates were present, representing bodies such as the political parties, local authorities, Scottish Council, the Confederation of British Industry, the Church of Scotland, and the universities. There was widespread support for devolution and for a strengthening of the Scottish Office's functions in industrial matters. A permanent Commission of 18 was established to represent the views of Scotland in the future, and the whole exercise was another example of the desire to fill the vacuum in the Scottish political system which is caused by the lack of an elected legislature or representative body (*Glasgow Herald*, 15 February 1972). A subsequent meeting of the Assembly took place in January 1973 but none have been called since then.

The outlook of the STUC seems at first sight to be strongly nationalist, but this should be seen in the context of the increasingly British character of industrial relations generally. The Industrial Relations Act 1971, the 'social contract' of 1974, and the disappearance of most purely Scottish unions indicate in different ways a shift away from Scotland as a focus of industrial decision-making.

The STUC remains an active pressure-group on behalf of Scottish workers' interests, and its lobbying in London is vigorous. Its annual congress receives considerable publicity in Scotland, and throughout Britain when Labour Party leaders speak at it. It is more to the left than the TUC, and so are such unions as the Scottish Area of the National Union of Mineworkers, in which Communist influence is strong. The STUC has fewer bureaucrats in its organisation than the TUC, and its congress is made up of rank-and-file union members to a greater extent than the official-laden congress of the TUC. Being more remote from government, the STUC has struck an independent line earlier on such subjects as the prices and incomes policy (1967), and entry to the EEC (1970).

But the real power has slipped to the big unions and the TUC, and trade unionists in Scotland increasingly look to them for support. This is all the more necessary as the control of industry in Scotland shifts to non-Scottish firms or public corporations, whose headquarters are in England, or abroad.

Scots want equal wages with workers in England and they stand to gain from British unions negotiating British rates. This tends to leave purely Scottish spokesmen somewhat on the sidelines.

At the same time, the STUC does draw attention to the particular needs of Scottish industry, which might otherwise be swamped within the all-British organisations. In the campaigning over Upper Clyde Shipbuilders and the Hunterston steel development in 1971, the STUC added an extra dimension to the activities of the unions involved by emphasising the needs of the whole Scottish economy. Thus particular Scottish disputes became enhanced with the aura of a national struggle.

A similar approach is adopted by the Scottish Council (Development and Industry). This is an 'omnibus' body made up of representatives of employers, unions, local authority associations, civil service 'assessors', and individuals. It originated in the 1930s, when Sir James Lithgow, the shipbuilder, established the Scottish Development Council to attract industry to Scotland. During the Second World War, a semi-official Scottish Council on Industry was set up by Thomas Johnston, the Scottish Secretary, as a substitute for a Scottish Board of Trade. These two bodies merged in 1946 to form the Scottish Council (Development and Industry).

Although not a government agency, it appears as such in the *Handbook on Scottish Administration* (HMSO, Edinburgh 1967). This illustrates the ambiguity of its position. It is a private body supported largely by subscriptions from its members but also in receipt of government grants. Since the Scottish Development Agency (SDA) was established in 1975, the Scottish Office has cut back its financial assistance, since the SDA has taken over much of the Scottish Council's function of attracting industry to Scotland. The Scottish Office used the medium of the Scottish Council to promote its ideas, most notably in the publication of the Council's *Report on the Scottish Economy* ('Toothill Report') in 1961. In form the work of the Council, the report was in fact written by Scottish Office civil servants, and one of its principal recommendations was the setting up of a Development Department within the Scottish Office. This was done in 1962. Later Reports, with titles such as *Oceanspan* and *Eurospan*, envisaged the central belt of Scotland as a bridge between North America and the continent of Europe. To some extent, Britain's entry to the EEC did stimulate American industries to settle in Scotland, but the Scottish Council is not influential in Whitehall, and has to rely on the Scottish Office to take up its ideas. It has also espoused a kind of Scottish nationalism (for example, in its 1969 Report, *Centralisation*, and in its annual International Forums at Aviemore), which does not generally accord with the views of Scottish business or of the Conservative Party.

The Scottish Council is not the only business-related group with a Scottish organisation and Scottish policy. The Scottish office of the Confederation of British Industry issues annual surveys of Scottish industry, and makes recommendations which, like those of the Scottish Council, call for special incentives for Scottish industrial development. So too do the recommendations of the Scottish Chamber of Commerce.

Scottish agriculture has been separately organised for many years. In part this is the result of the Scottish Office's responsibilities for the industry in the Department of Agriculture and Fisheries for Scotland. The department administers most of the agricultural support expenditure in Scotland, regulates farming and fishing, and even manages smallholdings and crofting estates of its own.

Scottish farmers have their own association, the National Farmers' Union of Scotland, which, along with the National Farmers' Union of England and Wales and the Ulster Farmers' Union has an office near the EEC Commission in Brussels, and is represented on the European farmers' organisation, COPA (in translation, Committee of Professional Agricultural Organisations). It is involved in the annual agricultural price settlement under the Common Agricultural Policy. In this negotiation, the Scottish Office is a participant. Farm workers are normally members of the Transport and General Workers' Union, although their wages are regulated by the Scottish Agricultural Wages Board. The rates have been higher than those in England in recent years.

Complaints are sometimes heard that Scottish farming interests tend to be swamped in the EEC review by the dominance of the English farmers, whose produce (e.g. wheat and pork) may not be important in Scotland. There are no separate subsidies for Scotland, and if the money goes on, for example, wheat, then oats and barley tend to suffer. Lately, however, Scottish farmers have appeared more content with the support schemes, and the strength of the Scottish Office here may be indicated by the fact that the ministerial team conducting negotiations in the EEC includes Scottish Office ministers. In 1982, these were prominent in the British delegation's negotiation of the Common Fisheries Policy. Scottish fishermen are organised in several localised bodies, but most combine in the Scottish Fishermen's

Federation, which speaks to the Scottish Office on European matters, and to the EEC directly.

Apart from these major economic interest groups, there are a whole host of Scottish organisations related to particular trades, businesses, and professions. That these should have a Scottish form is one of the minor puzzles of modern Scotland. The Glasgow telephone directory lists around 300 entries under 'Scottish . . .', ranging from the Scottish Opera Centre to the Scottish Bookmakers' Protection Association. While some of these can be related to a peculiar Scottish interest (e.g. the Scottish Football Referees' Association), others seem to have no Scottish character other than location (e.g. Scottish Window Cleaning Co.).

The reasons for using the word 'Scottish' vary from one body to another. The principal ones are *(a)* that the organisation is located in Scotland; *(b)* that the organisation's activities are confined largely to Scotland; *(c)* that the tag 'Scottish' is a trading advantage in a country with strong national consciousness; *(d)* that there are actual differences in the interests or services involved as between Scotland and elsewhere; and *(e)* that it is an expression of Scottish nationalism.

In some cases, only one of these factors is relevant, while in a few all characteristics are present. Many groups adopt a Scottish organisation because it is more convenient to do so than to be part of a British one. There is a close-knit pattern of trade and communication in Scotland, which is broken by the sparsely populated Border region between Scotland and England. Commercial and travel links in Scotland converge on Edinburgh and Glasgow, not on the main cities of England. Thus a Scottish network of organised groups develops almost naturally.

The relevance of convenience is clearly seen in such trade associations as the Scottish Commercial Travellers' Association and Scottish Federation of Meat Traders' Association. These bodies illustrate points *(a)* and *(b)* above. Under *(c)*, it is possible to trace a trading advantage in the use of 'Scottish' in enterprises such as the *Scottish Daily Express*, and in the various insurance companies such as Scottish Amicable, Scottish Provident, and Scottish Widows. The newspapers wish to impress their Scottish readers that they are predominantly devoted to Scottish affairs, while the insurance companies perhaps believe that they can attract customers on the strength of the popular belief in Scottish thrift and business acumen.

National differences in the interests or services of an organisation

190

(point *(d)*) occur principally among the historic or public sectors of Scottish life, such as the churches, education, law, and administration. Some of these have been discussed earlier in this chapter. They combine considerations of convenience with nationalist sentiment, and range very widely indeed from the relatively 'neutral' (as far as nationalism is concerned) promotional groups such as the Royal Scottish Society for the Prevention of Cruelty to Children[13] to the intensely nationalist Scottish Football Association and Scottish Football League.

It is obviously convenient to organise football on Scottish lines, as most of the teams are in the central lowlands of Scotland and would have to travel long distances to play English teams. But the origins of the Scottish Football Association (founded 1873) owe as much to the nationalism of Scottish football enthusiasts, who preferred to have nothing to do with English football. Football rivalry between Scotland and England is of course a large determinant of the nationalism of the working class in the twentieth century (see Ch. 7).

It might be deduced from this account of organised groups in Scotland that almost all the interests of the people of Scotland have taken on a Scottish form. As a corrective, it is necessary to balance the picture of apparent strength of such Scottish groups with an assessment of their importance relative to British groups operating in Scotland.

Interesting as it may be to discover that Scottish plumbers, motor traders, and tobacconists have their own national associations, and that those concerned about cruelty to children and animals also assert their Scottish identity, such facts tell us little about the real differences between these groups and the corresponding English groups.

In reality, a large number have identical interests and aims with those in England, and their Scottishness is the least important of their characteristics. It is doubtful whether it would make any difference if many of them merged with English groups, and some might gain financially if they were to do so. We have seen that Scottish trade unions have declined rapidly in recent years, as the benefits of membership of British unions have become apparent.

It is therefore true to say that the economic interests of the vast majority of the industrial working class of Scotland are represented and protected by British organisations, and that the Scottish bodies which remain are largely those of employers, farmers, and professional people. These three categories usually have good reason to preserve their Scottish identity, either because they pay their employees' lower wages than the average rates in England, or because they themselves have vested Scottish interests which they wish to maintain. Thus lawyers, teachers, and church ministers in Scotland defend a 'closed shop' which effectively excludes the English. In this way then, Scottish groups are predominantly middle class, with working-class Scottishness expressed in organised form through football, and the STUC.

As far as government and policy-making is concerned, the Scottish 'arena' is composed mostly of the former (middle-class) category of spokesmen. The vast apparatus of advisory councils and committees is dominated by professionals and businessmen (with an occasional STUC representative). On the other hand, Scottish working-class interests merge in the British 'arena', where the big, British unions negotiate for the Scottish workers in London, or at the factory.

Where Scotland appears to be defective in comparison with England is in the strength of its voluntary organisations in the field of citizens' rights. The political culture of Scotland is more authoritarian than that of England. This is in part because of the nature of the Scottish political system itself, which as we have seen is heavily weighted towards administrative and legal activities, without the underpinning of a legislative body to keep these in check. Beyond the political arena, other features of Scottish life illustrate authoritarian practices. Scottish state schools, for example, do not have Boards of Governors, as do English local authority schools. The institution of School Councils in Scotland in 1975, while appearing to give more power to parents, actually led to very little change, as curriculum, staffing, and discipline were excluded from the Councils' remit.

Nevertheless, there was in the 1970s an important assault on the traditional Scottish political culture by a variety of voluntary bodies, often led by English people. The Scottish Council for Civil Liberties, the Scottish Legal Action Group, and the Scottish Consumer Council tackled the question of the citizen's legal rights. As Scots Law was the target to a large extent, it is understandable that these groups took on a Scottish form. Similarly, welfare and conservation groups have been formed as Scottish organisations, perhaps because many of the relevant functions were exercised by the Scottish Office. Even where the functions (e.g. energy and social security) were not under the Scottish Office, the imperatives of Scottish organisation noted earlier have proved stronger than the forces for British unity. Thus British groups tend to have Scottish counterparts or branches: Shelter Scotland, Age Concern Scotland, Friends of the Earth Scotland,

Scottish Tenants' Organisation, and *ad hoc* bodies such as those against nuclear dumping, nuclear power stations, etc. Organisations concerned with homosexual or feminist rights (Scottish Minority Rights Group, etc.) are even further removed from traditional Scottish values, but this does not mean they are denied some success. Homosexual law reform did eventually (1980) come to Scotland, and the feminist movement has made its impact, notably in the teaching profession, where the word 'headmaster' has been replaced by 'headteacher'.

On balance, however, the Scottish political system is less 'open' than that of England to bodies of this kind. There is less of a tradition of citizen participation, and more 'élite' rule. These 'élites' have less to fear from grass-roots or radical pressures than their counterparts in England, and they are insulated from democratic politics because of the absence of a Scottish legislature. Their activities are discussed further in Ch. 12, where the policy-making process is examined.

Public bodies and advisory committees on which the STUC was represented in 1982

Source: *STUC 85th Annual Report*, pp. 7–15

Aberdeen Harbour Board
British Council for the Rehabilitation of the Disabled (Scotland)
Careers Service Advisory Council for Scotland
Central Advisory Committee for Scotland on Justices of the Peace
Cinematograph Films Council
City of Glasgow District Council Policy and Resources Committee:
    Subcommittee on employment
Community Education: Quality of Life for the Unemployed (committee)
Consultative Committee for Edinburgh Airport
Consultative Committee for Prestwick Airport
Council for Tertiary Education
Design Council: Scottish Committee
Duncan of Jordanstone College of Art
Economic and Social Committee of the EEC (J. Milne, General Secretary,
    serves as nominee of TUC General Council)
Education for the Industrial Society Project
Forth Ports Authority
General Teaching Council for Scotland
Highlands and Islands Development Board: Mull Development
    Committee
Highlands and Islands Development Board: Working Party on Higher
    Education
Highlands and Islands Development Board: Consultative Council
Livingston MOTEC: Board of Governors
Lothian Region Development Authority
Manpower Services Commission: Special Programme (representatives
    on five area Boards)
Manpower Services Committee for Scotland
Meat and Livestock Commission: Consumers Committee
Montrose Harbour Trust
National Advisory Committee on the Employment of the Disabled
Newbattle Abbey College
Nuclear Safety Advisory Committee
Open University
Parole Board for Scotland
Post Office Users' Consultative Committee for Scotland
Race Relations Board: Conciliation Committee for Scotland

Scottish Adult Literacy Agency Management Committee
Scottish Arts Council
Scottish Ballet Advisory Council
Scottish Business Education Council
Scottish Central Committee on Technical Education
Scottish Chamber of Safety
Scottish Cine Entertainment Association
Scottish College of Textiles
Scottish Cooperatives Development Committee
Scottish Community Education Centre Executive Committee
Scottish Council on Alcoholism
Scottish Council for Development and Industry: East of Scotland
    Committee
Scottish Council for Development and Industry: EEC Committee
Scottish Council for Development and Industry: Committee on In-
    dustrial and Social Conditions
Scottish Council for Development and Industry: Industrial Strategy
    Committee
Scottish Council for Development and Industry: Industry Committee
Scottish Council on Disability
Scottish Council for Educational Technology
Scottish Council for Racial Equality
Scottish Council of Social Sciences
Scottish Council for the Welfare of the Disabled: Employment Working
    Group
Scottish Development Agency (nominees of Secretary of State for
    Scotland)
Scottish Development Agency Consultative Committee
Scottish Economic Council (appointees of Secretary of State for
    Scotland)
Scottish Epilepsy Association
Scottish Gas Consumers' Council
Scottish Industrial Development Board
Scottish Industry/Education Micro-Electronics Working Party
Scottish National Orchestra
Scottish Opera Theatre Royal Board
Scottish Prison Industries
Scottish Records Advisory Commission
Scottish Technical Education Council
Scottish Tourism Consultative Council
Sea Fisheries Training Council
Sea Fish Industry Authority
7:84 Theatre Company
Shelter: Scottish Advisory Council
South of Scotland Electricity Board
Supplementary Benefits Appeal Tribunals: Training Advisory Group
Transport Users' Consultative Committee
Understanding British Industry: Scottish Advisory Committee
University of Strathclyde: General Convocation

Congress is represented by various trade unionists on:

College Councils
Careers Service Advisory Committee
Department of Health and Social Security Local Tribunals
Health Service Scotland: Area Health Boards; Local Health Councils
Industrial Tribunals
Manpower Services Commission District Manpower Committees
MacRobert Advisory Council
River Purification Board
Royal Blind Asylum and School
Scottish Business Education Council
Scottish Sports Council
South of Scotland Electricity Board
Supplementary Benefit Appeals Tribunals
War Pensions Committees
Ardrossan and Saltcoats and Stevenston Enterprise Trust
Clyde Port Authority
Countryside Commission for Scotland
North of Scotland Electricity Consultative Committee

11

Political communication and the mass media

Scotland has a strongly differentiated mass media network, which reflects and emphasises the particular characteristics of its society and its political system. It is one of the most active centres of newspaper-publishing outside London, with 6 daily morning, 6 evening, 2 Sunday, and around 100 weekly or twice-weekly newspapers. Many of these papers are independent, or are autonomous members of London publishing companies.

There is also a vigorous broadcasting output in Scotland, derived from BBC Scotland (principal studios in Glasgow, Edinburgh, and Aberdeen), Scottish Television (STV)(Glasgow and Edinburgh), and Grampian Television (Aberdeen). Border Television, which operates from Carlisle in England, transmits programmes to parts of the south-west of Scotland and the Borders, as well as to the extreme north-west of England and the Isle of Man. Independent local radio stations are (1983) Radio Clyde (Glasgow), Radio Forth (Edinburgh), Radio Tay (Dundee), North Sound (Aberdeen), Moray Firth Radio (Inverness), and West Sound (Ayr). Local BBC Radio is provided by Radio Highland (Inverness), Radio Nan Eilean (a Gaelic service for the Western Isles, from Stornoway), Radio Aberdeen, Radio Orkney, Radio Shetland, Radio Tweed, and Radio Solway.

All the communications media in Scotland assert varying degrees of independence from London, and they are able to achieve it to a greater extent than any other media output centres in Britain. Scots demand, and support, a separate newspaper press and separate broadcasting, and their tastes are reflected in the strongly Scottish content of the press, TV, and radio. The newspaper structure is shown in Table 25.

Table 25(a) gives the circulations (1981) of the principal newspapers in Scotland. The proprietors and dates of foundation are also given, where known. Table 25(b) gives the figures for adult news-

197

Table 25(a). *Place of publication, circulation (1981), founding date, and proprietor of principal Scottish newspapers*

	Circulation	Founding Date	Proprietor
Daily morning			
Daily Record (Glasgow)	727,506	1895	Mirror News- papers (IPC)
Scottish Daily Express (Glasgow/Manchester)	(*c.* 250,000)	1928	Trafalgar House
Courier and Advertiser (Dundee)	135,566	1801	D. C. Thomson
Glasgow Herald (Glasgow)	116,161	1783	Outram (Lonrho)
Press and Journal (Aberdeen)	113,038	1748	Thomson Region- al Newspapers
Scotsman (Edinburgh)	98,934	1817	Thomson Region- al Newspapers
Evening			
Evening Times (Glasgow)	211,229	1876	Outram
Evening News (Edinburgh)	113,346	1873	Thomson Region- al Newspapers
Evening Express (Aberdeen)	81,950	1879	Thomson Region- al Newspapers
Evening Telegraph (Dundee)	54,526	1877	D.C. Thomson
Greenock Telegraph (Greenock)	23,728	1857	Orr, Pollock
Paisley Daily Express (Paisley)	13,935	1874	Outram
Sunday			
Sunday Post (Glasgow and Dundee)	'Over 1,000,000'	1920	D. C. Thomson
Sunday Mail (Glasgow)	734,617	1914	IPC
Scottish Sunday Express (Manchester)	(*c.* 200,000)	1940	Trafalgar House
Principal Weekly			
Weekly News (Glasgow, Dundee, and Manchester)	1,156,324	1855	D. C. Thomson
People's Journal (6 editions) (Dundee)	53,400	1858	D. C. Thomson
Falkirk Herald	37,922	1845	F. Johnston
Hamilton Advertiser (Hamilton)	35,193	1856	Hamilton Advertiser
Perthshire Advertiser (Perth) (twice weekly)	28,902	1829	Scottish and Universal Newspapers
Dumfries and Galloway Standard (Dumfries) (twice weekly)	33,044	1843	Scottish and Universal Newspapers

Note: The Sunday Standard (circulation 127,000) was in existence from 26 April 1981 to 31 July 1983. The proprietor was Outram (Lonrho).
Source: Benn's Press Directory 1982, Vol. 1, UK (Benn, London 1982). Some circulations relate to 1980. Those in brackets are not listed in Benn, but are estimated by the author from the Readership figures in Table 25(b).

Table 25(b). *Readership of newspapers in Scotland, January–December 1981 (percentage of adults over 15 who read the following newspapers)*

	Scotland	GB	London and SE England	NE and North England
Daily Record (asked about in Scotland only)	52	5	*	*
Daily Express (Including Scottish)	17	14	14	14
Sun	17	27	29	26
Glasgow Herald	9	1	—	—
	(Glasgow area: 14)			
Press and Journal	8	1	—	—
	(Aberdeen area: 65)			
Star	8	11	7	15
Courier and Advertiser	7	1	—	—
	(Dundee area: 75)			
Scotsman	6	1	—	—
	(Edinburgh area: 19)			
Daily Mail	3	12	15	9
Daily Mirror	2	24	25	29
Daily Telegraph	2	8	12	5
Guardian	1	3	5	2
Times	1	2	3	1
Financial Times	*	1	2	1
Any National or Regional Morning	84	75	77	74
Evening Papers	35	32	13	46
Sunday Post	69	10	1	15
Sunday Mail	54	6	*	1
News of the World	12	26	25	28
Sunday Express (including Scottish)	10	18	20	16
Sunday People	10	24	22	28
Sunday Times	7	9	12	8
Observer	5	7	9	5
Sunday Mirror	5	25	28	26
Sunday Telegraph	2	6	9	4
Any National or Regional Sunday	88	78	75	79

*Under 1%; — not asked. In addition, the *Sunday Standard* (1981–3) had approximately 8% of Scottish adult readership.
Source: Joint Industry Committee for National Readership Surveys, *National Readership Survey 1981* (January–December 1981), Vol. 2 (London 1982).

paper readership (1981), covering Scotland, Great Britain, London, and the north-east and northern England.

The Scottish newspaper press has a long history, with four of its morning dailies dating back to the eighteenth or early nineteenth centuries. While few major papers published in Scotland are now Scottish-owned, all display distinctly Scottish characteristics. The *Scottish Daily Express*, though printed in Manchester, is published in Glasgow, and uses Scottish material, taking from London only major British and foreign stories, and some features. Editorial comment is shared between London and Scotland with effective power to differ where the Scottish editor thinks fit. The London editor does not see the *Scottish Express* before it is published, while the Scottish editor can pick and choose from the London edition. This arrangement had political significance during the 'D' notices affair in 1967, when the *Scottish Daily Express* printed the story about 'cable-vetting' before the English editions of the paper.[1]

The *Scottish Sunday Express* is less markedly Scottish, and uses more London features. The *Daily Mail* was published in Scotland as the *Scottish Daily Mail* until December 1968, but its poor circulation led to a retreat to Manchester. No daily newspaper published in England amounts to more than 17% of the Scottish adult readership (Table 25(b)), and that figure is reached only by the *Sun*, which in the late 1970s waged a successful campaign to break into the Scottish market. The *Daily Mirror* is replaced in most parts of Scotland by the *Daily Record* (sister-paper of the *Mirror*, but almost totally Scottish in content), and there is a very strong local readership for the Aberdeen *Press and Journal* and the Dundee *Courier and Advertiser*. The middle class in Scotland forsake the *Daily Telegraph, Times* and *Guardian* for the *Scotsman* and *Glasgow Herald*. Thus all social groups adhere on weekdays to the native press. On Sundays, the *News of the World* and *People* break through successfully, but no English Sunday matches the *Sunday Post* (69% of adults) and *Sunday Mail* (54%). Scots are more avid newspaper readers than people in the rest of Great Britain. The readership of morning daily newspapers in Scotland is 84% of the adult population, compared with 75% in Great Britain as a whole; that of Sunday newspapers is 88% compared with 78%.

In the Highlands, the strength of community interests, and the delay experienced in receiving newspapers from the south, makes the local press peculiarly important. The principal Highland newspapers are:

Highland News (Inverness)(1883) in a group with *Caithness Courier*
  (Thurso)(1866) and *John o'Groats Journal* (Wick)(1836), etc.*
Ross-Shire Journal (Dingwall)(1875)(15,000)
Inverness Courier (1817)(twice weekly)*
Oban Times (1861)(23,000)
Stornoway Gazette (1917)(13,000)
Orcadian (Kirkwall)(1854)(10,000)
Shetland Times (Lerwick)(1872)(11,000)
The Buteman (Rothesay)(1854)*
Campbeltown Courier (1873)(6,700)
West Highland Free Press (Kyleakin, Skye)(1972)(7,700)

These papers are widely read in the Highlands (and even outside)
and pay much attention to political reporting of constituency or
regional matters. Many are locally owned, and although most are
independent politically, the *Stornoway Gazette* and *Shetland Times*
describe themselves as Liberal, and the *Ross-shire Journal* is Unionist
(Newspaper Press Directory, 1982). The Stornoway paper has
recently been sympathetic towards Scottish nationalism, and is an
exponent of Gaelic culture. The *West Highland Free Press* is socialist.
  The politics of the principal Scottish newspapers have become less
static in recent years. Until the late 1950s, all except the *Daily Record*
and now-defunct *Bulletin* (Glasgow) were Conservative. After Lord
Thomson took over the *Scotsman* in the mid-1950s, that paper
became sympathetic towards the Liberal Party, and in the 1970 and
1974 general elections it favoured the SNP. Another Thomson Group
paper, the Aberdeen *Press and Journal*, deserted the Conservatives in
the late 1960s for the Scottish Nationalists, although it favoured the
Liberal-SDP Alliance in 1983.
  The *Scottish Daily Express* exhorted its readers to vote for Mrs
Winifred Ewing, the SNP candidate, at the Hamilton by-election in
November 1967. By the general election of 1970, however, it had
returned to the Conservatives, while stressing that devolution along
the lines of the Party's Scottish Convention was essential. It remained
strongly in favour of devolution until 1977, and indeed attacked
Labour's 1975 White Paper proposals as so weak as to be a 'black
betrayal of the people of Scotland who aspired to a greater say in the
running of their own affairs' (*Scottish Daily Express*, 28 November
1975). In 1977, however, after a change of ownership from
Beaverbrook Newspapers to Trafalgar House, the *Express* did a

*Circulation not available.

complete turnaround and followed Mrs Thatcher's anti-devolution line. The same is true of the *Daily Mail*, which in 1975 headlined its reaction to the White Paper as 'An Insult to Scotland!' (28 November 1975). On 1 March 1979, its headline ran 'No to this squalid manoeuvre!' (For an extensive discussion of the Scottish press and the devolution issue, see Chs. 5 and 6 of Bochel, Denver and Macartney; M. Brown, 'The Scottish morning press and the devolution Referendum of 1979', in N. Drucker and H. M. Drucker (Eds.), *The Scottish Government Yearbook 1980*, Paul Harris (Edinburgh, 1979).)

The D. C. Thomson papers (including the Dundee *Courier* and *Evening Telegraph* and *Sunday Post*) found the Nationalists attractive for a time. The last-named's colossal circulation (over 1 million; 69% of Scottish adult readership) requires some comment. The *Sunday Post* is probably the most 'Scottish' of the Scottish papers, although it circulates widely in the north of England (see Table 25(b)). Some of its writing and comic material is in Scots dialect. Most of the content consists of everyday stories about ordinary people. Politically, the paper is very right-wing. It abhors socialism, the welfare state, and trade unions (it will not recognise them among its own employees). But it stresses the peculiar virtues of Scottish character and independence of mind. This no doubt brought it close for a time to the SNP, and in general the paper helps to keep alive the differentiation between Scottish and English society, and the assessment of politics in terms of 'what is done for Scotland'.

Most Scottish newspapers take this line, and even when it was a Tory paper the *Glasgow Herald* on occasion proved critical of Conservative Governments' Scottish policies; in August 1971, for example, the paper persistently demanded more favourable treatment for Upper Clyde Shipbuilders, and the siting of a steel-works at Hunterston (Ayrshire). In 1983, the *Herald* supported the Alliance.

Scottish economic interests are identified and pursued by the Scottish press. Both the *Scotsman* and *Glasgow Herald* run Scottish financial supplements and trade reviews, and maintain industrial and agricultural correspondents. All Scottish papers are part of the economic log-rolling of the Scottish interest groups (among them the trade unions, employers associations, and the Scottish Council (Development and Industry)), who seek further government-aided development in Scotland. The political affiliation of the papers then becomes somewhat irrelevant.

The political preferences of the principal Scottish papers in the 1983 general election were as follows:

Scottish Daily Express	Conservative
Daily Record	Labour
Courier (Dundee)	Conservative
Press and Journal (Aberdeen)	Alliance
Glasgow Herald	Alliance
Scotsman	Alliance
Evening Times (Glasgow)	Alliance
Sunday Post	Conservative (but no specific recommendation on how to vote)
Sunday Mail	Labour
Scottish Sunday Express	Conservative
Sunday Standard	Alliance

During the election campaign of 1983 (as in other elections) a Scottish consciousness pervaded the press. In the *Scotsman*, all the Scottish constituencies were analysed, with profiles of the candidates. Thereafter, constituency reports were given, and the prospects weighed up. The dividing line between Scotland and England was again evident: the Scottish press had Scotland for its 'parish', and the English press, England. There were of course some overlapping interests, and the principal political speeches in England were reported in Scotland. But the Scottish campaign was seen as a unity, and was important material for readers in Scotland.

The 1983 general election was, however, much more 'British' than the elections of 1974, or even that of 1979. The SNP was highly visible in 1974, but less so in 1979 and 1983. Devolution and nationalism were burning topics in the 1970s, but after the 1979 Referendum the flame seemed to go out, and the press could not light it again. In fact, very few newspapers tried to do so. The Conservative press wished to be loyal to the party's anti-devolution policy, and all the newspapers in Scotland sensed that their readers were bored with the subject. The popular *Daily Record*, for example, kept up its pro-devolution coverage, but only on inside pages. By way of some redress, however, the *Glasgow Herald* swung round to supporting an Assembly after 1975 (this could be related to the fact that its owner at that time, Sir Hugh Fraser, joined the SNP for a time). The *Herald* remained sympathetic to devolution under its new ownership, and it was one of the many Scottish papers to support the Alliance in the election of 1983.

At non-election periods, too, the Scottish press presents a continuous service of reporting and commenting on Scottish political affairs. There is full coverage of Scottish parliamentary debates, parliamentary questions and even House of Commons Scottish committee work in the *Glasgow Herald* and *Scotsman*, which maintain their own parliamentary correspondents at Westminster. The popular papers also have parliamentary correspondents, and some have columns written by Scottish MPs. For the first year of her time in the House of Commons (from November 1967), Mrs Winifred Ewing, the SNP MP, wrote a weekly column in the *Daily Record*, and had one written *about her* in the *Scottish Daily Express* ('Winnie at Westminster').

Such journalism transmits the activities of the 'detached' portion of the Scottish political system in London to the grass-roots in Scotland. The reverse, however, is rarely the case. London prints very little political news from or about Scotland, except during such 'crisis' events as the collapse of Upper Clyde Shipbuilders (1971), or the Ravenscraig steel-mill (1983). The separate organisation of the press in Scotland is partly responsible for this, since it caters fully for Scottish readers. But a division of political interest between Scotland and England is also evident. What appears important in Scotland may have no meaning in London (examples are the Munn and Dunning reforms in Scottish education (see Ch. 12, p.227), Highland questions, and the Secretary of State for Scotland's conflicts with local authorities). So the press illustrates the separation of the Scottish and British segments of politics.

Scottish broadcasting does this also, although it is more homogeneous with that in the rest of the country than is the newspaper press. The main sources are BBC television, ITV, BBC radio, and local radio in ascending order of 'Scottishness'.

The BBC's television output in Scotland consists of around 130 hours a week (BBC 1 and BBC 2 combined). Of this, only about 10 hours originates in the studios at Glasgow, Edinburgh, and Aberdeen (see Table 26). Nevertheless, about half of the Scottish output has a bearing on politics. There is a daily Scottish news bulletin and magazine (25 minutes) at 6 p.m., and a late-night summary at around 11.30 p.m. These programmes include grass-roots and parliamentary material, with interviews of Scottish MPs and interest-group spokesmen. For nine months in the year there are two weekly current affairs programmes, devoted to Scottish problems. Special programmes are produced to report the party conferences in Scotland, the STUC conference, the Scottish local elections, and the general election campaigns and results (in the last case, Scotland 'opts out' of

Table 26.   *Broadcasting in Scotland*

	Coverage	Hours per week originating in Scotland
Television		
BBC Scotland	Most of Scotland	10
Scottish Television	Central Scotland, Oban, etc.	10
Grampian Television	North-east Scotland, Lewis, etc.	6
Border Television	South-west, Borders	4 (from Carlisle)
Radio		
BBC Scotland	All Scotland	100
Radio Clyde	Glasgow area	140
Radio Forth	Edinburgh area	130
Other independent and BBC local stations		variable

part of the network programme). Scottish schools programmes have series on Scottish history and affairs.

The BBC's Scottish headquarters in Glasgow maintains several experienced news and political commentators, whose contributions are equal in importance to those of the journalists in the Scottish press, if less partisan.

The ITV output is split between Scottish Television (STV) covering central Scotland, Grampian Television covering Aberdeen and the north of Scotland (and the north-west), and Border Television covering the south-west and Borders. The programme hours produced by these companies average 10, 6, and 4 hours respectively (Table 26). As with the BBC, about half the programmes are concerned with news, current affairs, and education. Unlike the BBC, however, ITV fragments Scotland into three, and combines the south-west with part of England and the Isle of Man. Moreover, about half the land area of Scotland (including most of the Highlands) does not receive ITV at all. Thus ITV programmes reflect a regional audience rather than an audience spread throughout the whole of Scotland. Grampian caters for Aberdeen and the north-east, STV for central Scotland, and Border for its 'multinational' community.

STV is the largest and most vigorous company, with an extended Scottish news programme daily (30 minutes for nine months of the year and 15 minutes for the remainder). It has a weekly 30-minute

205

political magazine programme, and as good a coverage of the annual political 'events' and elections as the BBC. It has one experienced political commentator, with supporting industrial and news staff.

Grampian and Border do not offer the same output of current affairs or political programmes, nor do they usually attempt to cover all the political conferences or elections. Border rarely bothers with the Scottish conferences, but Grampian and STV have reciprocal arrangements for reporting them. The smaller companies' strength lies in the news coverage and local magazine programmes. Grampian offers news (Monday to Friday) and a weekly magazine programme on the life of the area. It produces a monthly political programme involving a discussion between Scottish MPs. Other regular programmes deal with farming, religion, and education. There is also a considerable emphasis on Scottish-style light entertainment, with overtones of nationalism.

Border cannot afford to involve itself in Scottish nationalism, since 60% of its viewers are in England or the Isle of Man. In general, it does not offer a distinctively Scottish output, whether in news, politics, sport, or light entertainment. Nevertheless, its nightly news and magazine programme is very popular, as is its light entertainment. These programmes draw on local community interests. For 'Scottish' programmes Border viewers must turn to the BBC, especially for politics, sport, or religion.

BBC Scotland has a prolific radio output (around 200 hours a week including local radio) which is unmatched by any other region. Some of this is taken by the network, especially for the considerable amount of music. Much is Scottish news, comment, or educational material. The breakfast programme *Good Morning Scotland* (two editions) is important as it has a large audience and proclaims BBC Scotland's 'national network'. There is also an hour-long magazine and news programme at midday and another at tea-time. Radio caters for the Gaelic minority, with about $3\frac{1}{2}$ hours of broadcasting on weekdays and half-an-hour on Saturdays and Sundays. There are also occasional Gaelic programmes on television. The Gaelic radio output increased greatly in the late 1970s, as did that of BBC Scotland generally. The former owes much to the establishment of Radio Highland (Inverness) and Radio Nan Eilean (Stornoway) and the latter's expansion in 1978 was timed to correspond with the setting up of the Scottish Assembly. When that did not happen, BBC Scotland remained with a much-strengthened position, since BBC Radio Scotland was no longer an opt-out from Radio 4 UK but a 'network' in its own right for Scotland from six in the morning till after midnight. In fact, however, Radio Scotland now takes quite a few programmes from Radio 4 and some from Radio 2. It should also be noted that Gaelic broadcasting cannot compare in quantity with Welsh broadcasting in Wales, which includes BBC Radio Cymru and Channel 4 Wales with programmes predominantly in Welsh.

The picture of broadcasting in Scotland in the 1980s differs from that in England in several respects. The BBC has not in Scotland, as in England, largely replaced its regional broadcasting with local radio stations. This is because the National Broadcasting Council for Scotland vetoed such a proposal as being destructive of the national unity of the country.[2] The Council is charged with controlling BBC broadcasting in Scotland, and it is a buttress of national identity. At the same time, it is very much part of the Scottish Establishment, and consists of respected representatives of the Church, university, local government, and Gaelic communities. At the height of the SNP's first electoral success (1967–9) it refused to entertain the party's request that its political broadcasting time be increased beyond the 5 minutes on television and radio per year granted in 1965 although the ITV favoured this.

Party political broadcasting time is fixed by the Committee on Political Broadcasting, which consists of representatives of the Conservative, Labour, and Liberal Parties and, since 1974, the SNP, and the IBA and BBC (Butler and Pinto-Duschinsky, p. 201). The Committee meets annually to review, in the light of election results and other evidence, the ratio of time which will be allotted to the parties. It also devises separate ratios for Scotland and Wales, in view of the existence of nationalist parties in these areas.

The formula for allocating party political broadcasts during a general election campaign is ambiguous where Scotland. is concerned. The general rule is that if a party nominates 50 candidates or more it is entitled to a broadcast (Butler and King, p. 126). The Communist Party qualified in this way in 1966 and 1970, and the National Front did so in October 1974, 1979, and 1983. But the SNP did not qualify for a party political broadcast to be shown throughout Britain, despite putting up more than 50 candidates at every election since 1970. It did, however, qualify for one Scottish broadcast of 5 minutes each on TV and radio in 1966 and 1970, increased to two in 1974. The formula in the election of 1983 was as follows:

TV: Conservative and Labour, five 10-minute broadcasts; SDP-Liberal Alliance, four 10-minute broadcasts; SNP, two 10-minute broadcasts in Scotland only; Plaid Cymru, one 10-minute broadcast in Wales only.

BBC Radio 4 UK: Labour and Conservative, four 10-minute broadcasts; Alliance, three 10-minute broadcasts.

BBC Radio 2: Labour and Conservative, three 5-minute broadcasts; Alliance, two 5-minute broadcasts.

BBC Radio Scotland: SNP, two 10-minute broadcasts.

BBC Radio Wales/Cymru: Plaid Cymru, one 10-minute broadcast.

The SNP has attacked the arrangements at each election as unfair to it. It maintains that the transmission of party political broadcasts in Scotland should reflect only the Scottish balance of parties, and that on this basis (at least until 1979) it was under-represented and the Liberal Party was over-represented. It also claims the right to a UK broadcast, on the basis that it puts up the requisite number of candidates. It does not, however, put any candidates up outside Scotland. If it did, then the formula should entitle it to a UK broadcast.

About half of the party political broadcasts transmitted in Scotland on behalf of the British political parties are actually specially made for Scotland, and shown only there. Thus, the 'Scottish Conservative Party' has its own broadcasts, as does 'The Labour Party in Scotland', and the 'Scottish Liberal Party' (in 1983, the 'Liberal-SDP Alliance').

In the case of political programmes other than 'party politicals', yet another formula is in operation. In 1966 it was agreed that if a party contested one-fifth of the seats in a region, it was entitled to equal representation on programmes featuring party spokesmen. UK programmes were similarly dealt with, leaving the three main parties with assured seats on network coverage. As far as Scottish programmes were concerned, the formula secured representation for five parties in 1966 and 1970 since the Communists just qualified, with 15 candidates both times. Despite the fact that there were three ITV companies operating in Scotland, Scotland was treated as a unit for this purpose. This meant that Grampian and Border had to have Communist representation on all 'spokesmen' programmes despite the absence of Communist candidates in their areas. In other regions, each company's territory was used to compile the ratio. Since October 1974, the Communists have not qualified. On British network political programmes the Nationalists are naturally poorly represented. During the 1983 campaign, for example, the SNP and Plaid Cymru complained that in the BBC television *Election Call* series of interviews of party leaders, both parties had to share a single programme. Legal action was threatened, but was not actually taken.

Outside election campaigns, political discussion programmes are largely free from such formulae, although fairness, impartiality, and party balance must be observed. From 1966 to 1970 the SNP complained that their appearances on current affairs programmes were fewer than their popular support warranted (in 1968 they received 30% of the vote in the local elections). It is true that BBC Scotland veered away from all political subjects on television after mid-1968, and that SNP spokesmen were not seen for a year on that channel. While pressure from the major parties may have been partly responsible for this, there was also a feeling, reflected throughout the mass media, that the SNP was less newsworthy than it had been. The number of broadcasts and newspaper articles devoted to nationalism had been high to that point, and the subject was becoming over-exposed. Nevertheless, the building-up of the SNP by the media, followed by its comparative neglect, may have contributed to the rapid rise and fall of the party's fortunes at that time.

Scotland has a volume of broadcasting about politics in its area, both at election and non-election times, which is unmatched by any other part of Britain. The Scottish broadcasting media do not usually seek to produce programmes about other regions, or about British politics in general. Indeed, only a small proportion of Scottish programmes are seen outside Scotland. In 1981–2, 129 hours out of the 641 hours of television broadcasting originating in BBC Scotland went to the network. This should be compared with 545 hours of network television broadcasting out of 722 hours from BBC Manchester, and 513 out of 692 hours from BBC Pebble Mill (Birmingham). The only truly 'regional' services on BBC television are those of Scotland, Wales, and Northern Ireland. These provide 'opt-outs' from BBC 1 for their region of 512 hours, 840 hours, and 317 hours respectively. The highest 'opt-outs' for English regions are 179 hours (Pebble Mill), 177 hours (Manchester), and 175 hours (Bristol). The dominance of 'network' programmes on BBC television can be seen from the fact that these amounted to 8,419 hours in 1981–2. Current affairs, features, documentaries, and news accounted for 2,178 hours of network broadcasting.[3] Thus, the Scottish output in these political areas, while significant for Scottish politics, is tiny in comparison with the British output, and this must influence the Scots' consciousness of politics. Even smaller network contributions are made by STV and

209

Grampian. Scots watch network or other non-Scottish programmes for nine-tenths of the time. They are well-accustomed to such programmes as the network news and network political features (e.g. BBC's *Panorama* and ITV's *World in Action*). These programmes emphasise the British, not Scottish, aspects of politics, and during election periods rarely mention parties such as the SNP, or Scottish political issues. Broadcasting in general therefore goes some way to counteracting the otherwise divisive influence of the Scottish media, especially the press, which is much more completely Scottish.

The quality of Scottish political broadcasting is not equal to that of the best network productions. Its popularity in terms of audience ratings is also lower. There is a high rating for Scottish news productions, however, and Scottish light entertainment and sports programmes are as popular as those from the network. The expense and difficulty of producing good programmes in Scotland is greater than that of producing good newspapers. So there is more reliance on London in broadcasting than in the press.

Both branches of the communications media in Scotland play a vital part in the Scottish political system. Political information is now principally conveyed by television, and the Scottish channels have developed their own news and current affairs programmes. In the Scottish press, a vigorous and partisan political commentary is available, with the two 'quality' papers (*Scotsman* and *Glasgow Herald*) providing comprehensive reporting and analysis. There is ample support in the communications media for the operation of an autonomous Scottish political system.

And the links between the communications networks in Scotland and the decision-making machinery are also close. Scottish decision-makers in central and local government are as influenced by the *Scotsman* and the *Glasgow Herald* as their English counterparts are by *The Times*, *Guardian*, or *Daily Telegraph*. The prominence given to Scottish politics in the Scottish press shapes the attitudes of the electorate and the interest groups. Campaigns in Scottish newspapers (such as that to 'Save the Argylls' and the attack on the Highland Board in the *Scottish Daily Express* in 1967) have been important politically, and Scottish MPs avidly read the Scottish newspapers in the Library of the House of Commons for reports of their speeches. They are rarely disappointed, for Scottish papers carry an ample coverage of Scottish parliamentary activities. It must be presumed that the Scottish public shares at least some of their interest.

210

12

The policy-making process

The process of making policy is central to the working of a political system. In a democracy, it converts the political demands of society into governmental actions. If this job is done properly, the political system will be stable, and its activities will be beneficial to the social system (or systems) as a whole.[1]

The components of the Scottish political system have already been dealt with. They include those means which Scots have developed for articulating and aggregating their interests, such as the Scottish MPs, organised groups, and the media; those institutions which respond to such demands within the governmental structure, such as the Scottish Office; and those institutions which execute the decisions of government, or adjudicate disputes (i.e. the public service and the Scottish legal system). It is the thesis of this book that such activities constitute a Scottish political system, since the degree of interaction and interdependence of the components defines a boundary between the Scottish and English political systems, and that the range of activities which is involved makes it a relatively more important political system than those which could be analysed at (for example) the regional level in England or at the local (i.e. sub-state) level in countries such as the United States. It thus has feature of 'macro-politics', as well as 'micro-politics'.

In analysing these components, some attempt has been made to describe how they work, and to illustrate their dynamic qualities within the system. The question has been, 'What is the place of these institutions/organisations/people in the Scottish political system, and what are their characteristic activities?'

In this chapter, the question is rephrased to shed a different light on the system. Instead of asking what makes up the system, the enquiry is directed to the question of how decisions in certain fields of policy are made, and by whom. This involves a re-examination of the parts of the system, and reintroduces more forcibly the place of actors outside

211

the system who are important to it. In particular, it shows the place of the British political system in the decision-making process affecting Scotland.

Three broad areas have been chosen, for their importance and contrasting nature. They are (a) public finance and economic planning, (b) social services, and (c) law reform. Each has a measure of documentation, and a lively history. And in each there is a different relationship between Scottish and British decision-makers.

(a) Public finance and economic planning

Much attention in recent years has focussed on the financial and economic aspects of the Scottish political system. In part, this has been the result of the debate on devolution and independence which has included a discussion of devolved taxes and the economics of independence, etc.[2] Of more relevance to this chapter, however, are general studies of public expenditure in Scotland, which throw light on how the Scottish Office receives and spends its financial allocations from the Treasury, and how it in turn gives grants, etc., to local authorities and other bodies. From these sources, an assessment can be made of the nature and strength of part of the Scottish political system, for the getting and spending of public money is crucial to policy-making. It is difficult to assess the system as a whole on this basis, however, since public finance is only one aspect of it, and a rather special aspect. Even federal systems display a marked centralisation in financial and economic matters, and Scotland has neither federalism nor devolution. Most of the academic commentaries on the finances of Scottish government make comparisons between the present Scottish situation and what might be expected under devolution, federalism or independence, to point up what is seen as the lack of power or autonomy in the existing system. It is more realistic to examine the practices and outcomes of the Scottish political system in the context of conventional accounts of the British system of government. If this is done, what is noteworthy is not the lack of autonomy for Scotland, but how much independence there is within a so-called 'unitary' and homogeneous British constitutional and political framework.

In the first place, the concept of 'Treasury control' over public expenditure, when applied to Scotland, requires a modification which is not usually described in the standard British government textbooks. Although Scotland has no power to raise its own taxes (other than

212

local authority rates, which are significantly different in effect from those in England), public expenditure in Scotland is now governed in part by a formula which is reminiscent of those applied to central government grants in federal countries. This formula (nicknamed the 'Barnett Formula' after the Chief Secretary to the Treasury at the time, Joel Barnett) was introduced in 1978, and it was intended to be later used to determine the Block Fund allocations to Scotland and Wales under the devolution schemes which were then going through Parliament. When these schemes were not implemented, the Barnett Formula remained as the method by which the Scottish and Welsh Offices received most of their shares of public expenditure.

It is important to notice that the allocation of public expenditure in Britain is now based on the division of the country into its constituent nations, England, Scotland, and Wales (Northern Ireland is not covered by the Barnett Formula, but is equally separate in its treatment by the Treasury). The population of these nations determines the ratios adopted in the Formula. Thus, England represents 85%, Scotland 10%, and Wales 5% (these figures were based on the 1977 population estimates). It will be noticed at once that such a division is an arbitrary one, since it does not involve an assessment of 'needs' as between the different nations. It merely assumes that each nation is entitled to the share of public money which is proportional to its population. In politics, it is easier to divide up money in an arbitrary way than to engage in arguments about needs (for such an argument, see below, p. 215).

The Barnett Formula does not determine the entire amount of public expenditure in Scotland, nor even the entire amount of the Secretary of State for Scotland's expenditure. Moreover, it applies only to the *changes* (increases or decreases) in public spending within specified programmes under the Secretary of State's control. Despite these qualifications, it is a significant development within the Scottish political system, for it gives the Secretary of State an entitlement to a fixed share in British public spending, and a right to spend his 'block' in ways determined by him and not by the Treasury.[3]

In brief, the system works like this. Public expenditure is determined by the Government as a whole, on the basis of proposals by the 'spending departments' and the limits set by the Treasury for public spending. At this stage, the Scottish Office is merely feeding in proposals under 'functional' headings such as education, health, roads, etc., which will be taken into account in drawing up the functional totals for the whole country. Once these totals have been

Table 27. *Public Expenditure in Scotland, 1981–2*

1. Identifiable public expenditure in Scotland, 1981–2, £9, 661 m. (= 11% of UK identifiable public expenditure, and 123% of identifiable UK expenditure per head). £19,522 m of public spending in Britain was not identifiable as spending in England, Scotland, Wales, or Northern Ireland as such.

2. Total expenditure within the Secretary of State's responsibility, 1981–2: £5,763 m (i.e. 60% of total identifiable public expenditure in Scotland).

3. Secretary of State's Block (or 'comparable expenditure' covered by the Barnett Formula, 1981–2): £5,500m (i.e. 95% of the Secretary of State's expenditures).

4. Local authority expenditure (current and capital) in Scotland in 1981–2: £3,201m (i.e. 55% of the Secretary of State's spending programme, which covers not only the Scottish Office but public corporations linked to the Scottish Office and Scottish local authorities). Local authorities raise about half of the finance themselves to cover their expenditures.
    The amount handed on by the Secretary of State to local authorities in the form of Rate Support Grant, etc., was *c.* £1,650 m in 1981–2 (*c.* 30% of the Secretary of State's budget).

Sources: Parliamentary Debates, HC, 1 February 1983, cols. 85–96; *The Government's Expenditure Plans 1983–84 to 1985–86,* HMSO, Cmnd 8789 – II, pp. 76–7 (London, 1983). Further sources on Scottish public expenditure include SCSA 4, 5, and 6.

established, the Barnett Formula comes into operation. It applies to the changes in expenditure of those parts of the Scottish Office's functions which are deemed to be in his 'block'. These are basically the functions that would have been devolved to an Assembly under the Scotland Act, and they include education, health, housing, law and order, roads and transport, other environmental services, and tourism. Not included in the 'block' for formula purposes are the Secretary of State's functions in agriculture, fisheries, food and forestry, industry, energy, trade and employment, and some 'common services'. Some idea of the financial proportions involved in these categories and their relationship to all public spending in Scotland can be gleaned from Table 27.

As can be seen from the table, there are various types of public spending in Scotland, and each is subject to a different policy process. The Scottish Office accounts for 60% of the total of public spending in

Scotland. The remainder is provided by the British departments, such as Social Security, Employment, and Defence. These are 'non-comparable' expenditures, and are not included in the Barnett Formula. The policy process for determining these is a centralised one, in which the Scottish Office participates as a Cabinet Department, but without executive functions. This applies also to the raising of public finance through taxation, excise duties, and VAT. The Treasury is the government department which has the greatest say in deciding revenue matters and the size of public expenditure as a whole. It is also prominent in the decisions on the size of spending on the functions in the public expenditure programme. Lastly, the spending of British departments in Scotland is of course primarily their concern, not that of the Scottish Office, although the Scottish Secreatary will try to influence the decisions, and will be made aware of their effect on Scotland generally, and may even be held responsible by the public (e.g. for steel closures and unemployment).

Within the Scottish Secretary's responsibility for public spending, the split between 'comparable' (or block) spending and 'non-comparable' spending also means a split in the policy process involved. For the latter (amounting to 5% of all Scottish Office spending), the process is one which applied to all Scottish Office spending before 1978. It is essentially a negotiation between the Scottish Office and the Treasury and other departments for a share of the cake. Scottish Secretaries have been adept at these negotiations, described by one senior Scottish Office civil servant as 'table-thumping' (SCSA 4, p. 63, Q. 50). According to Rose (Rose 6, p. 138), about 7% of the 23% advantage which Scotland had over England in public spending per head in 1976–7 was due to 'political muscle' of this kind, and only 16% to greater needs. In this, he was following the Treasury *Needs Assessment Study – Report* (HM Treasury (London, 1979)), which tried to determine what the level of spending in England, Scotland, Wales, and Northern Ireland should be in certain services according to a 'needs' criterion. The exercise was naturally a controversial one, and covered only the functions which were to be devolved, not all public spending in Scotland (this is shown in Table 27 as running at 23% higher than UK identifiable expenditure per head in 1981–2).

The introduction of the Barnett Formula in 1978 meant a different policy process for the 95% of Scottish Office spending which was 'comparable' and thus included in the 'block'. It is essential to note that this block started with a 23% advantage per head over English spending in 1976–7, as mentioned above. This advantage was,

215

however, now subject to erosion under the Formula, for changes in spending within the 'comparable' services are allocated to Scotland by population (i.e. 10% of Great Britain), and this would threaten to cancel out the previous advantage negotiated by 'table-thumping' or by assessment of 'needs'. However, this erosion would be a lengthy process, and the Formula would have different effects depending on whether there were increases or cuts in public spending. In periods of increases, Scotland would lose, but only gradually – perhaps about $\frac{1}{2}$ or 1% over ten years (SCSA 4, p. 62, Q. 43). In periods of cuts, as experienced after 1976, the Formula actually protects Scotland, since the cuts are applied in a smaller ratio between Scotland and England (10/85) than the ratio of total 'comparable' spending (14/86). Moreover, according to the civil servant quoted earlier, 'the days of table-thumping were ceasing to have their effect' (*loc.cit.*). Thus, in a period of financial austerity, Scotland was guaranteed an advantage over England in certain areas of public spending without having to argue its case (its advantage over Wales was almost as great).

There is a drawback to this arrangement, however, with respect to the power of initiative in policy-making for the Scottish Office. In the areas covered by the Block, the Scottish Office cannot ask for expenditures for Scotland alone to take account of special programmes or needs. These can only emerge from the general share-out between England, Wales, and Scotland. With England making up 85% of the expenditures covered by the Formula, it is clear that proposals for England will largely determine what Scotland is to receive. Conversely, any special elements built into the British programmes to take account of Scottish programmes will also be distributed in part to England and Wales. What this means in policy terms is not clear, but it seems that the Scottish Office can be a 'free-rider' on English programmes, drawing a share of whatever is allocated to England, yet cannot be given much money for programmes peculiar to Scotland with no counterpart in England. As it happens, there are usually parallel policy developments in England to those proposed for Scotland, and, if there are not, the effect of 'swings and roundabouts' means that what Scotland loses because it cannot ask for specific funding for a Scottish programme it gains from the windfall attached to its share of British spending in general (and English spending in particular).

The advantage of the Formula is made more apparent when the Block allocation finally reaches the Scottish Office for spending. The Secretary of State can now rearrange his spending according to his own priorities. As an example, once he has earned a share of the 'roads' programme spending under the Formula, he can allocate it if he likes to education or health. So the English initiative in the build-up of the functional spending programme need not be followed in Scotland with regard to where the money is spent.

The Secretary of State for Scotland, Mr George Younger, was questioned on these arrangements by the Select Committee on Scottish Affairs in 1980. He explained (SCSA 4, p. 62, Q. 46) that he now possessed the ability to switch expenditures on his programmes without the Treasury's permission. When asked whether he was not worried that the Formula made it more difficult to get additional money for special programmes, he replied:

> I am not so worried, because if I were to get such a facility I would have to give up the ability to switch between my individual programmes; and that I do not wish to do, because Scottish needs are very often different; Scottish priorities are very often different. I would not wish to have my priorities dictated to me by my Whitehall colleagues. I now have complete control over these priorities myself (loc.cit., p. 63, Q. 47).

Despite these bold and rather nationalistic statements, it is usually the case that Scotland acts in parallel with departments operating in England, and priorities work out very similarly across the territorial departments. The reasons for this are not very far to seek. All government ministers subscribe to the Party manifesto, and collective responsibility in the Government means that ministers get together to avoid embarrassing clashes of policies between the different nations of the UK (see Keating and Midwinter, Chs. 2, 8, 9). The British civil service is a close-knit organisation which 'checks out' initiatives before they are adopted, and Scottish/English differences are often considered bad practice administratively. Despite these restraints, however, it must be emphasised that many such differences do emerge from the policy process, and the effect of the Barnett Formula for public expenditure is probably conducive to greater Scottish autonomy in policy-making, rather than less.

Some indication of this autonomy in the areas of public finance and economic planning can be seen with regard to local government finance and the operation of economic planning agencies in Scotland. The Secretary of State for Scotland determines how much of his expenditures will be allocated to local government, and how much aid he will give local authorities in the form of the Rate Support Grant and other grants. This policy process is contained within Scotland, as the money is part of his Block allocation. He thus has considerable freedom to determine priorities. He also has the freedom to devise his own system of grants to the local authorities, and to make allocations to each one of them, as well as to determine what rates they should levy in cases of 'unreasonable and excessive' expenditures (subject to Parliamentary approval). In the period 1979–83, the Scottish Office used these new legal powers against the 'overspending' of local authorities in ways which were not possible in England, although the central government in England began to seek similar powers after 1983. While the aim of cutting local spending was common to Government policy in Scotland and England, and the Scottish Office initiatives were approved by the Cabinet, the Secretary of State for Scotland acted in a way which he largely determined for himself. The Treasury's main interest was to contain Scottish public spending, leaving the method to the Scottish Office. Once the method was put into operation, the corresponding English departments began to imitate Scotland, and English local authorities made belated common cause with their Scottish counterparts, who had already suffered under the stronger central powers in Scotland.[4]

The other example presented here of the financial and economic policy process is that of regional economic planning. Regional economic planning in Britain has developed over the years from the piecemeal financial inducements given under the Special Areas Acts of 1934 and 1937 to encourage industry to come to depressed areas, to the armoury of regional policies which have been tried since the 1960s (see McCrone 1–3, especially 3, p. 12; Hogwood in Madgwick and Rose). From being a minor aspect of economic policy between the wars these regional policies have become a central interest of politicians and economists today. They have been accompanied by the setting-up of a number of government departments and public bodies in Scotland specifically concerned with regional economic policy. The effect of these developments has been to strengthen the power of the Scottish political system in economic policy-making.

Much of the impetus for regional policy in Britain came from Scotland. Economists working in Scottish universities in the 1950s and 1960s pioneered the subject, and reports such as the 'Cairncross Report' of 1952[5] and the 'Toothill Report' of 1961 (Toothill) helped to shape government policies regarding the Scottish economy and the 'growth areas' within it (McCrone 3, p. 209). According to Sir Douglas Haddow, then Permanent Under-Secretary at the Scottish Office, 'it is not in the least unfair to say Scottish thought and Scottish

218

practice pioneered in this country regional development policies' (SCSA 2, p. 23, Q. 54). Examples of Scottish initiatives were the *Central Scotland Plan 1963* (Cmnd 2188) and the formation of the Scottish Development Department in 1962. In 1965, the Highlands and Islands Development Board was established, to be followed in 1973 by the Scottish Economic Planning Department within the Scottish Office, and in 1975 by the Scottish Development Agency, a body 'linked' to that department.

The policy process in this area is obviously affected by the existence of these bodies. Each is empowered by law or by executive arrangements to take decisions within its allotted sphere of responsibility, and the establishment of the Scottish planning bodies meant that decisions which were previously taken centrally in Whitehall or, in the case of the HIDB and SDA, at St Andrew's House, were now decentralised. It is also likely, but not as clearly the case, that extra funds became available to justify the existence of the new bodies, and as a result of their 'empire-building'. Thus over time, the expenditures of the HIDB and SDA have grown in real terms.

What aspects of economic policy are within the sphere of the Scottish political system, and who are the decision-makers concerned with them? The formulation of the major decisions in economic policy is, of course, largely the prerogative of the Treasury and other Whitehall economic departments. The former fixes the rates of taxation, industrial financial incentives, and the level of government spending in the different departments. Clearly, the Scottish Office's functions and the general responsibility of the Scottish Secretary for the Scottish economy are here subsidiary to the powers of Whitehall, though Edinburgh has a hand in the decision-making.

The amount of consultation which the Scottish Office has with these departments depends on the subject-matter. As far as taxes are concerned, the Chancellor of the Exchequer consults no other minister (except the Prime Minister) before he lays his Budget proposals before the Cabinet. But arguments between ministers do take place over taxation, and one can be sure that the Scottish Secretary was vocal about the implications for parts of Scotland of the selective employment tax (introduced 1966), and about regional incentives. In 1967, a regional employment premium was brought in, which benefited manufacturers in development areas. It was abolished in 1977.

Contacts between the Scottish Secretary and the economics ministers are maintained through Cabinet meetings (including

Cabinet committees) and informal talks. It is difficult to evaluate these, since personal considerations (as well as secrecy) loom so large in their operation. A popular (and politically strong) Scottish Secretary can influence policy here, while a weak minister cannot.

The evidence to the Select Committee on Scottish Affairs and the Kilbrandon Commission shows that frequent consultations take place at the official (civil service) level, in interdepartmental committees. As far as these committees in Scotland are concerned, the Scottish Office is the dominant partner. Viewed from Whitehall, however, Scotland is only one of many claimants for scarce resources, and in terms of skilled negotiators the Scottish Office is no more than the equal of powerful departments like Trade and Industry, the Environment, and Employment.

The Select Committee reported that the Scottish Office had 'full opportunities for a distinctively Scottish view of administrative questions to be formed and to be pressed at all levels of central government from the Cabinet downwards', but it added that 'this is not to say that cooperation between the Scottish Office and the Great Britain departments is as effective a method of administration for Scottish purposes as that implied by the transfer of further functions to the Scottish Office' (SCSA 1, p. 21).

The evidence before the Committee showed that while interdepartmental coordination for Scottish economic planning has increased greatly since the early 1960s, the major British departments are still very much London-bound, and do not shape their policies to fit the needs of the Scottish economy as a whole, as opposed to the needs (as they see them) of particular industries throughout Britain, or of the general requirements of the British economy.

The Scottish Office may therefore find it difficult to present a convincing case for special expenditure in Scotland regarding the location of industry and the placing of government contracts. While the principle of parity of services throughout the UK is accepted by governments today, even if it means spending more in some parts of the country in proportion to population, it is not generally accepted that there should be equality of employment opportunities or of incomes as between all regions. The most favourable locations for some types of industry may be outside Scotland, and it would be economically foolish (in the conventional wisdom) to force industry into areas where it could not make a profit. If the growth industries are unwilling to come to Scotland, for reasons of distance from markets or lack of suitable labour, the regional policies of British government cannot compel them to do so, despite a wide range of regional incentives.

The Scottish Office, as the department held responsible for planning the Scottish economy, must involve itself in the decisions of the British departments and public corporations which determine or influence the location of industry. Quite often it has to fight a 'rear-guard action' against a decision which has ignored the interests of Scotland. In many instances, the Whitehall department or public corporation leaves the advocacy of the Scottish case to the Scottish Office, and presses for economic development in England. For example, the Ministry of Transport employed American consultants in 1967 to advise on the location of a container port. The ports examined were all in England, so the Scottish Office had to undertake its own survey, to make the case for a Scottish port. Its vigorous campaigning (and that of the Clyde Port Authority) for Greenock won the day, partly through the use of experts such as shipbuilder Kenneth Douglas, but also by the skill of Scottish Office civil servants, and the eternal nagging of Scottish Secretary William Ross. Ross and Barbara Castle, the Transport Minister, settled it between them.

Similar confrontations, at all levels of government, are repeated whenever a big decision has to be taken about industrial development. The energies of the Scottish Secretary, his Minister of State, and his top civil servants, are devoted to bringing more employment to Scotland, and to pressurising the departments which have it in their power to do so. The classic cases in recent years have been the motor-vehicle factories at Linwood and Bathgate, the Fort William pulp-mill, the Ravenscraig steel strip-mill, the Invergordon aluminium works, the Dounreay fast breeder reactor, Upper Clyde Shipbuilders, and the Hunterston deep-water port and steel-mill. For each, there is a story of reasoned persuasion, threats ('Scotland must have it or its economy will collapse'), political blackmail ('votes will be lost if it does not come'), and personal influence ('you know that I am one of your most steadfast allies, Mr Prime Minister'), almost monotonous in their similarity. The development of North Sea oil has involved the Scottish Office in a tussle with the Department of Energy. The Scottish Office handles infrastructure (housing, roads, water), local government, and planning permissions for onshore development, while the Department of Energy controls the oil production side. But the interaction of these responsibilities has given rise to many conflicts, for example, over planning permissions. The Scottish Office has to bear in mind sensitive Scottish opinion, while the London-based

Department is concerned mainly with the rapid development of the energy supply. To moderate this problem, a Scottish MP is usually appointed as minister at the Department of Energy.

Who are the key figures? Undoubtedly, the Secretary of State for Scotland is of the utmost importance in the decision-taking process. No other region (not even Wales) has so powerful a figure in the Cabinet, nor can any other Cabinet Minister claim to influence such a political fiefdom (72 seats). In return for getting his way on a development in Scotland, a Scottish Secretary will often pledge support for his Prime Minister in his battles in Cabinet, and will promise to deliver the votes of Scotland at the next election.

Next come the top civil servants in the Scottish Office, who brief their ministers and negotiate with other departments. The itinerant crew who commute from Edinburgh to London twice-weekly, and the 'Embassy' of 100 at Dover House, Whitehall, argue the case for Scotland in innumerable committees, Cabinet meetings, and through speeches prepared for ministers. In economic policy, the influence of civil servants such as Sir Douglas Haddow (Permanent Under-Secretary, 1964–73, biography on p. 77) and J.H. McGuinness (head of the Regional Development Division, 1964–72)[6] has been great. They have helped transform the Scottish Office from an administrative department into a planning department, and have added in effect to the responsibilities of the Scottish Secretary.

Then there are the other Scottish Office administrators who use the powers given directly to the Scottish Office. The development and range of these functions has already been discussed (Ch. 3). It is important to note that they cover several important activities such as roads, electricity, transport (except rail and air), local government, agriculture, and since 1975 industrial incentives and development. Decisions are taken in these areas not only by Scottish civil servants but also by bodies 'linked' to the Scottish Office, such as the electricity boards, the Scottish Transport Group, the Highlands Board, and the SDA. These are all part of the 'public sector', and decision-making in it is governed by law, patronage, and administrative practices. It is possible to interpret the public sector as a 'hierarchical' system in which government ministers at the top issue orders to lower-level bodies. It can equally be seen as a 'network' of decision-making, in which initiatives are taken and aims are voiced at all the levels, with no clear element of central leadership. Each interpretation may be seen to be correct in different circumstances. The Scottish Secretary can get his way, but he is often reacting to situations over which he has lost control. The affairs of public corporations and local authorities can lead to situations showing government ministers desperately trying to deal with awkward decisions which were not of their making.

Policy formulation also involves the 'pressure groups', such as the Scottish Council, the CBI, and the STUC, described in Ch. 10. The Scottish Council, in particular, has been closely associated with economic planning through its various reports (e.g. Toothill, 1961, and Oceanspan, 1970–1), and with the promotion of trade in missions to foreign countries undertaken jointly with the Scottish Office (e.g. Attraction of German Industry, 1971–2).

In examining the process of decision-making in Scottish economic policy, it is thus necessary to distinguish between the different types of decision. At the level of physical planning, the local authorities have discretionary powers to build council houses, schools, roads, and advance factories within the limits set by law and the supervision of the Scottish Office. They must draw up Regional and Strategic development plans to determine the use of land.

The Scottish Office possesses controls over local government (e.g. through grants and planning approvals), and can itself provide major public works such as roads, bridges, and hospitals (through hospital boards). While all these expenditures are subject to 'Treasury control', the formulation of specific proposals is very much in the hands of Scottish civil servants and ministers. As we saw earlier, the policy process for 95% of Scottish Office expenditure is now covered by the Barnett Formula, which gives considerable freedom for the Scottish Secretary to assess his priorities for spending within his Block. Of course, the room for change may be limited. 'When ministers consider the allocation of public expenditure each year, the choices before them relate to marginal changes' (SCSA 2, p. 59).

It can be argued that, since the main powers of economic policy (e.g. taxation, overall public expenditure, general level of industrial incentives, and location of industry) are wielded by non-Scottish bodies, the economic policy-process is essentially outside the Scottish political system. It is true that until 1975 the only direct powers of the Scottish Office in the field related to 'infrastructure' (roads, houses, etc.), and expenditure for these has to be negotiated with the Treasury.

Nevertheless, the 1960s began a new phase in the activities of the Scottish Office, so that economic planning was added to the already long list of its functions. It cannot compete with the Treasury or the

Departments of Trade and Industry, and Energy in its financial, professional, or political resources. It works entirely within the framework of British planning, and British thought on regional policy. But it can influence that policy more than other departments.

The Scottish Office pioneered the 'growth area' approach to development, in the Toothill Report, and its wide range of activities was reproduced in the Department of the Environment (1970). It was able to establish regional planning bodies (the HIDB and the SDA) with real powers to develop industry through grants, loans, and equity participation. In 1975, it gained the power to give selective regional assistance from the Department of Industry. In 1981 and 1982 it fought off an attempt by Whitehall to abolish the power of the SDA to attract inward investment from abroad through offices in foreign countries. A 'Locate in Scotland' investment bureau was established within the SDA to give a 'single door' for foreigners seeking to invest in Scotland. The offices of the SDA abroad were retained and expanded in number in 1982, despite the wish of the Foreign and Commonwealth Office to see them closed down and their functions taken over by themselves.[7]

The power of the Secretary of State for Scotland to influence decisions within the remit of other departments was strong in the 1970s and early 1980s, as it had been in the 1960s. Thus, despite the opposition of the Industry Secretary, Eric Varley, William Ross in 1976 was able to veto the closure of the Chrysler car factory at Linwood (it was closed under the Conservatives four years later). In 1982, George Younger prevented the closure of the Ravenscraig steel-mill, an action rumoured to be favoured by the Department of Industry and the British Steel Corporation chairman.

Even so, the contribution of the Scottish political system to the health of the Scottish economy has been only partly successful. While public expenditure per head has been kept in line with needs, or even above that line, regional policies have not been able to overturn a high rate of unemployment, urban deprivation, and continuing emigration. But from the 1970s, the gap between the unemployment rates in Scotland and England has narrowed, and the level of incomes of those in employment has been similar in Scotland and England. Emigration has not again reached the high level of the 1960s. The Scottish economy has undergone considerable restructuring, with the decline of traditional industries and the establishment of new ones, especially electronics, in which Scotland has been particularly successful. North Sea oil has provided employment and wealth for a considerable part of the Scottish economy.

There have been notable failures. The closure of major 'prestige' industrial plants such as the Linwood car factory, the Invergordon aluminium smelter, and the Fort William Pulp Mill, and the run-down and threatened closure of the Ravenscraig steel-mill and the Bathgate vehicles factory in 1983, and of numerous other smaller factories, coal-mines, etc., casts a cloud over the Scottish economy and the power of the Scottish political system to influence other government departments and stand against adverse international and British economic forces. The policies of the Thatcher Conservative Governments after 1979, moreover, have been unfavourable towards the *dirigiste* type of regional economic planning so fashionable in the 1960s and 1970s. But one should note that the Conservatives were prepared to retain the Scottish Development Agency and the Highlands Board despite their initial opposition to them. Indeed, these bodies have continued to expand, irrespective of which government has been in office.

This indicates the strength of the Scottish political system, and its ability to grow even in the most adverse economic and political conditions. Since it has been able to find a significant rôle in the financial and economic sphere, which in all countries tends to have a centralised policy process, the system is likely to be even more active within the area of social policy, which is the next area to be examined.

(b)   Social Services (education, health, social work, and housing)

The social services in Scotland are the responsibility of the Scottish Office (except for the social security cash payments made by the Department of Health and Social Security). The basic principles governing these services are common to the whole of the UK, and such variations from English practice as there are in Northern Ireland, Scotland, and Wales are considered to be adaptations of British policy to the particular needs of these areas.

In fact, these 'adaptations' constitute in many cases a radical departure from a uniform system. The most obvious example is education, where Scotland has had its own traditions in schools and universities for hundreds of years.[8] While the Scottish and English educational systems have grown closer together in recent years, there remains a strong contrast in the curriculum, the organisation of the

225

schools, and the training, remuneration, and careers of teachers. The universities, too, have their distinctive degrees and teaching methods.

The autonomy of the policy-process in Scottish education is based securely on the strength of the Scottish 'education world'.[9] It is this world which determines educational policy, although it is not impervious to outside influences and general social demands. As with economic planning, its main components are academics, pressure groups, and government departments.

The Scottish education world is remarkably insulated from that of England. This is due to the demarcation between the educational systems, especially at the school level, which inhibits mobility of the teaching profession. But the division also prevents a continuous discourse at other levels, for example, in the colleges of education and in the civil service.

The account of the policy-process in English education in *The Politics of Education* (see n. 9) reveals many contrasts with the corresponding process in Scotland. First, the influence of strong education ministers such as Boyle and Crosland was crucial to the development of the English system. These men gave practically their whole attention to education, and discussed its problems for hours with prominent educationists (see Crosland's accounts of evenings with John Vaizey, Michael Young, Noel Annan, etc., *The Politics of Education*, p. 185). They were strongly influenced by the current of academic work in the field, and sought to realise its conclusions in government policy.

Scotland has no education minister of this kind. The Scottish Secretary must deal with the economy, agriculture, health, and welfare (to name but a few of his responsibilities), as well as education. While he may be personally interested in the educational system, he cannot afford to devote too much time to it (neither can his junior ministers, who also have multiple briefs).

This means that the initiative tends to pass to the other parts of the education world (the professionals and the civil servants). But even this sector is unlike that in England. The long series of influential reports on education in England (e.g. the Plowden, Newsom, and Crowther Reports) have had less impact in Scotland because they dealt essentially with what were seen as English problems. The Robbins Report on Higher Education (1963), on the other hand, was as important for Scotland as it was for the rest of the UK.

The Scottish educational world has produced its own Reports, which to some extent parallel those for England and Wales. They are the work of academics, inspectors of schools, and teachers working in Scotland. In recent years, the most important have been the Munn Report on the Curriculum[10] and the Dunning Report on Assessment[11] (i.e. examinations), both concerned with the third and fourth years of secondary education. These Reports have formed the basis for a major reform in Scottish education in the 1980s, involving a new curriculum and national examination, replacing the 'O' grade examination in 1986. While there are similar reform movements afoot in England, the Scots have taken their own decisions and have ended up with a curriculum and examination structure which is still different from that in England. There is little evidence here of any pressure being exerted on Scotland from the Cabinet or the Department of Education and Science in Whitehall. The Scottish educational system at the school level is able to act in virtual isolation from that of the English system, and along lines of its own choosing.

In effect, Scottish traditionalism in education is perpetuated by the lack of communication between the Scottish and English education worlds. At ministerial level, the discourse concerns only those aspects of education which raise political implications. Thus, the decision to 'go comprehensive' in England in 1965 (DES Circular 10/65) was automatically followed by a corresponding circular from the Scottish Education Department (Circular 600). In 1970, with the return of a Conservative government, both education departments issued similar circulars allowing local authorities the freedom to reject comprehensivisation (DES Circular 10/70; SED Circular 762). Clearly, it was party politics which drew the countries together in this case. The Labour and Conservative philosophies were shared by the Scottish and English members of the parties, who therefore demanded uniformity of policy.

Another example of concerted action is that of the school-leaving age. It is unthinkable that this should have been raised in England but not in Scotland, although the problems of doing so might be different if the supply of teachers and school buildings were different in the two countries (no clear evidence exists on this). According to the SED's written evidence to the Constitutional Commission (Kilbrandon 2, p. 25), 'Where the Government take major decisions of policy, which may be social as well as educational . . . they apply to Scottish schools as well as to schools in England and Wales'. Such matters include the two mentioned above, and items like schools meals and school milk.

The introduction of the 'Youth Training Scheme' of the Manpower Services Commission (MSC) showed a more subtle interaction of the

Scottish and British political and educational systems. This Scheme (framed in 1982 and inaugurated in 1983) was the creation of the 'British' MSC, under the Department of Employment, a body which is, however, also responsible to the Scottish Secretary in Scotland for its functions. The Scheme is as much a social and economic one as an educational one, since it aims to give training to unemployed school-leavers in the hope that jobs will later be obtained. Clearly, this training has to be available throughout the country and the subject of youth unemployment is highly political. Nevertheless, the educational system of Scotland is different from that in England, and is subject to the Scottish Office. Here was an educational initiative of major importance coming from England which would affect the activities of Scottish schools and further education colleges. Could this be 'managed' by the Scottish political system so as to preserve its independence in matters relating to Scottish schools and colleges (universities and CNAA degrees were already subject to a British policy process)? By 1983 it seemed that the Scottish system was showing its superiority. The Scottish Office issued its own 'Action Plan', which laid down the types of courses to be taught ('modules') and the qualifications to be obtained (a Scottish 16–18 certificate). Schools and colleges in Scotland would remain responsible to the Scottish Office and would not report to any body or department in England.

The Employment Secretary was planning a somewhat different kind of Youth Training Scheme in England from that of the Scottish Office: the English scheme would cover the age group 14–18, while the Scottish one was limited to 16–18. In England, technical and vocational colleges were to be created to teach such pupils, thus threatening the ideal of comprehensive schools for all pupils. In Scotland, the Scottish Office announced that it would not be following the English example, since the Munn and Dunning reforms were the Scottish equivalent.[12] This effectively preserved the traditional position of the all-through secondary comprehensive school, a position already eroded in England by the setting up of Middle Schools and Sixth Form Colleges (neither of which are to be found in Scotland). In 1983, the Junior Minister responsible for Education at the Scottish Office, Mr Allan Stewart, pledged that he would protect the system of Scottish comprehensive education from developments taking place south of the Border. 'My objective is to improve the Scottish education system in accordance with its own traditions', he said.[13] In this way, a

Conservative Scottish politician defended both comprehensive schooling and Scotland from English Conservative ideology.

This 'victory' of the Scottish school system and the Scottish Office was, however, less clearly seen with regard to further education colleges. With the MSC (along with business firms, etc.) providing the finance for the Youth Training Scheme, a new link opened up between the essentially 'British' MSC and the local authorities and further education colleges. For if a considerable source of educational finance was to come via a route which was beyond the control of local authorities or the Scottish Office, then there was at least the potential of a new 'British' policy network in Scottish education similar to that already present in the universities. But with the Scottish Office Action Plan already under way, and the Scottish Secretary closely linked with the MSC's Scottish organisation, the likelihood was that even here the Scottish political system would preserve Scottish autonomy. This has proved to be the case.

On most topics there is probably no conflict between Scottish and English ministers, and over the whole gamut of educational policy outside the 'social' sphere, the Scottish education world rules supreme. According to the then Secretary of the SED, Mr (now Sir) Norman Graham, 'I cannot think offhand of any important matter on which Scotland has been prevented... from taking a decision that ministers wanted to take' (Kilbrandon 4, p. 103).

It is easy to produce evidence that Scotland has gone its own way in educational policy in such matters as the curriculum, examinations, age of transfer to secondary education, Roman Catholic schools, the binary system of higher education, and even university degrees. To call these 'educational' decisions as opposed to 'social' decisions, is to make a fine distinction which becomes increasingly difficult to sustain as the links between education and socialisation become daily more clear.

All of the so-called 'educational' decisions about Scottish education are made within the Scottish political system. The legislation governing education in Scotland is Scottish legislation which has been drafted in the SED, with the help of Scottish educational organisations, and debated largely by Scottish MPs. Its administration is in the hands of the Scottish Office.

Contact between civil servants of the SED and DES rarely concerns substantive matters of policy. It is assumed that each department has its own educational system to administer, and that the one should not get in the other's way. The closest liaison is on the resources of education (e.g. the Buildings and Finance Divisions) and on some 'new' areas of education such as further education where there are British examinations, and where the different traditions of school education in the two countries begin to lose their distinctive characteristics. In fact, most SED trips to London are to the Treasury, or to Parliament, when legislation is being pushed through.

The principal policy-makers in Scottish education today are the permanent officials at the SED (especially the Secretary), the Inspectors of Schools (a more powerful body in Scotland than in England),[14] the local authority directors of education, and the teachers' organisations. Since 1965, the General Teaching Council for Scotland has headed the list of official bodies representing the education world, but the Scottish Examination Board and the Consultative Committee on the Curriculum are also as important. In the late 1950s and early 1960s, a strong influence was that of the senior Chief Inspector of Schools, John S. Brunton.[15] He dominated the department and much of educational thinking in Scotland; the Brunton Report, *From School to Further Education*, was published in 1963, and was the Scottish counterpart of the Newsom Report, *Half Our Future*, also issued in 1963.

What is lacking in this network is the influence of the layman. The politicians (including ministers) are weak, and the consumers (parents and pupils) are almost totally excluded. The forces for change come indirectly from English and foreign examples, partly through inter-communication, and partly from the need for Scots to get jobs outside Scotland (see Kilbrandon 4, p. 104, for a Scottish trade unionist's distaste for separate Scottish qualifications which prevent Scots getting into English universities and colleges). Education is one of the best-defined 'arenas' of Scottish life, and one which most strongly maintains the boundary of the Scottish political system.

A rather less well-defined Scottish arena is that of health and welfare. The National Health Service is a British scheme, and the principles of the welfare state (like the so-called social aspects of education) are uniform throughout the country.

Yet here too one discovers marked divergencies in Scotland. The medical profession must deal with Scottish government agencies, especially the Scottish Home and Health Department, and the health boards. The Scottish Secretary appoints these boards (just one aspect of his vast patronage), and administers the Health Service with the assistance of such powerful professionals as the Chief Medical Officer at the Scottish Office (e.g. Sir John Brotherston, who held the office from 1964 to 1977). Scottish doctors rarely see anything of the Department of Health and Social Security, except when Scottish officials of the British Medical Association are negotiating scales of remuneration and general conditions of service.

The Scottish medical world (like that of education) has its own distinctive history. The teaching of medicine has been an outstanding tradition. Scottish universities and their medical schools cooperate with the health boards in the teaching of medical students, and the teaching hospitals are relatively more numerous than in England. All such hospitals in Scotland come under the health boards, while in England they have their own boards of governors. The position of the teaching hospitals was one of the strongest reasons for a separate administration of the Health Service in Scotland.[16]

Since its establishment in 1948, the National Health Service in Scotland has developed along lines appropriate to the needs of the country. Decisions about charges and remuneration are taken on a British basis, but hospital organisation and general medical practice continue to show differences in Scotland. There are more GPs, hospital beds, nurses, and hospital medical staff in proportion to population in Scotland than in England and Wales. More is spent *per capita* over all the health and welfare services. Scotland has pioneered some aspects of medical administration, notably training for hospital administrators.[17] The reorganisation of the health service into area health boards has a special form in Scotland. The principal difference between Scotland and England is that in the former country a single-tier structure of health boards has been adopted, while in the latter a two-tier system of area and regional boards has been established. While the English area boards have boundaries corresponding to the counties and metropolitan districts in the local government structure, 6 of the 15 boards in Scotland do not correspond to the regional authorities in local government. Moreover, in England the local authorities appoint some of the members of the area boards, but all the members of the Scottish boards are chosen by the Secretary of State for Scotland. There is a common service agency for the whole of Scotland, while the English regional boards have their own agencies.[18] It is worth noting that the Scottish legislation went ahead in 1972, a year before the corresponding English reform.

Social work is another area in which Scotland has pointed the way for

England. The Social Work (Scotland) Act 1968 established social work departments in counties, cities, and large burghs in Scotland. The new departments brought together services previously exercised in local authority departments such as the children's, welfare, and education departments, and the probation service. One director of social work now takes charge of these services in each authority (since 1975, the regions and islands).

The process of policy-formulation for the Social Work Act involved a subtle interaction of Scottish and English decision-makers.[19] Discontent with the state of local authority social work services had been expressed in reports of official committees in England and Scotland in the 1950s and early 1960s. The first positive move was made by the Home Office over a matter of law reform relating to juvenile courts. In 1960, a report appeared on the subject (*Children and Young Persons*, Cmnd 1191) which covered England and Wales. The subject was taken up in Scotland by a committee under Lord Kilbrandon,[20] which reported in 1964 (*Children and Young Persons (Scotland) Report*, Cmnd 2036). Meanwhile, an interdepartmental committee covering all Great Britain reported on the probation service (Cmnd 1650, 1962).

From being a matter of law reform, the question became one of reforming local authority social services (including probation) to make one social work department. The Scots and English now went separate ways. A Scottish White Paper was issued (*Social Work and the Community*, Cmnd 3065, 1966) which recommended the setting up of social work departments, and led directly to the introduction of the Social Work (Scotland) Bill in March 1968.

The English, on the other hand, did not begin their enquiry until December 1968 (the Seebohm Committee), and excluded any examination of the probation service. This was because there was much opposition in England to the reform of the juvenile courts and to the merging of the probation service with social work departments.

The Scottish legislation was essentially different from that which was eventually produced in England and Wales. Apart from the omission of the probation service in the English and Welsh social services departments, these departments also suffered in comparison with the Scottish social work departments in their lack of powers. Section 12 of the Social Work (Scotland) Act gave local authorities a duty to provide generally for social welfare, while the English and Welsh Act merely brought together existing statutory functions. One example of the implications of this was that Scottish social work departments could give cash assistance to persons in need, while in

232

England such payments were restricted to needy children. The drafting of the Bill was a matter for Scottish decision-makers. An account of this process was given to the Constitutional Commission by the Secretary of the Scottish Education Department (N. W. Graham):

> The framing of this was entirely in the hands of the Scottish Office. All the preliminary work, stemming from Lord Kilbrandon's committee, was done in Scotland. There was a working party with local authorities, with which three social work professional advisers were associated. Then there was a White Paper, and then there was the legislation. All this was done in Scotland. Naturally in the ordinary course of business the English departments interested were kept in touch. At a point along this line the Seebohm Committee was set up to look at more or less, but not quite, the same territory, in England and Wales, and the English Departments have known throughout what we were doing, and were very interested in what we were doing. But the decisions which were taken were in the Scottish context, with the Secretary of State of course consulting his colleagues, who were thus aware of the proposed legislation (Kilbrandon 4, p. 109).

It was possible to move faster in Scotland than in England towards the reform of social work because the Scottish Office had a more comprehensive range of functions than any department in England. It could therefore deal intra-departmentally with problems which in England had to be negotiated between several ministers. The Scottish Office ministers (particularly Judith Hart, then a Parliamentary Under-Secretary in the department) gave the subject a political impetus which it could not obtain in England. They were able to convince anxious English ministers that an experiment could be made in Scotland which need not be a precedent for England or Wales. It would provide Whitehall with the evidence of a 'pilot project', from which they could learn valuable lessons. Nevertheless, the Home Secretary attacked the Bill in the Cabinet, and William Ross, the Scottish Secretary, had to fight for its survival.

There were other factors in Scotland favouring acceptance of the Bill. The local authorities and pressure groups have a much closer liaison with the Scottish Office than the corresponding English bodies have with the Department of the Environment.[21] This smoothed the way for a radical change, and reduced the need for prolonged discussions.

One of the virtues of the Scottish political system is that its small size enables most of the policy-formulators to know each other personally. This is especially true of central–local government relations. Negotiations between governments and local authorities can proceed more quickly in Scotland, while in England they can get bogged down as a result of the scale involved and the more entrenched power of local government in the political system. Thus the regionalisation of water supplies took place in Scotland in 1968, years before it happened in England. Another illustration of this difference was found in the negotiations over the Countryside Bills for Scotland and England and Wales (1967). The Scots proposed a strong Bill which encroached on the power of local authorities. In England, the resistance of these authorities was so great that the Government threatened to drop both Bills. The Scots insisted on theirs, thereby forcing the English to produce a stronger Bill (Countryside (Scotland) Act 1967, and Countryside Act 1968). Yet even in Scotland the local authorities can show their power, for during the Social Work Bill discussions they insisted that Large Burghs should have social work departments, although the 1966 White Paper had restricted these to Counties and Cities. The Government gave in on this point.

A policy area where local authorities and central government in Scotland do not have smooth relations is that concerning council-house rents. Scottish local authority housing rents are much lower on average than those in England. At the same time, council houses make up twice the proportion of the housing stock. In some local authorities, the proportion of houses rented from the council is over three-quarters of the total housing stock, and the issue of 'council' rents is always a matter of politics. The Labour Party maintains power in many of these councils because it is the party which will guarantee low rents and build a large number of council houses (whose tenants usually then vote Labour).

The central government (i.e. the Scottish Office) has only limited powers to raise the level of rents, desirable as this may be from the point of view of economic allocation of resources and the health of the private sector in housing. Over the years, public enquiries have been held to determine whether certain authorities have fulfilled their statutory duties to review regularly the level of rents, and some authorities have been forced to make increases (e.g. Glasgow, Dundee, Dunbartonshire, and Coatbridge). By the late 1970s, other weapons were brought into play by the central government to achieve this end (the reduction of the Housing Support Grant and of Capital Allocations where rents were considered to be too low)(see Keating and Midwinter, pp. 193–4).

234

Throughout the 1970s successive governments (especially Conservative ones) tried to bring Scotland into line with England on public housing. Yet most of the differences remain, although council house rents have risen in Scotland, and private housing has increased while council housing building has slowed down considerably. It is clear that the different conditions in Scotland in housing tenure have made it necessary for governments to seriously modify their policies for the two countries (counting England and Wales as one country in this respect). The party philosophies remain the same for both, and the direction of the legislation is similar, but the problems of implementation are very different. They will not be ironed out for a generation at least (see Keating and Midwinter, Ch. 8, for further discussion of housing policy-making).

These examples of Scottish policy-making in the social services show that a separate political decision-making network is involved from that which operates in England. This is partly the result of the existence of the Scottish Office, the separate system of local authorities, and the differences between Scots and English Law. The case-studies also bring in a separate 'Establishment' of professionals such as educationists and doctors, who belong to their own Scottish world, one stage removed from the political system. And the case of housing points to the importance of the social structure of Scotland in conditioning policy.

In none of these areas do Scottish decision-makers work in total isolation from those in England. Indeed, we have seen that as regards the Social Work Act, the repercussions for England were appreciated up to Cabinet level, and some argument took place. Yet the outcome was two Acts of Parliament, with separate provisions for Scotland and for England and Wales. The same applies to the Housing Acts. Thus in the social services, the principle of uniformity for the whole of the UK must be flexible enough to allow for substantial variations between Scottish and English practice.

(c) Law reform

Scotland and England have separate legal systems, and much of the separateness of their political systems stems from this fact. All the while, however, the law is undergoing change, and some of this process has led to a greater correspondence between the Scottish and English systems. There is a greater area of so-called 'British' law today than there was fifty years ago, because of the development of the welfare state, government regulation of the economy, and the large area of commercial and public law which is common to both countries.

All law in Scotland is technically 'Scottish' law, since it is subject to interpretation by the Scottish Courts (and in civil cases to the House of Lords, sitting, some say, as a Scottish court).[22] But in substance, much law is British in that it lays down the same rights, duties, and conditions for citizens throughout Great Britain.

The area of law reform which concerns us here is that area where the special characteristics of Scots Law remain so strong that separate Scottish legislation is required to deal with them. Many Scots lawyers would maintain that far more separate Scottish legislation should be passed, to take account of the separate legal system.[23] And they would be willing to reform that system without reference to English developments.

What has happened is that only certain areas of law and legal administration in Scotland have developed along totally indigenous lines (notably property law, much personal law, and the organisation of the courts). Reform proposals here come largely from the 'legal world', with some prompting from Scottish politicians. For example, the system of feudal land tenure was attacked by radicals in the Labour and Liberal Parties over the years. It also stood in the way of Conservative Government plans for land use and economic development in the early 1960s. In 1964, a committee under Professor J. M. Halliday of Glasgow University was set up by Conservative Scottish Secretary Michael Noble to investigate and report. The result was a series of sweeping proposals for the abolition of feu-duties and of the power of feudal superiors over development.[24]

The subject was so complex that the incoming Labour Government was reluctant to tackle it. Considerable drafting problems arose, and legislative time had to be found. Scottish law reforms have often been held up because of the apparent lack of time in the Scottish committees of the House of Commons.

Pressure continued from back-benchers, and a Liberal MP, James Davidson, introduced his own Bill on the subject. Eventually the government brought forward a Bill in 1969 (the Conveyancing and Feudal Reform (Scotland) Bill) which tackled some of the problems involved (but not the redemption of feu-duties). In the Scottish Standing Committee of the House of Commons, the debates were severely handicapped by the technical nature of the legislation and the almost total absence of lawyer MPs from Scottish constituencies. Even the government speakers were at a loss during much of the

236

discussion (at this time the Scottish Law Officers were not in the Commons), though the Conservatives had at least one articulate Scots lawyer, Norman Wylie, QC, among their MPs (later Lord Advocate, 1970). Total reform followed in 1974 (Land Tenure Reform (Scotland) Act).

The less political areas of Scots Law, such as the organisation of the Sheriff Courts and the law of succession, have been reformed by the familiar method of a report by a professional committee of enquiry, and a non-contentious law reform bill.[25] Since 1965, Scotland has had its own Scottish Law Commission, which has issued several reports on the more technical aspects of law reform. Some of these subjects have also been dealt with by the (English and Welsh) Law Commission, and occasionally a joint report is issued by the two Commissions. In such cases, there is a cross-fertilisation of ideas between Scotland and England, and this has also been in evidence in several law reforms (or proposals for reform) which have taken place in England. The subjects include majority verdicts, pre-trial publicity, public prosecutions, and private bargains before house purchase. In all these, Scottish practice has been commended by English reformers. Organisations such as Justice (the British section of the International Commission of Jurists) have been especially aware of Scots Law, despite its traditional neglect in England.[26]

Scots, for their part, have not been immune to English influence. The feudal reform legislation brings Scotland more into line with the freehold tenure of England, and in personal law the example of English reforms has been powerful. The passing of the Divorce Reform Act 1969 (a Private Member's Bill which applies only to England and Wales) opened up a gulf between the two legal systems in that subject, which had previously been narrowing in the direction of Scotland. The Law Commissions had recommended reform throughout Great Britain, and in Scotland the Church of Scotland gave qualified support. Yet Scottish Private Members' Bills between 1970 and 1975 failed to get the support of enough Scottish MPs in the House of Commons to survive the difficulties placed in the path of such non-government Bills. (A Bill was passed in 1976.)

This was not only because of the difficulty of steering Scottish Private Members' Bills through the House of Commons, but also because the Scottish MPs themselves were ambivalent about divorce law reform. It would seem that religious pressures played a large part in the attitude of many Scottish MPs, especially those who were Roman Catholics[27] and puritanical Kirk members (a similar coalition developed over homosexual law reform, which was not introduced in Scotland alongside the English Bill in 1967, but was passed eventually in 1980 as an amendment proposed by Robin Cook, the Labour MP, to the Conservative Government's Criminal Justice (Scotland) Bill; they failed to prevent David Steel's Abortion Bill being passed in 1967, largely because that was a British measure).

Decision-making in law reform therefore involves a different set of actors according to the amount of controversy which is aroused. The most technical questions are settled in the 'legal world', in much the same way as technical matters in education and medicine are left to the relevant professions. Usually this means a committee of enquiry, followed by consultation with government over legislation. Scots lawyers show a high degree of independence from England in this sphere, though some apparently accept assimilation cheerfully. But they complain that the processes of reform are slow, and that MPs are ignorant of legal matters.[28]

The MPs come into their own, however, when political, religious, or social considerations are involved. Land reform and 'permissive' legislation (including also liquor licensing, Sunday observance, and family planning) are traditional battlefields where Scottish MPs have strong prejudices. They are often able to veto the extension to Scotland of English Private Members' legislation, and a puritanical (or politically sensitive) Scottish Secretary can delay the application of a government 'permissive' Bill to Scotland. Thus William Ross stopped the application of the National Health Service (Family Planning) Act 1967 to Scotland, ostensibly on economic grounds. This Act allowed local authorities to provide free contraceptives and was opposed by Roman Catholics and some Kirkmen. Public and medical opinion was mobilised, however, and the Health Services and Public Health Act 1968 (sec. 15) extended the 1967 provisions to Scotland.

Opinion in Scotland about such matters is expressed through the channels of representation analysed in the last two chapters. Some of these channels go no further than the Scottish political and social systems, and a solution is found in purely Scottish terms. But many bring in communication between Scotland and England, and involve a comparison of the legal developments in the two countries. The influence of television in publicising English law reforms (often without explaining that they do not apply to Scotland) makes citizens in Scotland restless when it is discovered that such measures are purely English. Conversely, discussion of the flaws in English law nowadays increasingly draws upon the lessons to be learnt from Scottish experience. In this way, a gradual assimilation takes place.

Conclusion

The three policy areas chosen for discussion in this chapter provide illustrations of the varying degrees of autonomy possessed by decision-makers in the Scottish political system.

In public finance and economic planning, the major decisions are taken by the British departments such as the Treasury, Trade and Industry, and Energy. Yet the policy formulation is influenced by Scottish academics, pressure groups, administrators, and ministers (not of course in that order of importance!), and its execution is coordinated by the Scottish Office. There are signs that the Scottish political system is increasing its hold over this sector.

Education, health, social work, and housing have strong Scottish traditions, with separate 'worlds' of their own. The British system of government, and the philosophies of the parties, allow Scotland scope to experiment and go its own way, as long as general standards are maintained and the repercussions for England are not too grave. There is perhaps more autonomy in large matters such as the curriculum in the schools, than there is in 'social' or financial matters such as youth training or school milk, which are politically sensitive and must be seen to be uniform throughout Britain.

Finally, law reform also illustrates the different decision-making processes which operate within the system. At one extreme there is the self-contained world of the Scottish lawyer, with his ability to control the technical aspects of Scottish law reform. At the other, there is the political discourse between MPs and the public on divorce, abortion, and other 'moral' issues. While each process belongs inside the Scottish political system, in the sense of being primarily a matter of communication among those in Scotland with only incidental references to England, the boundaries break down to some extent through the awareness of English practices, the increasing assimilation of Scottish society to that of England, and the desire in Great Britain to establish 'equal rights' for all citizens.

The philosophies of the political parties are conducive to the principle of legal and social equality in this sense. In Britain, diversity in policy-making between parts of the country is only tolerable if it concerns 'means' rather than 'ends'. The distinction is not easy to draw in many cases, but there is no doubt that the central

239

government can, if it wishes, impose its will to secure uniformity even in minor matters.

What holds back an even tighter centralisation of power in Britain is the historic strength of the nations and regions, with their vested professional interests in law, education, medicine, etc., the sentiment of nationalism and the lingering ideology of local self-rule derived in part from thinkers such as John Stuart Mill (a Scot by paternal parentage).

The policy process in Scotland is based on these foundations of opinions and power, and its autonomy shows few signs of weakening, despite the general movement towards social homogeneity in Britain.

13

*The Highland periphery**

The Highlands of Scotland[1] form part of the northern periphery of Europe, an area which extends in an arc from Ireland in the west, through northern Scandinavia, to arctic Russia. The periphery is distinguished from the rest of the continent by its cool climate, its difficult soil, its proximity to the sea, its sparsity of population, its culture, and its ethnic composition. Distance from cities and from centres of industry and government gives a special character to its societies. They are Europe's most isolated and most individual peoples.[2]

There are around 330,000 inhabitants in the seven 'crofting counties' of Scotland, and 353,000 in the area covered by the Highlands and Islands Development Board. They live in an area of over fourteen million square miles, at a density of around twenty people to the square mile. Although 40% live in towns, the largest of these is Inverness (population *c.* 40,000) and the next in size are Dunoon (*c.* 10,000) and Thurso (*c.* 10,000). There are only eight other towns with over 4,000 people (these figures are approximate, since the new local government Districts are larger than the old towns, and the latter are not now enumerated separately). The Highlands contain 7% of the population of Scotland and 47% of its area (16% of the area of Great Britain).

They are an important political region in Scotland, and deserve to be treated separately, since they are so untypical. They have for hundreds of years been the object of interest and concern on account of their romantic and tragic history, which has included such events as the Jacobite rebellions of the eighteenth century and the

---

*The Borders are to some extent a second Scottish periphery. They include the constituencies of Roxburgh and Berwickshire; Tweeddale, Ettrick and Lauderdale; and Dumfries. Like the Highlands, they have been strongly Liberal, and a Liberal MP (David Steel) has sat for Roxburgh/Tweeddale since 1965. The areas is much closer to population centres than the Highlands, and there is no crofting economy. The Gaelic culture is absent, so that cultural cleavages with the rest of Scotland are much less marked.

clearances in the eighteenth and nineteenth centuries. The sympathy aroused in the Lowlands of Scotland and even in England on account of these happenings is still very much alive today. It can be seen in the numerous books and articles written about the area, and by such practical political measures as the setting-up in 1965 of the Highlands and Islands Development Board. The Board took its place at the end of a series of special government agencies for the Highlands, of which the Crofters Commission (1886–1911; 1955–), the Congested Districts Board (1897–1911), and the Advisory Panel on the Highlands and Islands (1947–65) are the other principal examples.

Many of the symbolic aspects of Scottish nationality are derived from Highland, rather than Lowland, culture. Tartans, kilts, clans, bagpipes, and country dancing are now built into the Scottish image, although before the nineteenth century Lowland Scots despised the 'barbaric' Highlanders and supported the suppression of the kilt and the clans by the government after the 1745 Jacobite rebellion.

Sir Walter Scott in his novels converted most people to a romantic view of the Highlands, and George IV was prevailed upon to wear the kilt in Edinburgh in 1822, a precedent for the Royal Family ever since. It can be claimed that the Highlands now occupy in Scottish mythology something of the character of the 'Wild West' in America: an ideal landscape ('land of bens and glens') peopled with rugged individualists. Much of the sympathy for the Highlands is based on the feeling that if its way of life were to perish, Scottish nationality itself would be in danger. This accounts for the adoption of pseudo-Highland ways in the Lowlands, and for the support given for public expenditure to prop up the Highland economy.

The political history of the Highlands shows that for 150 years it has been a distinct region in terms of electoral behaviour. Until 1884, when the franchise in the counties was extended to male householders, the number of voters in Highland constituencies was extremely small. For example, Sutherland had 104 electors in 1832, rising to only 325 in 1880. There were no contested elections in that county until 1885, and in other Highland seats contests were rare. Ross and Cromarty went uncontested from 1837 to 1852, and from 1857 to 1884. Inverness-shire was similarly dormant from 1838 to 1865, and from 1868 to 1880. Some of these seats could be considered to be 'rotten counties', in the gift of a landed patron, or at most a bone of contention between rival landowners. Highland seats controlled by patrons between 1868 and 1885 were Argyllshire (Duke of Argyll), Orkney and Shetland (Earl of Zetland), and

242

Sutherlandshire (Duke of Sutherland) (Hanham 1, pp. 407–8). (For the period 1885–1910, see also Henry Pelling, *Social Geography of British Elections 1885–1910*, Macmillan (London, 1967), pp. 37–96.)

The extension of the franchise in 1884 revolutionised Highland politics. The crofters were given the vote, and at one stroke the electorate in some constituencies rose dramatically (e.g. in Sutherland to 3,185; in Ross and Cromarty from 1,720 to 10,265). In the election of 1885, a Highland political party, the Crofters' Party, ousted the landlords' nominees from five of the Highland seats. These 'Crofter' MPs retained their position as an 'independent Labour party' in Parliament until 1895, when they merged with the Liberals.[3] They gave an early indication of the Highlanders' disregard for the conventions of the British two-party system.

That system has never been strong in the crofting counties, since its principal basis, an identification of each of the principal parties with the interests of a social class, has had little relevance to Highland society. Class divisions do exist in the Highlands, but they are unlike those in the rest of the country (especially in the urban areas). Until the oil developments of the 1970s, only 10% of the employed people were engaged in manufacturing (SCSA 3, p. 29) Oil has provided about 10,000 jobs directly, and perhaps the same again indirectly, especially in Shetland and in Highland Region, but many of these have gone to incomers. There is little urbanisation, and the main divisions tend to be diffused and personalised. Landlord and tenant conflicts produced social and political cleavages in the nineteenth and early twentieth centuries, of which the Crofters' War (1882–8) and the Crofters' Party are examples. But the effect of the Crofters Acts, and of public ownership of much of the land through the Department of Agriculture and Fisheries for Scotland and the Forestry Commission, has been to diminish greatly such conflicts. Crofters' security of tenure and low rents have transformed Highland politics from latent revolution into peaceful 'pressure' politics. Such politics involve playing one party off against another to secure greater attention for the Highlands.

This strategy is politically both conservative and swift to change, in terms of voting loyalties. Its conservatism was first seen in the lingering strength of the Liberal Party, after it had declined in most parts of Britain. This strength was partially maintained during the 1930s and 1940s, and revived in the 1950s and 1960s. Jo Grimond, the leader of the Liberal Party from 1965 to 1967, represented Orkney and Shetland in Parliament from 1950 to 1983. In 1983 he was succeeded by another Liberal, James Wallace. In 1964, Liberals took four of the six Highland seats. In 1983, the Liberal-SDP Alliance took four seats in the Highlands, and two seats in the Borders (out of eight Alliance seats in Scotland as a whole).

No party can rely entirely on Highland loyalty, for that is often given to outstanding candidates irrespective of political allegiance, or to candidates who will upset political predictions, and thereby attract publicity. This is the second Highland strategy: the unexpected result.

Table 28 shows the political 'fickleness' of the Highland seats from 1959 to 1983. Although the constituencies are broadly similar in social and economic terms, their political allegiances vary considerably, as does the progression of each party's support from election to election. Some of these seats reveal examples of the 'unexpected change'. Caithness and Sutherland became Independent (Conservative) in 1959 as a result of the resignation of the Conservative whip by the sitting member, Sir David Robertson, and his subsequent re-election at the general election of that year. In 1964 the seat went Liberal, and in 1966 it became Labour, which it remained until 1983, when the sitting member was elected for the SDP-Liberal Alliance. While some of the change in voting behaviour in that constituency is due to the industrial developments round Thurso (Dounreay atomic research station), much seems to be the result of a desire to choose the best candidate, irrespective of his party, and thereby create the maximum political effect (Grimble, in Butler and King, pp. 227–32).

Other examples of unexpected change are the SNP gain in the Western Isles in 1970 and the SDP gain in Ross, Cromarty, and Skye in 1983, neither of which was foreseen by their respective party headquarters. Such dramatic switches may, however, indicate that these are 're-aligning' elections, and that stability will follow as a result of the emergence of a new majority party (see Grimble, *op. cit.*, p. 232). The SNP retained the Western Isles in the four subsequent general elections.

In the absence of academic research into Highland electoral politics, any hypotheses about electoral behaviour there have yet to be tested. At this stage, it is worth pointing to certain features of Highland elections, and to the assumed perceptions Highlanders have of elections and parties.

The importance of the candidate is probably greater in the Highlands than in other areas, even in other rural areas (Grimble, *op. cit.* p. 230). A local man, or a man with local connections, is almost

Table 28. *Election results in Highland constituencies, 1959–83*

Constituency	1959	1964	1966	1970	1974 (Feb.)	1974 (Oct.)	1979	1983
Argyll (Argyll and Bute, 1983)	Con	Con	Con	Con	SNP	SNP	Con	Con
Caithness and Sutherland	Ind Con	Lib	Lab	Lab	Lab	Lab	Lab	SDP-Lib All
Inverness (Inverness, Nairn, and Lochaber, 1983)	Con	Lib	Lib	Lib	Lib	Lib	Lib	Lib-SDP All
Orkney and Shetland	Lib	Lib	Lib	Lib	Lib	Lib	Lib	Lib-SDP All
Ross and Cromarty (Ross, Cromarty, and Skye, 1983)	Nat Lib and Con	Lib	Lib	Con	Con	Con	Con	SDP-Lib All
Western Isles	Lab	Lab	Lab	SNP	SNP	SNP	SNP	SNP

Key:

Con	Conservative
Nat Lib and Con	National Liberal and Conservative
Ind Con	Independent Conservative
Lab	Labour
Lib	Liberal
Lib-SDP All	Liberal-Social Democratic Party Alliance
SNP	Scottish National Party
SDP-Lib All	Social Democratic Party-Liberal Alliance

Note: In the elections to the European Assembly in 1979, the SNP won the Highlands and Islands seat.

essential, and such a person should have a strong personal connection, through kinship or face-to-face contacts, with the electorate. Something of the 'clan' loyalties of bygone years is still present in the Highlands, and votes may go to a Macleod or a Campbell through such ties. This may mean supporting a Conservative laird, or it may mean voting for a Labour schoolteacher.

The localism of the election is further stressed by the absence of interest in great national issues. Such issues are often considered foreign to the Highlands, where the sole demand is for increased aid. To some extent the candidates differ as to what use should be made of such aid, and the activities of the Highland Board have become controversial. But it is usually impossible to put a party label to such differences, especially since the Conservatives now fully accept the powers of the Board and its strategy, which they did not in 1965.

An exception to the absence of national issues in Highland elections are questions relating to the EEC. These are widely discussed, and the prevailing opposition to entry helped to win votes for the SNP, as the only party which sympathised with that view. The EEC is seen as a threat to the fishing industry and to the subsidies given to marginal farmers. It threatens to remove the centre of government even further from the periphery. These feelings were not adequately represented by the main parties nationally (though candidates did voice them locally), and the Highlanders felt no compunction in giving strong support to a fourth party (the SNP) which had previously been largely inactive in the area. In 1979, they elected Mrs Winifred Ewing as their representative to the European Assembly. But the strength of feeling for nationalism and self-government apparently expressed in such support is not clear. In the EEC Referendum in June 1975, Shetland and the Western Isles were the only regions in Britain to vote 'No'. But while the SNP continued to represent the Western Isles in the House of Commons, Mrs Ewing came a poor third in Orkney and Shetland in the general election of 1983.

The pattern of communications is a crucial factor in Highland elections. Local newspapers and election meetings play a greater part in shaping opinion than they do in the rest of the country. The London (or Glasgow) media are relatively less important, and give a very inadequate coverage of Highland news. Large areas of the Highlands have poor or non-existent television reception, especially of ITV, and newspapers are often delivered late.

Candidates must cover vast areas during election campaigns, so that they can make appearances in all communities, no matter how

246

small. Failure to cultivate support in this way between elections, as well as during election campaigns, can prove fatal for a candidate or sitting member. (Labour's loss of the Western Isles in 1970 was probably related to this factor.)

The influence of local notables on political behaviour is important, if little understood by political scientists at present. Traditionally, the laird commanded a following from his tenants and employees, but his influence is now on the wane (see Grimble, in Butler and King, p. 228). The schoolteachers of the Western Isles were the bulwark of Labour support there, until many revolted in 1970 to join the SNP. Ministers and priests have their say in elections, and in 1970 the 'permissive' legislation of the Labour government was strongly attacked in the Western Isles and in other Highland constituencies. The strictly puritanical Free Church of Scotland is influential in some places, but television and tourism have successfully challenged its power.

The role of the 'political entrepreneur' is essential in peripheral areas.[4] He is the man who links the local community with the centres of government, and so has a foot in both worlds. He has a necessary function in the Highlands, since the Highlander feels isolated and culturally distinct from the major part of the population, especially from government decision-makers.

The western Highlands and Islands contain the bulk of the Gaelic-speaking community, rising to over 80% of the population in parts of the Western Isles (they almost all speak English as well) (Thomson and Grimble, p. 178). This linguistic characteristic is accompanied by others of a cultural, ethnic, and economic nature. The Gaelic Highlands are dependent on the political entrepreneur, as the man who can move freely between the Celtic and non-Celtic communities, and can communicate the demands of the grass-roots to the government, as well as the government's response to such demands.

The eastern Highlands do not possess the same cultural distinctness, though it should be said that Orkney and Shetland have traditionally been considered by their inhabitants to be outside Scotland altogether, as part of Scandinavia. They resisted merging with a Highland local authority, for they do not feel 'Highland' (Thomson and Grimble, pp. 268–9). Most easterners find no difficulty in communicating with outsiders, and are not averse to cultural change. They are more inclined than their western neighbours to take the hard, materialist view of life, and to seek means of providing for rapid commercial advancement. Significantly, the Highland Board

247

has promoted most of its industrial development policies in the eastern Highlands, partly because of natural resources, but also because the population there is more responsive to industrialisation.

But the political entrepreneur is needed in the east as well as in the west. Both parts are recognisably Highland, and are far from London and Edinburgh in spirit as well as in geography. Sir David Robertson, MP for Caithness and Sutherland from 1950 to 1964, typified the role of entrepreneur, for he sought government recognition for Highland problems while maintaining a firm base of support against the neglect of the Highlands by the Conservative Government. His successors have also been independents in action if not in form. Most Highland MPs are constituency men first, and party men afterwards, and even Jo Grimond (Orkney and Shetland 1950–83) retained most of his electoral support through his Orkney lineage and his constant advocacy of local interests.

Other entrepreneurs are the councillors and local government officials, the schoolteachers, doctors, and hoteliers. The landowner is prominent in some areas (e.g. Argyll, Inverness-shire, and Ross and Cromarty), though in the Western Isles and Caithness and Sutherland his influence has waned (Grimble, in Butler and King, p. 228). An analysis of Highland county councils in January 1967 showed that landowners and farmers accounted for only 84 out of 317 Highland councillors, while there were 132 businessmen and miscellaneous white-collar workers. But there were only 20 crofters and 20 manual workers, and lairds held convenerships in several counties (Magnusson, 'Highland Administration', in Thomson and Grimble, p. 301).
· The average age of councillors in the seven counties in 1967 was 57.7 years, with an average length of residence in their respective counties of 43.7 years, and an average term of council service of 11.5 years (Magnusson, op.cit., p. 300). Even more than most rural areas, the Highland councils seem dependent on retired or self-employed persons of advanced years and comfortable financial means. (Unfortunately, there is no more recent survey of Highland local government known to the author.)

Party politics is not usual in local government in the Scottish 'periphery'. Most councillors are independents, and represent their own constituents before all else. Moreover, contested seats are more unusual there. In Highland Region, for example, in the Regional Council elections in 1982, only 28 of the 52 seats were contested (the Council retained a large 'Independent' majority). In the Western Isles in the same election only 12 of the 30 seats were contested (by 30 candidates), all on a non-party basis. In Orkney, 12 of the 24 seats were contested, three by Labour and one by the Orkney Movement. In Shetland, 9 of the 25 seats were contested, and all but two candidates (Labour) stood without political affiliations.[5] While the Islands authorities remain staunchly Independent in local politics, there is some evidence of a slow movement towards party politics in the Highland Region, where the number of party candidates has risen. In the 1978 elections, Independents won 40 seats out of the total of 47 seats on the Council. In 1982, Independents won 42 of the 52 seats, with the remainder shared by Labour (5), Liberal (2), SNP (2), and Conservative (1).[6] On a turnout of 41% the party share of the vote was Labour 15%, Alliance 5%, SNP 9% and Independents 71%. In 1978, on a 43% turnout, the party share was SNP 6%, Labour 5%, Conservative and Liberal each $2\frac{1}{2}$%, and Independents $83\frac{1}{2}$%.[7]

Attempts to reform Highland local government met with strong resistance. The Wheatley Report proposal to create one large Highland Region from Argyll to Shetland was bitterly attacked, and in 1971 the Conservative government gave large concessions to Highland opinion. Orkney, Shetland, and the Western Isles were each made virtually all-purpose authorities, cooperating with other authorities only for some aspects of education and social work, and for police and fire services. The Wheatley Highland Region was further reduced in size by extracting most of Argyll and adding it to the Strathclyde Region.

Such successes achieved by Highland pressure groups can be related to the precarious politics of the area, and to the desire of governments to win marginal seats there. Other examples have been the postponement of rail closures, first in the early 1960s, when the 'MacPuff' campaign and the protests of the Highlands and Islands Advisory Panel stopped the 'Beeching Axe' falling on Highland lines, and then at the end of 1971, when the Dingwall-Kyle of Lochalsh line was reprieved for two years, at a net cost of about £200,000 per annum (*Glasgow Herald*, 23 December 1971).

The establishment of the Highlands and Islands Development Board (HIDB) in November 1965 was a sign that political pressures from the area were at last beginning to lead to strong executive action. Not the least of Highland problems has been the chaotic administrative problems endured by the region (Magnusson, 'Highland Administration', in Thomson and Grimble, pp. 243–96; also Farquhar Gillanders, 'The Economic life of Gaelic Scotland Today', *ibid*. pp. 95–105). Around fifty government agencies, as well as the local authorities, have a hand in Highland development, a fact that makes the Board's functions a little difficult to isolate (see SCSA 3, pp. 18–20, for a list of government and other agencies operating in the Highlands at that time).

The HIDB was created by Act of Parliament, and vested with executive powers to acquire land, erect buildings, carry on business, give grants and loans, and provide a wide range of advisory and publicity services. Its finance comes from a grant-in-aid on the vote of the Industry Department for Scotland (IDS) and some projects need the Secretary of State for Scotland's approval, or must be sanctioned by the Treasury. The grants which the Board can give to firms are similar to those given by the government in development areas. The Board can, however, give assistance to 'non-economic' projects which are social or partly social in character, and special assistance to other projects which will eventually become successful economically. Loans offered at preferential rates of interest, and grants, which are repayable in certain circumstances if the project does not proceed, are the Board's main forms of assistance.[8]

The Highlands must compete with other development areas in the attraction of industry. Their position in this respect has of course been transformed since the advent of North Sea oil. International companies have flooded into the area, with platform sites, supply bases, and pipeline and oil-rig construction camps. The challenge to the traditional way of life has been severe, and campaigns were mounted by certain interests to prevent developments taking place. Other sections of Highland opinion were strongly in favour of oil-related industry, and the Scottish Office had to take the final decisions on planning approval, often after lengthy public enquiries. The Board has been something of a bystander in this area, since its powers do not extend into town and country planning, nor has it played any important part in shaping the oil developments which have taken place largely over its head. Local authorities such as Shetland have made their own deals with the oil companies, and have acquired special powers by Act of Parliament. At the other end of the governmental spectrum, the Department of Energy in London has handled most of the relations with the oil companies, and the Department of Industry (now Trade and Industry) the relations with the onshore companies.

The chief advantage in having the Board is that the region possesses a government agency dedicated to attracting industry to it, and to no other. The Department of Trade and Industry gives no priority to the

250

Highlands (SCSA 2, p. 127, Q. 610), and the Scottish Office has often proved sceptical of many Highland developments. The SDA does not operate in the Highlands as far as industrial estates and small businesses are concerned, but does deal with large projects, along with the IDS (Keating and Midwinter, p. 39). The Board has a large team (7 members and 257 staff in 1982) and its combination of powers is unique to any regional development agency in the United Kingdom.[9] Yet some of these powers have been potential rather than actual, and its expenditures, though growing, are small in relation to those of other public bodies in the Highlands. Nevertheless, the Board estimates that in the ten years to the end of 1982 it has helped to create more than 22,000 jobs, and spent £160m, spread over land development, fisheries, manufacturing and processing, construction, and tourism.

Controversy surrounded the Board from its inception. Its strategy for developing the Highlands was initially one of bold thinking directed towards the establishment of large industrial development 'growth areas' (three were chosen). One of these areas, the Moray Firth (the others were Lochaber and Wick/Thurso) was given special attention, and a plan to make the area a metropolis with half a million people was suggested by the first chairman, Professor Sir Robert Grieve[10] (*Scotsman*, 22 April 1966). Invergordon was to be developed as a deep-water port, with large aluminium and petro-chemical works. Inverness was to be the administrative centre, with a new university.

Such schemes soon aroused the opposition of Highland traditionalists, such as lairds and Gaels, who feared that the Highland way of life was being threatened. Many on the west coast wondered whether the Board had their interests at heart, and they did not relish emigrating to the east coast to get work, any more than having to go to Glasgow or London. Sniping at the Board became a popular pastime (and spread even to commentators such as Grimble, in Butler and King, pp. 230–1), and the *Scottish Daily Express* waged a campaign against some of its members. One member resigned, in March 1967, on account of the outcry about his personal commercial interest in the establishment of a petro-chemical works by a particular firm at Invergordon. Another went in July of the same year, bitter about the poor support which he said the Scottish Office was giving to the Board (*Scotsman*, 8 July 1967).

With the passage of time, these events can be seen as teething troubles. The Board was an administrative invention, and such animals are not welcome to traditional politicians and civil servants. Its members were chosen from academic, commercial, and public life, and they did not always understand the diplomatic subtleties (hypocrisies?) of government.

Nor were they 'political entrepreneurs' of the kind understood in the Highlands. They were neither local men (on the whole) nor government men, and so fell between two stools. They spoke out boldly for their schemes, and so offended the vested interests of the counties, St Andrew's House, and Whitehall. At one point, they were rebuked by the Scottish Office Minister of State for dealing with big developments. These were the government's concern, said St Andrew's House, and the Board's rôle was to help small industrial concerns, and to deal with land use, forestry, fishing, tourism, and agriculture. The Board telegrammed its chairman, Professor Grieve, who was abroad: 'Continue to think big. Staff behind you' (*Glasgow Herald*, 2 September 1967).

There followed something of a lull under the next Chairman, a retired diplomat, but the third Chairman, Professor Kenneth Alexander, a left-wing economist from Strathclyde University, revived the bold approach, when he sought legislation to give the Board powers to purchase land compulsorily if it appeared to the Board that such land was being poorly used.[11] The Labour Government, however, took no action, and the old radical call for land nationalisation, dating from the nineteenth century Clearances, remained unanswered. Another notable failure of the Board was the closure of the Invergordon aluminium smelter in 1982. Here the Board got into conflict with another Highland agency, the North of Scotland Hydro-Electric Board. The Hydro Board supplied power to the smelter, but not at a cheap enough rate to keep it economically viable. The Highland Board attacked the Hydro Board for its prices, which were higher, it was claimed, than those charged to similar smelters in England and Wales.[12] But the Board had no powers in the matter, and the smelter (one of the Board's original prestige projects) closed.

These examples illustrate the institutional problems facing the Board, as well as the considerable cultural and political ones. It is only one of many public bodies operating in the Highlands, and it is not elected. The new local authorities established in 1975 have had the advantage of such election by the Highlanders themselves, and they possess greater powers and territorial scope than the old authorities. They alone have the legal powers over land use, which many see as the real key to the Highland problem.

It is difficult to be confident about the future of the Highlands, and perhaps even of the Board. The population of most rural areas continues to decline, and is only offset by the increase in the 'growth areas'. While many applaud this development, it does nothing to maintain isolated communities in their traditional way of life. Without such communities, the Highlands will become pockets of industrialisation surrounded by emptiness. These industries are sometimes commercially precarious, and even the stupendous impact of oil wells off the coasts of northern Scotland may be an insecure basis for the Highland economy in the long run, despite considerable activity related to the construction and maintenance of oil rigs, platforms, and pipelines. Much the same could be said for the fishing industry, which is subject to periodic depressions, and EEC policies over which it has no control.

The Board's future as an agency of government is probably assured, but its character changes with its personnel. Its Chairmen have been two university professors, a retired diplomat, a Rear-Admiral, and, since 1982, a management consultant whose last post was in Hong Kong. Highlanders have been notable for their absence. The Highland Board thus represents another example of the power of outsiders in the Highlands and Islands, to set beside English landlords, American oil companies, lowland environmentalists and 'white settlers'.

Yet the Board is also the culmination of years of pressure for a strong body to develop the resources of the area. In part, this campaign has been realised. The Board has brought employment and money to the Highlands, and a new form of public administration to the Highland capital. It has proceeded carefully with a strategy which balances the different claims of small and large industry, agriculture, fisheries, and tourism, west coast and east coast, and so on. It is doubtful whether any human agency could satisfy all the diverse elements in this part of Scotland, nor would it be politic (or politics!) to try to do so.

Highlanders are in many ways dependent on the rest of the country. This is part of the price of living in the periphery, with its problems of remoteness and underdevelopment. Yet in their politics they show a sturdy independence and an unwillingness to conform to Scottish (let alone British) norms. Their local authorities are non-partisan, yet powerful. The only all-purpose authorities in Britain are the three Islands Authorities of the Western Isles, Orkney, and Shetland. The last two have special powers over industrial development not possessed by any other local governments. Highland and

253

Islands MPs are among the most independent in the House of Commons, and they frequently belong to 'minor' parties. All this serves to make up a political identity as resilient as that of Scotland itself.

14

Conclusion: Scotland in a comparative context

There are two important questions which have to be asked, and, if possible, answered, at the end of this study of the Scottish political system. The first relates to the position of Scotland within the UK. Is the Scottish political system merely a sub-system of the British political system without independent means of support, and without effective power over the 'allocation of values'? Second, how does one relate the study of Scottish politics to that of comparative government as a whole? Such basic problems, which must arise from the material which has been presented, ought to engage the attention of any political scientist who carries forward the study of the Scottish political system.

Since this work first appeared in 1973, many political scientists have carried forward this study, even if they have not all approved of the concept of a 'Scottish political system'. John Mackintosh, for example, in a review[1] of the Second Edition(1975), wrote:

> to talk of a Scottish politics as a 'system' suggests that there is a focal point in Scotland where the various Scottish pressures meet and are resolved before the Scottish input is made into the British political system. In fact this is not the case.

Richard Rose, in his *Understanding the United Kingdom* (Rose 6), remarks:

> Kellas speaks of a 'Scottish political system', but the phrase begs the question: What is its government? The answer is very clear: British government is the dominant force in the Scottish political system... Scottish politics is best conceived as a *subsystem* of United Kingdom politics and government (Rose 6, p. 52).

In their *The Government of Scotland*, Michael Keating and Arthur Midwinter write:

> We rely heavily on the concept of 'policy networks', seeing Scottish government not as a 'political system' since ultimate authority lies

255

outwith Scotland, nor as simply part of the 'British political system' since it is undeniably different, but rather in terms of a series of complex networks, linking Scottish actors to one another and to non-Scottish networks (Keating and Midwinter, pp. 3–4).

The reasons for calling Scotland a 'political system' are first presented in Ch. 1 of this book. The rest of the book is devoted to different aspects of Scottish politics and government, which are to be understood in conjunction with this organising concept. The main alternatives to such an organising concept seem to be that of a Scottish input to the British political system (Mackintosh, and Rose, quoted above), or a series of Scottish and Scottish/British policy networks, with 'ultimate authority' elsewhere (Keating and Midwinter, above). It is maintained here that these models or approaches to Scottish politics are not inconsistent with the concept of a Scottish political system, but do not in themselves provide an adequate alternative to it. For Mackintosh only devolution can provide Scotland with a political system of its own (*loc. cit.*). Keating and Midwinter are also devolutionists, but for them even with devolution Scotland would not possess a political system, since 'ultimate authority' would still lie in London (Keating and Midwinter, p. 210). Similarly, Rose writes that 'The proposed devolution assemblies for Scotland and Wales were completely consistent with the doctrine of the unitary state', and only federalism would alter that (Rose 6, p. 53). But Rose's concept of the UK unitary state is unorthodox, since he sees it as a 'multinational political system' (*ibid.*, p. 17).

There is no doubt that devolution or federalism would strengthen the Scottish political system, and perhaps make it a different kind of political system. It is possible to support the 'prescriptive' parts of these works, without accepting their 'analytical' conclusions about the existence of a Scottish political system. Nationalists (not quoted above) would deny that anything short of total independence for Scotland would produce a political system in their terms, and some political scientists would argue that even the nation-state has lost its independence as a political system to multinational or supra-national 'systems'.

The evidence of this book demonstrates the existence of a Scottish political system comprising a large number of actors engaged in a wide range of political activities. These activities or functions are partly exercised through the medium of political structures such as the Scottish Office and the organised groups, and partly through the expression of public opinion in the media, or by direct action. Such activities are recognisably Scottish because they take place within a political and social system which history has differentiated at many key points from that of England. Most relevant, of course, are Scottish national consciousness, the religious, educational, and legal institutions, and the socio-economic conditions (e.g. in housing), which have led to the setting up of Scottish political institutions. In the Highland periphery, cultural and linguistic characteristics, crofting, and separate administrative agencies make up a sub-system of the Scottish system.

The Scottish system can be defined by the flow of communications. In Table 24, Ch. 10, a diagram was drawn to show the principal channels of communication in the Scottish system, and between Scotland and London. While the flows could be charted in all directions, there were two basic patterns, that within Scotland towards St Andrew's House, and that from Scotland to the Government in London. The former was a Scottish communications system, the latter a British one.

In political terms, these systems are less easy to separate. The Scottish communications network which focusses on the Scottish Office involves the British political system, for the Scottish Office is a department of the British Government, with a minister in the British Cabinet. Decisions of that Cabinet are binding on the Scottish Office, and the Scottish communications network must therefore be finally dependent on the vital link between London and Edinburgh.

Conversely, the activity of Scottish MPs in Parliament with regard to Scottish legislation and Scottish administration, though geographically in the British system (or London 'activity area') is more sensibly seen as being within the Scottish system in a 'detached portion'. This is because communication here is almost entirely between the Scottish MPs, who are primarily involved in the Scottish committees and in Scottish question time. Even on British issues, their main interest is in the Scottish aspects.

One can move from a communication model to a decision-making model. In Ch. 12, the policy process was examined to discover who the principal decision-makers were in specified areas of policy. Once more, the question of system and sub-system was involved, for in some areas of policy the Scottish system was dominant, while in others it was dependent. The chief examples of the former were education, social work, and law, and of the latter, economic policy and the financial aspects of welfare. The crucial function of allocation of resources was in the British system, with Scottish influence nevertheless asserting itself to a remarkable degree.

Was 'allocation of values' British? If so, the idea of a political system in Easton's terms[2] is not present in Scotland. But we have seen that in the crucial areas of education, religion, and law, Scotland stands apart from England, and these institutions represent values. Many were, of course, 'allocated' in the distant past, when Scotland was an independent state, but they have grown autonomously since then within the structure of the British state. This is because Scots have been able to allocate the values within Scotland to their own satisfaction, usually without let or hindrance from London. Clearly a conflict may develop when the party majorities in Scotland and in Britain as a whole are at variance. Even then, the British government must adapt its policies to take account of the demands of the Scottish system.

Scots have shaped the style of Scottish government to their own taste. They created the Scottish Office in the 1880s by their demands, and have added continuously to its functions. The Scottish committees of the House of Commons established a sort of 'parliament within parliament'. In the 1970s, they adopted a local government system significantly different from that of England.

In all these political institutions there is an element of strong, centralised government, based on Edinburgh (not London). The Scottish Office is an 'omnibus' department encompassing functions distributed among several departments in England. This naturally concentrates power in the hands of one minister. Similarly, the regional structure of local government and the tradition of strong central government control over local authorities limits the scope of local self-government. Finally, the Scots have shown themselves to be fickle over devolution and nationalism. While apparently demanding an Assembly with some vigour in the mid-1970s, and giving strong support to the SNP in elections at that time, their vote in the Referendum of 1979 was ambiguous, and their interest in the subject since then has not been great. Perhaps the 'civic culture' of Scotland is rather more of a 'subject political culture'[3] than that of England (itself more 'subject' than that of the USA), since its citizens have delayed in insisting on a democratic institution to underpin the administrative and legal autonomy of the system. But this may be because they have been able to get their own way by other means.

There are now only a limited number of policy areas where Scots are determined to act independently of England. Thus the allocation of 'British' values is acceptable to Scotland in many important respects. Despite its divergencies from England noted above, the Scottish political culture is essentially at one with that of England on fundamentals. That this is so can be seen clearly by comparison with the political culture of Northern Ireland, where 'Governing without Consensus' (Rose 4) is the norm. In Scotland, there is no fundamental challenge to the constitution (despite the SNP), and politics is not dominated by religion, although there are special correlations between religion and voting in Scotland (see Ch. 6). Religious issues, especially denominational education, have been as important in English politics in the twentieth century as they have been in Scottish.

Some say that a separate parliament in Scotland would undermine the consensus. But this seems to be an exaggerated fear. Political tensions usually manifest themselves independently of the existence of legislatures, and Ulster's problems were obvious long before the Parliament of Stormont was set up in 1920. What is likely to happen under devolution in Scotland is a new confidence that Scots can take decisions for Scotland which in the past have been left to London.

If the political cultures of England and Scotland are similar, and many of the basic values are allocated by the British system of government, does this not reduce the present Scottish political system to the level of a sub-system?

This is obviously a matter of definition and a matter of opinion as to what is sufficiently important to constitute a system. The discipline of political science is not precise enough to distinguish clearly between a system and a sub-system in politics,[4] and all systems are sub-systems of some greater system (e.g. Britain is a sub-system of the EEC for economic planning). But just as Britain lost some of her independence as a system ('sovereignty' in old-fashioned language) by entering the European community, she undoubtedly remains a strong political system in other respects. The analogy with Scotland and the Union of 1707 is not completely satisfactory, but the implications are similar. Scotland and England came under one government with shared values, but each retained its identity and something of its political system. The evidence in this book shows how much has been retained over the past 276 years, and how much has been added.

It hardly needs demonstrating that people in Scotland ought to know about the government of the country they live in. If it is said that they can do so from what has already been written on British government, then it is the purpose of this book to challenge such a view, and to present Scotland as a definable political system with its own characteristics.

This interpretation has implications for the study of British government, and for comparative government. The simplistic view of the British system as a unitary, homogeneous, and stable polity faltered in the late 1960s. First the Welsh and Scottish Nationalists, then the Irish, showed how 'multinational' the UK was, and how divergent were many of its regional political cultures. At the time it was not clear whether the British system was being fundamentally challenged in Wales and Scotland, or whether the people in these nations wished for marginal improvements that could be negotiated (by 1970, the latter seemed to be the case yet in 1974 the challenge had reappeared in Scotland, to disappear again in 1979). In Northern Ireland, a fundamental constitutional and religious conflict flared up, which upset the British system profoundly. An alternative view, rejected by Richard Rose (Rose 4, p. 73), is that the British system was not upset, since Northern Ireland was not a part of it. British governments, however, consistently act as if Northern Ireland were part of the UK. As a result of the nationalist movements of the 1960s, and 1970s, the meaning of the British system altered, and England and English nationality came to be seen as something different from British nationality.[5]

Interest in Scotland within the field of comparative politics and government increased in the 1960s and even more so in the 1970s, when Scotland's potential contribution to the discipline began to be realised. At first, it was the rise of the SNP which attracted scholars throughout the world. Scottish nationalism had long had its place in the literature of nationalism,[6] and its ups and downs in the 1960s and 1970s proved as inexplicable as ever. The literature suffered from an analytic confusion which did not relate the nation-building process in Scotland, Ireland, Wales, and England to that of Britain as a whole. Karl Deutsch had attempted an analysis of Scottish nationalism in the early 1950s,[7] but most of his attention was focussed on the Gaelic language. By 1983, most scholars were still unable to explain the meaning and strength of Scottish nationalism, although a considerable amount had been written on the subject (see Ch. 7).

The study of Scottish voting behaviour, which the successes of the SNP largely inspired, led to much academic and journalistic writing. Some of the authors of these have produced work with an international reputation (e.g. Rose, and Miller). The Scottish universities now take a serious interest in Scottish politics and government generally, where for years they neglected these subjects in favour of British (i.e. without Scottish aspects) politics. The University of Edinburgh established a Unit for the Study of Government in Scotland in 1976, and in the same year the University of Strathclyde began a Centre for the Study of Public Policy, with a strong Scottish focus. In 1976 too, the International Political Science Association met in Edinburgh, amidst considerable interest in Scottish politics.

The contribution of Scotland to the study of political science has thus become known throughout the world in the last ten years. In Scotland itself, Scottish students are now generally required to study some Scottish politics, a subject totally ignored until the late 1960s. Students in the rest of Britain are also taught something about Scotland within their British politics courses. Among the subjects which can be studied with advantage on a comparative basis, using Scotland as an example, are nationalism and ethnicity, devolution, federalism, electoral behaviour, and decentralised public administration. The Highlands also offer a potential area of study in the political ecology of peripheries, building on the work of the late Stein Rokkan of Bergen University in Norway, and others.[8] The political cleavages in the Scandinavian peripheries resemble in some respects those in the Scottish Highlands, and detailed cross-national comparisons can be made. North Sea oil gives added importance to studies of this kind.

Scotland as a whole, as a periphery of the European 'heartland', gives scope for comparative work with the other 'smaller European democracies'. Countries of between five and ten million people, with a high degree of sophistication of political culture, provide an alternative model of development to the giant states of western Europe and America.

If it be argued that it is invalid to bring Scotland into such comparisons, since it is not a state, the reply of this book is that it is nevertheless a political system. There are features of statehood in that system, such as separate laws, administration, church, and education. Through these, the system allocates the values which maintain its identity. Political science can learn from studying such a nation and its political system, and the system itself can be improved on the basis of the knowledge so generated.

Postscript

The General Election of 1987

The result of the 1987 election gave further evidence of the distinctive character of the Scottish political system. It revealed an increasing gap between Scottish and English voting behaviour and produced a strain in the workings of the Scottish political institutions, since the Conservative MPs in Scotland were reduced to ten from their previous total of twenty-one. This was barely sufficient for the Government to provide ministers for the Scottish Office and the Law Departments, let alone make any other ministerial appointments from their Scottish MPs (George Younger was the only Scottish MP appointed to a non-Scottish post, as Defence Secretary). It was to prove particularly embarrassing for the Government in the Scottish Committees of the House of Commons which require a Government majority (the Scottish Standing Committees and the Select Committee on Scottish Affairs). The former, with a minimum of 16 Scottish MPs, tied up nearly all the Scottish Conservative MPs, and the latter had to be reduced from 13 MPs to nine, since only backbenchers can serve on Select Committees. Even then, the Government was unable to find the five MPs required for a majority, since three at first refused to serve, claiming it was a 'waste of time'. By June 1988, the Committee had still not been appointed.

The electoral polarisation between Scotland and England can be seen from Table 29 (this should be taken as an addition to Table 15 at p. 107).

The difference between the Scottish and English results is striking, and the Scottish Conservative total in terms of seats is the lowest since 1910, when seven were returned in the election in December (there were, however, four Liberal–Unionist allies returned as well). The decline of the Conservatives in Scotland has been proceeding steadily since 1955, although it is exaggerated in terms of seats by the electoral system. Thus, while the party lost 11 seats from its 1983 total, its share of Scottish vote declined by only 4.4%, and was only 0.7% lower

Table 29   *General Election Result, 1987*

1987 Election	UK		Scotland		England	
	% of vote	MPs	% of vote	MPs	% of vote	MPs
Con	42.2	376	24.0	10	46.2	358
Lab	30.8	229	42.4	50	29.5	155
All	22.6	22	19.2	9	23.8	10
SNP/PC	1.7	6	14.0	3	—	—
Others	2.7	18	0.4	0	0.5	0

than in October 1974. Nevertheless, the difference from England is very marked, where the Conservatives in 1983 won 46.2% of the vote. While there is a 'North–South' divide in voting in Britain generally, even the North of England, with a greater working class population than Scotland, was 32.0% Conservative (Labour, 47.0%; Alliance 20.8%), and Wales managed 29.5% Conservative (Labour 45.1%; Alliance 17.9%). The Welsh Nationalists (Plaid Cymru) with 7.3% (down 0.5%) compared unfavourably with the SNP (14.0%; up 2.3%), although the SNP result was not good, since it lost Dundee East, seat of the Chairman, Gordon Wilson, and the Western Isles, seat of the retiring President, Donald Stewart. These were both lost to Labour, while the SNP gained three seats from the Conservatives, equivalent to those it had held between 1974 and 1979, Moray (= Moray and Nairn), Banff and Buchan (= East Aberdeenshire), and Angus East (= Angus South).

The social characteristics of the vote in 1987 can be compared with those in 1983 from MORI surveys conducted at both elections (see Table 18(c), p. 141, for the System Three Scotland survey at the 1983 election).

The most striking features of these findings are the low Conservative support in all classes; the strong relationship between housing tenure and Conservative and Labour support, with surprising gains for Labour and the SNP among owner-occupiers; the large rise in Labour support among young and male voters; and the increasingly middle class (ABC1) character of the SNP. A detailed comparison between Scottish and English voting behaviour is not attempted here. In the 1987 election Scottish and English voters moved even further apart and explanations based on class, unemployment, housing, etc., could

263

Table 30 *Voting intention, 1987 (change from 1983 in brackets)*

		Class			Housing Tenure	
					Owner-Occupied	Council Tenants
	Total %	ABC1 %	C2 %	DE %	%	%
Con	24.1	33(−9)	21(−4)	16(−2)	36(−8)	12(−4)
Lab	42.4	25(+6)	48(+10)	54(+5)	27(+8)	55(+7)
Alliance	19.2	22(−7)	19(−3)	17(−5)	19(−7)	19(−5)
SNP	14.1	18(+8)	12(−3)	12(−1)	17(+6)	13(+1)
Other	1.2	2(*)	0(*)	1(*)	1(*)	1(*)

	Age				Sex	
	18–24 %	25–24 %	35–54 %	55+ %	Male %	Female %
Con	15(−13)	18(−4)	26(−1)	30(−4)	22(−4)	25(−5)
Lab	43(+11)	44(+7)	42(+6)	40(+5)	45(+10)	39(+4)
Alliance	22(−1)	20(−7)	18(−7)	18(−4)	19(−5)	19(−6)
SNP	16(−1)	18(+4)	13(+1)	12(−4)	12(−2)	16(+7)
Other	4(*)	*	1(*)	*	2(+1)	1(0)

Source: MORI. The data were weighted to reflect the actual election results.
(*=less than 1%)

explain only part of the difference. The Scottish dimension to Scottish voting strengthened, and threatened to polarise the British political system along national lines.

The 'Doomsday Scenario'

In 1987 Scottish political commentators began talking of the 'Doomsday Scenario', in which Scotland would be governed for the foreseeable future by a Conservative Government, while voting increasingly against the Conservatives.

This interpretation of electoral trends seemed plausible in the light of the 1987 election result, with the prediction that the Conservatives might win future elections because of the weakness of the opposition parties in England.

The SNP and Labour (and to a lesser extent the Alliance) proclaimed that the Conservatives had no 'mandate' to govern Scotland. A survey conducted at the beginning of 1987 found that only 31% thought that

264

the Conservatives would be 'entitled to govern Scotland' with fewer MPs in Scotland, and 64% approved action by the other parties to 'set up a Scottish Assembly to handle Scottish business, even if the Tories opposed it' (quoted in the *Scotsman*, 6 February 1987, from *Radical Scotland*, No. 25 (February/March 1987), p. 9).

The Conservatives for their part denied that the results in Scotland affected the legitimacy of the British results which had given them the right to govern Scotland as much as other parts of the United Kingdom. The Scottish Labour leadership, sensing the dangers of using a 'nationalist' argument, soon backtracked on the 'mandate' approach, preferring to say that the Conservatives lacked a 'moral' mandate in Scotland. This was not strong enough for some Scottish Labour MPs, who wanted to take action of some kind, whether parliamentary obstruction of Scottish business or the calling of a Scottish Constitutional Convention to draw up plans for a Scottish Assembly.

Devolution

Electoral support for devolution has remained strong since 1983. In 1987, MORI conducted two surveys on the subject (and on independence) comparable to those in Table 20(d). p. 150.

The May 1987 survey showed that only 4% named devolution as one of 'the two most important election issues', with unemployment at 63% and the Health Service at 29% as the top two. However, this response does not necessarily indicate a lack of strong support for devolution, and it is notable that support for 'independence' (if that is really meant) was running at its highest level. It is also seen that half the Conservatives supported either devolution or 'independence', despite that party's opposition to any form of Home Rule. Perhaps as worrying for the Labour Party is the 36% for 'independence' among Labour supporters, and for the SNP the mere 55% for 'independence' among their supporters. Alliance supporters back their party's devolution policy only to the extent of 60%.

The Labour Party produced a new Scotland Bill in November 1987. This was a stronger version of the Scotland Act 1978, for it now devolved a power to vary the level of personal income tax, control over the universities, police, electricity, manpower and training, and stronger executive power over the enonomy. It is arguable that had this been the Bill before the electorate in the 1979 Referendum it would have passed the '40% Rule' requirement (see p. 153). But in the

265

Table 31   *Attitudes towards constitutional change in Scotland, May 1987*

	Con %	Lab %	Lib/SDP %	SNP %	Total %	Total (March 1987) %
A completely independent Scottish Assembly separate from England	11	36	18	55	29	32
A Scottish Assembly as part of Britain but with substantial powers	39	41	60	41	41	50
No change from the present system	48	20	18	4	25	15
Don't Know	2	3	4	—	5	3

Source: MORI, *Scotsman*, 15 May 1987.

context of a Conservative Government the Bill had no hope of success, although a few Scottish Conservatives were now openly supporting devolution again, if not the Labour Bill. Indeed the cross-party Campaign for a Scottish Assembly continued to find party loyalties a stumbling-block to united action for devolution.

Nationalism

Evidence of Scottish nationalism was seen in a more sophisticated survey of national identity, reported in the *Glasgow Herald* (18 August 1986). In response to the question, 'Which of the statements best describes how you regard yourself?', 69% gave a predominantly or exclusive Scottish identity, with only 10% a predominantly or exclusively British identity (see Table 32, below). Even Conservative supporters preferred a Scottish to a British identity, with only 20% predominantly or exclusively British.

Parliament

The profile of the Scottish MPs elected in 1987 is shown in Table 33, which corresponds to Table 11, p. 83.

Table 32 *Nationality in Scotland*

	Total %	Con %	Lab %	Alliance %	SNP %	Other %
		Party supported				
Scottish, not British	39	27	37	34	58	45
More Scottish than British	30	29	35	26	29	20
Equally Scottish and British	19	22	20	28	7	18
More British than Scottish	4	10	2	3	3	5
British, not Scottish	6	10	4	7	2	9
Don't know	2	2	2	1	1	4

Source: System Three Scotland.

The turnover of MPs in 1987 was considerable, with 25 new MPs elected, and 14 seats changing parties. The profile of MPs, shown on p. 268, shows no great change from 1983, and is even more dominated by Labour.

The problems for the conduct of Scottish parliamentary business of the small number of Scottish Conservative MPs have already been referred to. With only ten MPs, including five backbenchers, the composition of Scottish Committees was broadened to include MPs from non-Scottish seats. It also became more common for Scottish legislative provisions to be added to English/Welsh Bills, thereby avoiding the need to go through the Scottish procedures. Of course, this practice was attacked by the Opposition parties, and by informed opinion in Scotland. Scottish business in Parliament became fraught with tensions as Labour used obstructive tactics such as all-night sessions, and tabling thousands of written Questions. The Select Committee on Scottish Affairs had already broken up in disarray in December 1985 over the Gartcosh Steelmill inquiry, when the Conservative side split over whether to oppose closure. This split carried over into the 1987–8 Session, when three Conservatives refused at first to serve on the Committee. Two relented under pressure, but the remaining MP, Bill Walker, would not. He had been involved in the Gartcosh revolt, and led the extreme right-wing Conservative backbenchers. The Committee had not been re-established by June 1988.

As with the 'Doomsday Scenario', the crisis of Scottish politics in

Table 33 *Scottish MPs, 1987*

	Con	Lab	Alliance	SNP
No. of MPs	10	50	9	3
Average Age	49	45	43	39
Non-Scots	—	3	—	—
Educated outside Scotland	3	7	—	—
University education	8	29	8	3
Former Councillor	4	24	—	1
Women	—	1	1	1
Occupation				
Land/farming	2	2	—	—
Business	5	4	1	—
Professions (incl. TU officials, etc.)	1	23	5	3
Scots lawyers	3	4	3	—
Unskilled/skilled	—	12	—	—

Parliament highlighted the powerlessness of those opposed to the Conservative Government. Short of independence, Scotland was still subject to the overwhelming constitutional supremacy of the British Government, and could rely only on 'pressure politics'. But the frustration of Scottish MPs of all parties was more marked in the late 1980s because of 'Doomsday' than ever before.

The Scottish Office

The process of adding functions to the Scottish Office continued. The administration of Regional Development Grants (RDGs) was transferred from the Department of Trade and Industry in late 1984. This consolidated the position of the Locate in Scotland bureau and the SDA (see p. 224). However, RDGs were abolished in 1988, and all regional aid became selective. This did not affect the powers of the Scottish Office, as selective aid was within its remit. The wider implications of the changed regional policy, however, might diminish the power of the Scottish Office to attract industry to Scotland.

Malcolm Rifkind replaced George Younger as Secretary of State for Scotland in January 1986, and he continued after the 1987 election. His team was drawn from the remaining eight Scottish MPs, and Scots in the House of Lords (two Ministers of State and two Parliamentary Under-Secretaries). The Lord Advocate was in the House of Lords and the Solicitor-General for Scotland was outside Parliament altogether.

The Conservatives were barely able to fill their Scottish ministerial positions, and mobility for these ministers would obviously be limited.

Local Government

Central–local relations continued to dominate Scottish politics in the late 1980s. A Conservative central government faced an almost totally non-Conservative local government system in Scotland. The Regional Council elections in 1986 gave Labour control of four Regions (Strathcylde, Lothian, Central and Fife) and the largest number of seats in two other big Regions, Tayside and Grampian. There were no Conservative-controlled Regions. Of the District Councils elected in 1988, 53 in number, the Conservatives controlled only three, although many rural Districts were non-partisan and generally sympathetic to the Conservatives. They represented however under a quarter of the Scottish population. The Convention of Scottish Local Authorities, which speaks for all Scottish local authorities, became increasingly anti-Government and obstructive.

To counteract the opposition of local government, central government obtained new legislative powers to control the revenue and spending of local authorities, notably by the Rating and Valuation Amendment Act (Scotland) 1984, and by the introduction of the 'community charge' under the Abolition of Domestic Rates, etc. (Scotland) Act 1987. These, taken together with Acts passed earlier in the 1980s (see p. 172), signalled a significant centralisation of power, especially in finance. The former Act gave the Secretary of State effective power to set the level of rates and council house rents, and to penalise 'overspending' on housing and services generally. The latter Act heralded the introduction of the flat-rate 'community charge' which was to replace the rates in 1989.

Conflicts between the Scottish Office and local authorities reached a peak in 1985, with Edinburgh and Stirling District Councils in open defiance of the Scottish Office. Last minute climbdowns by the councils prevented local bankruptcies and surcharges on councillors, as had happened in parts of England.

Rate Support Grant was cut back as a percentage of relevant local spending from 68.5% in 1979–80 to 55.5% in 1987–88, but the control of local spending was only partly effective, since it remained at much the same level as in 1979. At the same time, central government had intervened to reduce council housing expenditure severely; to facilitate the sale of council houses and the setting-up of new types of

269

housing association; to open local contracts to competitive tender; to assess local spending on a 'client group' basis, etc. There were also significant interventions in education, with school boards, made up largely of parents, given powers which had previously been exercised by local authorities. Scottish opinion largely opposed these changes, and the Convention of Local Authorities and the teachers' unions, etc., waged campaigns against them. This could be seen as not just a central–local conflict, but also an English–Scottish one, since many of the innovations were based on English practice. Moreover, it could be seen that had there been devolution, the changes would probably not have taken place, as they were in the devolved field, and the Conservatives were unlikely to have been able to control a Scottish Assembly. However, some local government leaders, such as Charles Gray of Strathclyde Regional Council, considered devolution to be of low priority, and local government, especially the Regions, feared that a Scottish Assembly would abolish one of the tiers of local government and transfer some local powers to Edinburgh.

The policy-making process

The Thatcher Governments have attacked the consensus which has traditionally underpinned the Scottish policy process. That consensus operated through a 'Scottish lobby' which defended Scottish interests in the UK Parliament and Government, often on a cross-party basis, and combining business and labour in support of Scottish industries and public expenditure in Scotland. There was also agreement that Scottish institutions such as education, law, and public administration should be organised separately from those in England, and should pursue distinctive policies to take account of the special needs and traditions of Scotland.

Mrs Thatcher and her radical Conservative supporters were unsympathetic to this Scottish consensus, because it stood in the way of policies they wished to introduce for the whole of Britain. In particular, her Governments wished to reduce public expenditure, transfer activities from the public to the private sector, and abolish the dependence of Scottish industry on the state. She was also adamantly opposed to devolution, and to the powers of local government which stood in the way of Conservative policies.

Conservative policies which had proved popular in England (especially the South) were now to be applied in Scotland, although the low vote for the Conservatives there might indicate lack of support.

A wide range of radical reforms was introduced during the second and third Thatcher administrations, which hit at many time-honoured traditions of the Scottish consensus. Local government powers were curbed, rates abolished and a community charge introduced. Regional development grants were abolished and regional aid in general cut; nationalised industries such as the electricity boards were to be privatised; important state industries were closed or threatened with closure. Council and SSHA housing was attacked through spending limits and rent rises, sale of council houses, and the establishment of a new agency, 'Scottish Homes', to speed the privatising process. In education, 'Parent power' was introduced to give choice of school, and later, new 'school boards' were proposed with powers over staff, finance and curriculum. The funding and staffing of the Scottish universities were severely cut back by the UGC, and no special Scottish or regional factors were taken into account in this process. The Manpower Services Commission, based in England, increased its hold on Scottish further education through its funding and supervision of various youth training programmes. Even Scottish schools linked up to the MSC through the Technical and Vocational Education Initiative (TVEI).

All this pointed to an increasingly centralised, London-dominated policy-making process and to assimilation with England. Yet the Scottish system remained resilient, if no longer confident that it would be respected in London. On many fronts it fought back, with some victories, and a few tactical retreats. Ravenscraig steelmill was guaranteed, at least in the short term, despite determined efforts by the British Steel Corporation and the Department of Trade and Industry to close it. The SDA, Locate in Scotland, and the HIDB continued to operate, with higher funding, and the Scottish Office promised in 1988 to retain the level of regional aid. Council house sales proceeded at only half the rate of those in England, and the management of council houses remained overwhelmingly in the hands of the local authorities. Scottish teachers won an independent inquiry into pay, and retained their negotiating machinery, unlike their English colleagues. English examination and curriculum reforms, announced in 1987, were not replicated in Scotland, nor were City Technology Schools. The Scottish Office withdrew much of its original school board scheme, after extensive consultation had revealed strong opposition. For example, schools would not be able to opt out of local government control. The Scottish universities obtained recognition of their special status through the establisment of a Scottish sub-committee on the UGC.

271

Finally, the funding of the Scottish Office, through the 'Barnett Formula' (see p. 213) protected Scotland from drastic differential cuts, and continued to give the Department the power to order its own priorities within its Block. Public expenditure levels per head in Scotland in services covered by the Block remained at a level around one-fifth higher than those in England, despite the criticism of some English Conservative MPs. The Conservative Scottish Office thus defended the Scottish political system when vital Scottish interests were at stake.

Notes

Chapter 1

1 For Scottish Office expenditure, see House of Commons Committee on Scottish Affairs, *Scottish Aspects of the 1982–85 Public Expenditure White Paper*, Minutes of Evidence, 16 June 1982. HC (1981–82) 413, p.5.

2 See for example T. B. Smith, 'The Union of 1707 as fundamental law', *Public Law* xcix (1957).

3 Lord Cooper in the case *MacCormick and another* v. *The Lord Advocate*, 30 July 1953. Report in *Scots Law Times*, 17 October 1953, p. 262

4 M. Keating and A. Midwinter, *The Scottish Office in the United Kingdom Policy Network*, Studies in Public Policy No. 96, Centre for the Study of Public Policy, University of Strathclyde (Glasgow, 1981), pp.1–2.

5 K. W. Deutsch, *Nationalism and Social Communication*, MIT Press (Massachusetts, 1953), p. 70.

6 For a detailed account of Scottish social institutions, see J. G. Kellas, *Modern Scotland*, 2nd edn, George Allen and Unwin (London, 1980).

7 J. M. Bochel and D. J. Denver, 'Religion and voting: A critical view and a new analysis', *Political Studies* xviii (1970), 205–19.

8 Readership figures are from the *National Readership Survey 1981*, Joint Industry Committee for National Readership Surveys (London, 1982).

9 *Annual Report and Accounts of the British Broadcasting Corporation, 1969–70*, HMSO, Cmnd 4250 (November 1970), p. 127.

10 *Household Food Consumption and Expenditure; 1967*, Report of National Food Survey Committee, 1967, HMSO (London, 1969), pp. 19–23, 39–40.

11 K. W. Deutsch, *Nationalism and Social Communication*, p. 71.

12 P. Self and H. J. Storing, *The State and the Farmer*, George Allen and Unwin (London, 1962), p. 194. See also R. W. Howarth, 'The Political strength of British agriculture', *Political Studies* xvii (1969), 458–69.

13 See D. I. MacKay and G. A. Mackay, *The Political Economy of North Sea Oil*, Martin Robertson (London, 1975).

14 The concept of 'arenas' in politics is adapted from F. G. Bailey, *Stratagems and Spoils*, Blackwell (Oxford, 1969), p. 153.

15 D. Easton, *The Political System*, Alfred Knopf (New York, 1953), pp. 134–40.

16 D. Easton, *A Systems Analysis of Political Life*, John Wiley (New York, 1965), p. 61. Easton, however, goes out of his way to exclude Scotland as a political system, since it has been 'absorbed into an alien system' (*A Framework for Political Analysis*, Prentice-Hall (New Jersey, 1965), p. 83). That this contradiction is unresolved is discussed by Michael Evans in 'Notes on David Easton's model of the political system', *Journal of*

Commonwealth Political Studies vııı (1970), 133, n. 69.
17 K. W. Deutsch, *Politics and Government,* Houghton Miflin (Boston, 1970), pp. 126–7.
18 Talcott Parsons *et al., Theories of Society,* Free Press (New York, 1961), ı, 30--79. A general discussion of the concept of the political system is found in Peter Nettl, 'The concept of system in political science', *Political Studies* xıv (1966), 305–88.

Chapter 2

1 On this, see T. B. Smith, 'The Union as fundamental law', *Public Law* xcıv (1957), and *Scotland,* Stevens (London, 1962), p. 52.
2 A. V. Dicey, *Introduction to the Study of the Law of the Constitution,* first published 1885. Tenth edition, London, 1959, especially introduction by E.C.S. Wade, pp. lxiv–lxvi.
3 Reported in *Scots Law Times,* 24 October 1953, p. 262.
4 T. B. Smith, *Scotland,* p. 32.
5 *Scotsman,* 5 May 1967.
6 *Scotsman,* 12 March 1975; *Scots Law Times,* Reports, 1975, pp. 134–8.
7 'The prosecution process in England and Wales', *Report by Justice* (London, 1970).
8 But see T. B. Smith, *Scotland,* 'Special Aspects of Scottish Constitutional Law', pp. 61–79.

Chapter 3

1 Other boards, such as the Board of Manufactures (1726–1906) and the Fishery Board (1808–1939), were not as closely linked to local government, and the Registrar General for Scotland (1855–) conducts the Census of Scotland as well as supervising local registrars. The Lord Clerk Register (Scottish Record Office) and Lord Lyon King of Arms (heraldry) are medieval survivals.
2 Scottish Secretaries from 1955 to 1970 had a year's extra stay in office, compared with the ministers in charge of other major departments. R. Rose, 'The making of Cabinet ministers', *British Journal of Political Science* 1 (1971) 408.
3 A considerable literature is devoted to evaluating the performance of the Scottish Office. See in particular, J. M. Ross, *The Secretary of State for Scotland and the Scottish Office,* Studies in Public Policy No. 87, University of Strathclyde (Glasgow, 1981); M. Keating and A. Midwinter, *The Scottish Office in the United Kingdom Policy Network,* Studies in Public Policy No. 96, University of Strathclyde (Glasgow, 1981); J. G. Kellas and P. Madgwick, 'Territorial Ministries: the Scottish and Welsh Offices', in Madgwick and Rose; Rose 6. An ex-civil servant, George Pottinger, has written critical and entertaining sketches of *The Secretaries of State for Scotland, 1926–76,* Scottish Academic Press (Edinburgh, 1979).
4 Statement by Michael Noble (Secretary of State for Scotland, 1962–64), *Scotsman,* 19 September 1966.
5 *Scotsman,* 16 November 1966, 10 March 1970, 30 April 1970.
6 John Warden, 'Scotland at Westminster', *Glasgow Herald Trade Review,* January 1972, p.24.

Chapter 4

1 In January 1982 local government employees in Scotland numbered 258,500 (*Scotsman*, 12 January 1982). This is a high figure relative to England. In 1977, local government employment in Scotland was 11% above the UK average, while in England it was 2% below. In Wales it was 18% above, and in Northern Ireland it was 26% above. (Richard Parry, *The Territorial Dimension in United Kingdom Public Employment*, Studies in Public Policy No. 65, University of Strathclyde (Glasgow, 1980), p. 7.)

2 According to Parry (*op. cit.*, p. 4), Scotland in 1977 had 765,000 workers in public employment, or 34.3% of the employed workforce. In England the proportion was 30.0%, in Wales 38.0%, and in Northern Ireland 40.5%. The UK figure was 31.4%. The total is made up of the civil service, local government, nationalised industries and publicly-owned companies, the National Health Service, The Armed Forces, and others.

3 Defined here as those receiving at least part of their education in Scotland. This is obviously only a rough indication of whether an applicant is Scottish or not, but it is the only available criterion for this purpose given in the Civil Service Commissioners' Reports. A Scottish school is probably a better guide to 'Scottishness' than a Scottish university.

4 *6th Report from the Estimates Committee*, HC 308 (1964–5), p. 29.

5 *Ibid.*

6 Civil Service Commission, *Civil Service Recruitment of Graduates, 1971–4 Statistical Tables* (for Conference for University Careers and Appointment Secretaries, 24–6 September 1974).

7 See the general discussion by J. G. Kellas and P. Madgwick, 'Territorial Ministries: the Scottish and Welsh Offices' in Madgwick and Rose. An interesting quantitative analysis of the Scottish Office is to be found in C. C. Hood, A. Dunsire and K. S. Thompson, 'Comparing the Scottish Office with "Whitehall": A Quantitative approach', *British Journal of Political Science* 9 (1979), 257–80.

8 *P.E.P. Planning* xxiv, No. 444 (12 September 1960), 'Local self-government: the experience of the United Kingdom, the Isle of Man, and the Channel Islands', p. 245. See also the 'Hardman Report', *The Dispersal of Government Work from London*, Cmnd 5322, 1973, p. 197.

Chapter 5

1 J. M. Bochel and D. T. Denver, *The New Scottish Constituencies: A Guide and an Analysis*, Election Studies, Department of Political Science, University of Dundee (Dundee, 1983).

2 Michael J. Keating, *A test of political integration: the Scottish Members of Parliament*, Studies in Public Policy No. 6, University of Strathclyde (Glasgow, 1977).

3 Only 21 Scottish Labour MPs made four or more speeches covering at least ten lines in Hansard in 1969–70. Most of these speeches were on topics relating to Scotland. Fifteen Conservatives and 4 Liberals also made speeches, making a total of 40 Scottish MPs. The Scottish party distribution at this time was Labour 44, Conservative 21, Liberal 4, and SNP 1 MPs. In the whole House, 358 were frequent speechmakers in the

same period. (R. Oakley and P. Rose, *The Political Year 1970*, Pitman (London, 1970), pp. 204–10. See also Keating, *op. cit.*)

4 Compare the *Memorandum of Evidence of the Law Society of Scotland to the Commission on the Constitution* (Edinburgh, 1970), p. 6, para. 17.

5 *Scotsman*, 25 April 1975.

6 J.H. Burns, 'The Scottish Committees of the House of Commons, 1948–59', *Political Studies* VIII (1960), 272–96.

7 Sir Ivor Jennings, *Parliament*, 2nd edn, CUP (Cambridge, 1957), p. 272

8 See 'The Scottish Penitentiary', in Emrys Hughes, *Parliament and Mumbo-Jumbo*, Hillary (London, 1966).

9 *Parliamentary Debates* HC, 1st Scottish Standing Committee, 18 January 1972, cols. 7–8, 26–7.

10 The Law Society of Scotland's Evidence to the Commission on the Constitution (1970) cites seven examples of delays in Scots Law reforms. These are:

    1. Mackintosh Report on Succession (1951); legislation 1964.

    2. McKechnie Report on Diligence (1958); legislation, none.

    3. Guest Report on Licensing Law (1963); legislation, partial 1969.

    4. Reid Report on Registration of Title to Land (1963); legislation, none.

    5. Hunter Report on Salmon and Trout Fisheries (1965); legislation, none.

    6. Halliday Report on Conveyancing (1966); legislation, partial 1970.

    7. Grant Report on the Sheriff Court (1967); legislation, none.

Commission on the Constitution, *Written Evidence 5* (Scotland), HMSO (1972), p. 20.

11 *Glasgow Herald*, 24 February 1971.

12 Law Society of Scotland's Evidence, p. 1·5.

13 *Hansard*, 5th Series, vol. 756, cols. 1375–6, 20 December 1967.

14 Some of the most prolific questioners in Parliament are the Scottish MPs. In Session 1968–9, for example, Mrs Ewing (SNP) asked 516 questions (for oral and written answer). This was the second highest for any MP. Other notable questioners in Scotland were Bruce-Gardyne (Con) 387, Dalyell (Lab) 386, Taylor (Con) 335, and Eadie (Lab) 224. These were all in the 'top ten' of the House of Commons. (*The Political Companion, No. 1*, October–December 1969 (Glasgow, 1969), pp. 149–67.)

15 Michael J. Keating, *Scotland in Parliament: Options for Reform*, Studies in Public Policy No. 45, University of Strathclyde (Glasgow, 1979).

Chapter 6

1 A. J. Beattie, *English Party Politics*, Weidenfeld and Nicolson (London, 1970), 2 vols.

2 A. H. Birch, *The British System of Government*, 1st edn, Allen and Unwin (London, 1976), p. 17.

3 G. Moodie, *The Government of Great Britain*, 1st edn, Crowell (New York, 1961), p. 1n.

4 Cf. H. J. Hanham, *The Scottish Political Tradition*, University of Edinburgh, Inaugural Lecture No. 19 (1964), pp. 17–18.

5 J. G. Kellas, 'The Mid-Lanark By-election (1888) and the Scottish Labour Party (1888–1894)', *Parliamentary Affairs* xvⅢ, No. 3 (1965), 318–29.

6 E.g. Sir Ivor Jennings, *Party Politics*, Cambridge University Press (Cambridge, 1960–2), 3 vols.; J. Blondel, *Voters, Parties and Leaders*, Penguin Books (London, 1963); S. H. Beer, *Modern British Politics*, Faber (London, 1965); and Butler and Stokes.

7 The description of the Conservative and Labour Parties as class parties is obviously an over-simplification. For the relationship between class and party see Butler and Stokes, Chs. 4–5.

8 His argument can only be briefly summarised here. Under (1) he illustrates the territorial and social diversity of Britain (covering 'natural frontiers', ethnic groups, competing forms of centralisation in the four nations, institutional decentralisation, and subjective national identification). The difficulty here is evaluating the pull of these centrifugal forces as compared with those leading to homogeneity. Under (2) he shows the different religious profiles of the nations, but admits that 'religious issues as such rarely become prominent in British politics today' (p. 13). For (3) he says much the same, since the politics of agriculture is a 'matter in which English and non-English farmers can both press claims'. Under (4) he gives interesting evidence that working-class consciousness and trade union affiliation are stronger in Scotland and Wales than in England. (In Northern Ireland class consciousness is weak, though trade union affiliation is high.) Variations in electoral behaviour between the nations are also examined (Rose 3, pp. 4–19).

9 For this period, see particularly, Henry Pelling, *Social Geography of British Elections, 1885–1910*, Macmillan (London, 1967), Ch. 16; and J. F. McCaffrey, 'The origins of Liberal Unionism in the West of Scotland', *Scottish Historical Review* L, No. 149 (1971), 47–71.

10 James G. Kellas and Peter Fotheringham, 'The Political Behaviour of the Working Class' in A. Allan MacLaren (Ed.), *Social Class in Scotland: Past and Present*, John Donald (Edinburgh, 1976), pp. 154–8. See also Miller, pp. 210–16. Miller estimates that in elections between 1923 and 1979 the average difference between the Conservative lead in Scotland and England (8%) was due entirely to the class difference between Scotland and England. But individual elections (e.g. 1955 and 1979) deviate considerably from this average.

11 J. M. Bochel and D. J. Denver, 'Religion and voting: A critical review and a new analysis', *Political Studies* xvⅢ, No. 2 (1970), 205–19.

12 The principal towns in Scotland with a strong Catholic population are Coatbridge (43% of population RC), Port Glasgow (42%), Dumbarton (40%), Rutherglen (38%), Greenock (36%), Airdrie (36%), Glasgow (30%), Motherwell and Wishaw (27%), Hamilton (26%), and Paisley (22%) (*The Western Catholic Calendar*, John S. Burns (Glasgow, 1970)).

13 Cf. George Scott, *The Roman Catholics*, Hutchinson (London, 1967). Constituencies most affected were Coatbridge and Airdrie, Motherwell, Glasgow Bridgeton, and Glasgow Gorbals.

14 R. T. McKenzie, *British Political Parties*, 2nd edn, Heinemann (London, 1964), p. 488.

15 These are listed in the annual *Reports* of the Labour Party (Scottish Council).
16 D. W. Urwin, 'The development of the Conservative Party organisation in Scotland Until 1912', *Scottish Historical Review* XLIV. No. 138 (1965), 90–111.
17 D. W. Urwin, 'Scottish Conservatism: A party organisation in transition', *Political Studies* XIV, No. 2 (1966), 145–62.
18 F. Bealey and H. Pelling, *Labour and Politics, 1900–1906*, Macmillan (London, 1958), pp. 293–7.
19 Labour Party (Scottish Council), *Constitution and Standing Orders*, p. 12.
20 Labour Party (Scottish Council) *Report 1969*, pp. 6–7; *Report, 1970*, p. 8. From 1972, the Labour Party Constitution allowed regional councils (including the Scottish Conference) official freedom to discuss any issue except international affairs.
21 *Report 1970, loc. cit.*
22 Labour Party (Scottish Council), *Report of the Executive Committee 1981*, pp. 92–100.
23 Labour Party (Scottish Council), *Interim Policy Statement on Devolution* (1981).
24 *Scotsman*, 27 March 1982.
25 Michael Rush, *The Selection of Parliamentary Candidates*, Nelson (London, 1969), p. 289.
26 *Ibid.* p. 135.
27 Labour Party (Scottish Council), *Constitution and Standing Orders*, p. 11.

Chapter 7

1 G. Jahoda, 'The development of children's ideas about country and nationality', *British Journal of Educational Psychology* XXXIII (February and June 1963), 47–60, 143–53.
2 English nationalism has not yet attracted the attention of political sociologists. English children (and most adults) call their country 'England' rather than 'Britain', but this is partly the well-known confusion regarding the use of England to include Scotland, Wales, and even Northern Ireland. See J. Dennis, L. Linberg, and D. McCrone, 'Support for nation and government among English children', *British Journal of Political Science* 1 (January 1971), 25–48, and comments by A. H. Birch, *ibid.* (October 1971), 519–20.
3 In Jahoda's survey of Glasgow children's ideas about country and nationality (*op. cit.* p. 149) a picture of Burns was recognised by 88% of children aged 10–11. Jahoda remarks, 'Evidently Burns constitutes one of the most potent Scottish national symbols, as early as childhood.' Other symbols of Scottishness (costumes, landscapes, buildings, songs, and emblems) were readily identified as such.
4 The nineteenth-century debate between Anglicisers and nationalists in the Scottish universities is dealt with in G. E. Davie, *The Democratic Intellect*, Edinburgh University Press (Edinburgh, 1961).
5 See J. Highet, *The Scottish Churches*, Skeffington (London, 1960),

pp. 153–9; and I. Henderson, *Power without Glory*, Hutchinson (London, 1967).

6 The Law Society of Scotland stated in evidence to the Commission on the Constitution that 'further developments towards the assimilation of the law and legal systems of Scotland and England are inevitable and desirable' (*Memorandum of Evidence*, p. 8). Yet a large number of Scots lawyers have argued to the contrary.

7 W. L. Miller, with B. Sarlvik, I. Crewe, and J. Alt, 'The Connection between SNP voting and the demand for Scottish self-government', *European Journal of Political Research* 5 (1977), 83–102; W. L. Miller, 'What was the profit in following the crowd? Immigration and devolution strategy since 1970', *British Journal of Political Science* 10 (1980), 15–38.

8 For this, readers should consult L. A. Pollock and I. McAllister, *A Bibliography of United Kingdom Politics: Scotland, Wales and Northern Ireland*, Centre for the Study of Public Policy, Vol. III (Glasgow, 1979); and C. H. Allen, 'Recent Publications in Scottish Government and Politics', in *The Scottish Government Yearbook*, Paul Harris and Unit for the Study of Government in Scotland, Edinburgh (annual).

9 Discussion of these can be found in J. G. Kellas, 'Review article: Political science and Scottish politics', *British Journal of Political Science* 10 (1980), 365–79; and C. H. Allen, 'The Study of Scottish Politics: A Bibliographical sermon', in N. Drucker and H. M. Drucker (Eds.), *The Scottish Government Yearbook 1980*, Paul Harris (Edinburgh, 1979).

10 Tom Nairn, *The Break-up of Britain*, Verso (London, 2nd edn 1981).

11 M. Hechter, *Internal Colonialism: The Celtic Fringe in British National Development, 1536-1966*, Routledge and Kegan Paul (London, 1975).

12 W. Miller, J. Brand, and M. Jordan, *Oil and the Scottish voter, 1974–79*, Social Science Research Council (London, 1980).

13 W. L. Miller, with B. Sarlvik, I. Crewe, and J. Alt, *op. cit.*, p. 99.

14 Robert M. Crawford, 'The Scottish National Party, 1960–1974: an investigation into its organisation and power structure', unpublished PhD thesis, University of Glasgow, 1982.

Chapter 8

1 H. M. Drucker, *Breakaway: The Scottish Labour Party*, EUSPB (Edinburgh, 1978), p. 12

2 Tam Dalyell, *Devolution: The End of Britain?*, Cape (London, 1977), pp.97–9.

3 Barbara Castle, *The Castle Diaries, 1974–76*, Weidenfeld and Nicolson (London, 1980), p. 153.

4 *Ibid.*, p. 179.

5 Peter Kellner and Lord Crowther-Hunt, *The Civil Servants*, Macdonald and Jane's (London, 1980), pp. 217–8, 235; Drucker and Brown, pp. 98–101.

6 *The Times*, 16 May 1981.

7 David Heald, *Financing Devolution within the United Kingdom: a Study of the Lessons from Failure*, Research Monograph no. 32, Centre for Research on Federal Financial Relations, The Australian National University (Canberra, 1980).

8 V. Bogdanor, *The People and the Party System*, Cambridge University Press (Cambridge, 1981), p. 55. The Yes Vote was 1,230,937, and the 'correct' electorate was 3,163,760.

Chapter 9

1 The Maud Report (Cmnd 4040) called for indirectly-elected provincial councils, but its main proposal was for 58 'all-purpose' authorities throughout most of England. Three conurbations would have a two-tier structure, and London would continue to have a separate system. The Government in February 1971 decided to introduce a two-tier structure of 38 counties and 300 districts, which appeared to resemble that proposed by Wheatley. But there were to be six metropolitan areas, and the provincial level was dropped. The English reform remained a much less drastic revision than the Scottish, and was essentially one of amalgamated counties. The Local Government Act 1972 established 39 non-metropolitan counties and 296 county districts, 6 metropolitan counties and 36 metropolitan districts. The London system was retained as were about 10,500 parish councils and meetings.
2 I am indebted to Professor W. J. M. Mackenzie for this insight. He developed it in a paper delivered to the Royal Institute of Public Administration Glasgow and West of Scotland Regional Group Conference in 1970. See its published *Report*, Glasgow, 1970.
3 For an assessment of the development of corporate management in Scottish local authorities, see Arthur Midwinter, *Management Reform in Scottish Local Government*, Department of Administration, University of Strathclyde (Glasgow, 1982). Also Keating and Midwinter, Ch. 6, for an extensive discussion.
4 For a critical yet approving account of the effects of the new system on democratic accountability, etc., see Edward C. Page and Arthur F. Midwinter, *Remote Bureaucracy or Administrative Efficiency? Scotland's New Local Government System*, Studies in Public Policy no. 38, University of Strathclyde (Glasgow, 1979). Also Keating and Midwinter, Ch. 5.
5 See D. A. Heald, C. A. Jones, and D. W. Lamont, 'Breaking Mr. Younger's Runaway Train: The Conflict between the Scottish Office and Local Authorities over Local Government Expenditure', in H. M. Drucker and N. L. Drucker (Eds.)., *The Scottish Government Yearbook 1982*, Paul Harris (Edinburgh, 1981). Also A. Midwinter, *Conflict and Confusion: the Politics of Rates*, Strathclyde University, Department of Administration (Glasgow, 1981); Keating and Midwinter; A. Midwinter, M. Keating, and P. Taylor, '"Excessive and unreasonable": The politics of the Scottish hit list', *Political Studies* xxxi (1983), 394–417.

Chapter 10

1 Interest groups as here defined are organisations formed to defend the (generally economic) interests of their members. Examples are trade unions and employers' associations. Attitude (or promotional) groups draw support from the public generally in pursuit of a cause. Examples are the Lord's Day Observance Society and Oxfam.

2 These include the Scottish Council of Social Service, the Standing Council on Youth and Community Service in Scotland, the Transport Users Consultative Committee for Scotland, the Advisory Council on Education in Scotland, the School Broadcasting Council for Scotland, the Scottish Hospital Scientific Council (established 1971), and the Scottish Economic Council (downgraded in 1970 from the Scottish Economic Planning Council). See also Appendix to this chapter.

3 Cf. J. T. Cox, *Practice and Procedure in the Church of Scotland*, 5th edn, Church of Scotland (Edinburgh, 1964).

4 Robin F. Cook, MP, 'Parliament and the Scots Conscience', in H. M. Drucker and M. G. Clarke (Eds.), *The Scottish Government Yearbook 1978*, Paul Harris (Edinburgh, 1977), pp. 99–112.

5 *Scotsman*, 6 January 1979.

6 See Sister Martha Skinnider, 'Catholic Elementary Education in Glasgow, 1818–1918', in T. R. Bone (Ed.), *Studies in the History of Scottish Education*, University of London Press (London, 1967). Also Rev. Brother Kenneth, 'The Education (Scotland) Act, 1918, in the making', *Innes Review* xiv, No. 2 (1968), 91–128; J. H. Treble, 'The Development of Roman Catholic Education in Scotland, 1878–1978' in D. McRoberts (Ed.), *Modern Scottish Catholicism, 1878–1978*, Burns (Glasgow, 1979).

7 A survey in Glasgow in 1967 found that 63% of Glasgow Catholics favoured integrating Protestant and Catholic schools (*Glasgow Herald*, 29 April 1967). This fell to 56% in 1979 (*Scotsman*, 4 October 1979), and 47% in 1983 (*Sunday Standard*, 24 April 1983). Protestants favour religious integration in the ratio of 9:1, but the Church of Scotland has shown sympathy towards the system of Catholic schools, mainly because it fears that mixed schools would have to be completely secular in their teaching. As it is, so-called 'non-denominational schools' have religious teaching along Church of Scotland lines, sometimes by ministers.

8 The movement for religious integration in the Labour Party began in Glasgow City Labour Party, which voted for it in March 1970 (*Scotsman*, 16 March 1970). The Scottish Executive of the Labour Party endorsed religious integration in 1972 (*Glasgow Herald*, 22 February 1972), and this was supported by Labour Scottish conferences in 1976 and subsequently (*Scotsman*, 29 March 1976).

9 *Scotsman*, 9 June 1979.

10 *Scotsman*, 1 December 1980.

11 In 1971, the last major Scottish industrial union, the Scottish Commercial Motormen's Union (21,000), merged with the Transport and General Workers' Union. By 1982 there were only two Scottish industrial unions affiliated to the STUC, the Scottish Carpet Workers' Union (2,900 members) and the Scottish Lace and Textile Workers' Union (1,200 members). There were five Scottish teachers and lecturers' unions affiliated, and the NAS/UWT Scottish membership, in total over 60,000 members: *STUC 85th Annual Report 1982*, STUC (Glasgow, 1982).

12 Scottish Trades Union Congress, *Submission to Royal Commission on Trade Unions and Employers' Associations*, Glasgow, 6 May 1966, p. 1. Compare the STUC General Council *Memorandum of Evidence to the Commission on the Constitution*, May 1970, p. 3: 'It may be appropriate to recall that

when the Scottish Trades Union Congress was formed in 1897 the circumstances surrounding its formation reflected the uneasiness in Scottish trade union circles about the "remoteness" of London, the inability of the people there, including trade union people, to understand or be interested in the Scottish scene, especially with regard to the unfair interpretation by the Sheriff Courts of the law as it affected workpeople and their dependents.' Wherever Scots Law is involved, there is a strong impetus to establish a separate Scottish organisation.

13 Cf. The National Society for the Prevention of Cruelty to Children. Other groups of this type in a Scottish form include the Scottish Society for the Prevention of Cruelty to Animals (England, RSPCA), the Scottish Temperance Alliance, the Saltire Society (promotes Scottish culture), the National Trust for Scotland, the Scottish Band of Hope Union, etc.

Chapter 11

1 *Report of the Committee of Privy Councillors Appointed to Inquire into 'D' Notice Matters*, HMSO, Cmnd 3309, 1967, pp. 180, 206.
2 *Annual Report and Accounts of the British Broadcasting Corporation, 1969–70*, HMSO, Cmnd 4520, p. 127.
3 *BBC Annual Report and Handbook 1983*, BBC (London, 1982), pp. 115–7.

Chapter 12

1 The distinction between a social and political system is not always clear (cf. G. A. Almond and G. B. Powell, *Comparative Politics*, Little, Brown (Boston, 1966), p. 20): 'The same individuals who perform roles in the political system perform roles in other social systems such as the economy, the religious community, the family, and voluntary associations.' Since most of these 'social systems' are heavily dependent on the political system it is difficult to draw boundaries round them.
2 See in particular, David Heald, *Financing Devolution within the United Kingdom: a Study of the Lessons from Failure*, Centre for Research on Federal Financial Relations, The Australian National University (Canberra, 1980); Donald MacKay (Ed.), *Scotland 1980: the Economics of Self-government*, Q Press (Edinburgh, 1977).
3 Descriptions of this system and assessments of its effects are to be found in SCSA 4, 5, and 6; Keating and Midwinter; D. A. Heald, *Territorial Equity and Public Finances: Concepts and Confusion*, Studies in Public Policy No. 75, University of Strathclyde (Glasgow, 1980); Richard Parry, 'Public Expenditure in Scotland', in D. McCrone (Ed.), *The Scottish Government Yearbook 1983*, Unit for the Study of Government in Scotland, University of Edinburgh, (Edinburgh, 1982).
4 For an early assessment of the Scottish system see references in Ch. 9, n. 5.
5 *Report of the Committee on Local Development in Scotland*, Scottish Council (Development and Industry)(Edinburgh, 1952).
6 J. H. McGuinness, Assistant Under-Secretary of State, Scottish Office, until 1972. Born 1912, Leeds. Educated, St Aloysius College, Glasgow, Glasgow University, and Trinity College, Oxford. Ministry of Transport before 1939; Scottish Office since 1946.

7 *Scotsman*, 6 March 1981, 11 August 1982; B. W. Hogwood, 'The Regional Dimension of Industrial Policy', in Madgwick and Rose, p. 48.
8 Works comparing the Scottish and English educational systems are G. S. Osborne, *Scottish and English Schools*, Longman (London, 1966), and R. Bell and N. Grant, *Patterns of Education in the British Isles*, George Allen and Unwin (London, 1977).
9 For the English education world see Edward Boyle and Anthony Crosland in conversation with M. Kogan, *The Politics of Education*, Penguin Books (London, 1971).
10 *The Structure of the Curriculum in the Third and Fourth Years of the Scottish Secondary School* (Munn Report), Scottish Education Depart ment/Consultative Committee on the Curriculum, HMSO (Edinburgh, 1977).
11 *Assessment for All. Report of the Committee to Review Assessment in the Third and Fourth Years of Secondary Education in Scotland*, Scottish Education Department, HMSO (Edinburgh, 1977).
12 *Scotsman*, 13 November 1982.
13 *Scotsman*, 6 July 1983.
14 T. R. Bone, *School Inspection in Scotland, 1840–1966*, University of London Press (London, 1968); Charles D. Raab, 'Mapping the boundaries of education policy systems: The case of Scotland', *Public Administration Bulletin*, No. 39 (1982), pp. 52–5.
15 John S. Brunton, Born 1903, died 1977. Educated, Albert Road Academy, Glasgow, and Glasgow University. HM Inspector of Schools 1932–51; Assistant Secretary, Scottish Education Department 1951–5; HM Senior Chief Inspector of Schools 1955–66. 'Brunton Report', *From School to Further Education*, Scottish Education Department (Edinburgh, 1963).
16 *Hansard*, 5th Series, vol. 431, col. 1003, 10 December 1946.
17 L. A. Gunn and R. Mair, 'Staffing the National Health Service', in J. Revans and G. McLachlan (Eds.), *Challenges for Change: Essays on the Next Decade in the National Health Service*, Oxford University Press (London, 1971), pp. 277–8.
18 National Health Service (Scotland) Act 1972; National Health Reorganisation Act 1973. See also, R. Mair, 'Health Services', in J. English and F. M. Martin (Eds.), *Social Services in Scotland*, Scottish Academic Press (Edinburgh, 1979).
19 I am indebted to Robert Mair of Glasgow University for permission to draw upon his unpublished case study of the Social Work (Scotland) Act.
20 Lord Kilbrandon, Scottish Law Lord since 1959 and Life Peer, 1971 (Charles J. D. Shaw). Born 1906, Ayrshire. Educated, Charterhouse, Balliol College, Oxford, and Edinburgh University. Scottish Bar, 1932; Sheriff, 1954–9; Chairman of Scottish Law Commission, 1965–71, and member of (Crowther) Commission on the Constitution, 1969; Chairman of Commission on the Constitution, 1972–3.
21 Up to 1970, the Ministry of Housing and Local Government was the relevant department in England. For this aspect of central–local relations, and further discussion of the formulation of the policy relating to social work in Scotland, see Kilbrandon 4, pp.109–10, also, p.37.

22 But see T. B. Smith, *British Justice: The Scottish Contribution*, Stevens (London, 1961), p. 84.

23 Law Society of Scotland, *Memorandum of Evidence to the Commission on the Constitution* (Edinburgh, 1971), p. 5.

24 *Conveyancing Legislation and Practice*, Cmnd 3118, 1966.

25 *Sheriff Courts: Report of the Grant Committee*, Cmnd 3248, 1967, followed by Sheriff Courts (Scotland) Bill 1971. *Law of Succession: Report of the Mackintosh Committee*, Cmd 8144, 1950, followed by Succession (Scotland) Act 1964.

26 Justice, *The Prosecution Process in England and Wales* (London, 1970), pp. 9–12.

27 But there were only four of these in the Parliament elected in 1970 (House of Commons Debates, *Hansard*, 5th Series, vol. 809, 1970–1, col. 1507, 22 January 1971). Robin Cook, the MP who sponsored the divorce and homosexual law reforms in the mid-1970s, tends to discount the influence of religious pressures in his account of the legislative history of Scottish divorce law reform, licensing reform and homosexual law reform. (Robin F. Cook, MP, 'Parliament and the Scots Conscience. Reforming the law on Divorce, Licensing and Homosexual Offences', in H. M. Drucker and M. G. Clarke (Eds.), *The Scottish Government Yearbook 1978*, Paul Harris (Edinburgh, 1977) Ch. 8.

28 Law Society of Scotland *op. cit.*, p. 4.

Chapter 13

1 The old counties of Argyll, Inverness, Ross and Cromarty, Caithness, Sutherland, Orkney and Zetland (Shetland). These are also known as the seven 'crofting counties', from their inclusion in the Crofters Acts. There are, however, only about 15,000 people out of the total of around 330,000 living in crofts. The parliamentary constituencies until 1983 were Argyll, Inverness, Ross and Cromarty, Western Isles, Caithness and Sutherland, and Orkney and Shetland. Since 1983, Inverness has become Inverness, Nairn, and Lochaber; Argyll has become Argyll and Bute; and Ross and Cromarty has become Ross, Cromarty, and Skye. The area covered by the Highlands and Islands Development Board includes the old crofting counties plus Nairn, Arran and Bute.

2 Political studies of the European periphery are contained in Basil Chubb, *The Government and Politics of Ireland*, Oxford University Press (London, 1970); Henry Valen, *Regional Contrasts in Norwegian Politics*, Chr. Michelson Inst. (Bergen, 1964); Stein Rokkan, 'The Mobilisation of the Periphery', in *Citizen, Elections, Parties*, Universities Forlaget (Oslo, 1970), pp. 181–225; and articles in *Scandinavian Political Studies* (1966–   ). See also Ch. 14, n. 8. A survey of social anthropological work on the Highlands is included in Edward Condry, *Scottish Ethnography*, Association for Scottish Ethnography, Monograph No. 1, Social Science Research Council/Department of Social Anthropology, University of Edinburgh (Edinburgh, 1983). Condry and others reject the 'periphery' interpretation of the Scottish Highlands, and its associated 'romantic' view of Highland

history and culture. They see the Highlands as an integral part of British capitalism, as 'modern' as the rest of the country. How far this applies to its politics is not clear.

3 J. G. Kellas, 'The Crofters' War, 1882–1888', *History Today*, April 1962; 'Highland migration to Glasgow and the origin of the Scottish Labour movement', *Bulletin of the Society for the Study of Labour History*, No. 12 (1966), 9–12; D. W. Crowley, 'The Crofters' Party, 1885–1892', *Scottish Historical Review* xxxv (1956), 110–26; H. J. Hanham, 'The Problem of Highland discontent, 1880–85', *Transactions of the Royal Historical Society 5th series* xix (1969), 21–65; J. Hunter, *The Making of the Crofting Community*, John Donald (Edinburgh, 1976).

4 Frederik Barth (Ed.), *The Role of the Entrepreneur in Social Change in Northern Norway*, Norwegian University Press (Bergen/Oslo, 1963).

5 *Glasgow Herald*, 14 April 1982.

6 *Scotsman*, 6 May 1982, 8 May 1982.

7 *Scotsman*, 8 May 1982; and N. Drucker and H. M. Drucker (Eds.), *The Scottish Government Yearbook 1979*, Paul Harris (Edinburgh, 1978) p. 239.

8 *HIDB 17th Annual Report 1982* (Inverness, 1983), p.2.

9 *Ibid.*, p. 51

10 Professor Sir Robert Grieve. Born 1910. Educated, North Kelvinside School, Glasgow, and Royal College of Science and Technology, Glasgow (now Strathclyde University). Civil engineer with Glasgow Corporation and Renfrew County, subsequently Chief Planning Assistant, 1927–39; Regional Planning Officer, Department of Health for Scotland, 1946–60; Chief Planner, Scottish Office, 1960–4; Professor of Town and Regional Planning, Glasgow University, 1964–74; seconded to Highland Board, 1965–70. Recreations: mountaineering, skiing, and canoeing.

11 *Scotsman*, 9 June 1978.

12 James Grassie, 'Invergordon: a question of power politics', *Scotsman*, 19 January 1982. See also that author's *Highland Experiment*, Aberdeen University Press (Aberdeen, 1982), for a book-length critique of the record of the HIDB.

Chapter 14

1 *Round Table*, January 1976. John P. Mackintosh was Professor of Politics at Edinburgh University and MP for Berwick and East Lothian from 1966 until his death in 1978 at the age of 48. He was a prolific writer on Scottish politics, and a leading campaigner for Scottish devolution. See H. M. Drucker (Ed.), *John P. Mackintosh on Scotland*, Longman (London, 1982).

2 David Easton, *The Political System* (New York, 1953), pp. 134–40.

3 A 'subject political culture' is one in which the citizens have no great urge to participate in government themselves (G. A. Almond and S. Verba, *The Civic Culture*, Princeton University Press (Princeton, New Jersey), p. 19). It is difficult to apply this idea to Scotland, since it depends on whether the appropriate centre of government is London or Edinburgh. Scots participate in the British Parliament but do not have a parliament in Scotland.

While they seek greater devolution, it is not usually a political priority for them.

4 Cf. K. W. Deutsch, *Politics and Government*, Houghton Mifflin (Boston, 1970), pp. 126–7, where all levels of politics from the individual to the UN are described as 'systems'.

5 Julius Gould, 'A sociological portrait: nationality and ethnicity', *New Society*, 30 December 1971, p. 1282. 'Unlike America, Britain does not give any structural supremacy to White Anglo-Saxon Protestantism, but outsiders, even British "nationals", can feel and can be made to feel, selectively excluded. It is often a tacit major premise, but at times it can become almost whimsically articulate. During the revivals of Welsh and Scots nationalism in the late 1960s, Englishmen were heard to say, half-seriously, that they too, should strive for autonomy via regional devolution.'

6 E.g. Hans Kohn, *The Idea of Nationalism*, Macmillan (New York, 1944).

7 K. W. Deutsch, *Nationalism and Social Communication*, MIT Press (Massachusetts, 1953).

8 S. Rokkan and D. W. Urwin (Eds.), *The Politics of Territorial Identity. Studies in European Regionalism*, Sage (London, 1982); S. Rokkan and D. W. Urwin (Eds.), *Economy, Territory, Identity. Politics of West European Peripheries*, Sage (London, 1983).

Bibliography

Balfour, Royal Commission on Scottish Affairs, 1952–4 (Balfour Commission), *Report*, HMSO, Cmd. 9212, 1954.

Bochel, J., Denver, D., and Macartney, A. (Eds.), *The Referendum Experience. Scotland 1979*, Aberdeen University Press (Aberdeen, 1981).

Bogdanor, Vernon, *Devolution*, Oxford University Press, (Oxford, 1979).

Brand, Jack, *The National Movement in Scotland*, Routledge and Kegan Paul (London, 1978).

Budge, I. and Urwin, D. W., *Scottish Political Behaviour*, Longman (London, 1966).

Butler, D. and Kavanagh, D., *The British General Election of 1979*, Macmillan (London, 1980).

Butler, D. and King, A., *The British General Election of 1966*, Macmillan (London, 1966).

Butler, D. and Pinto-Duschinsky, M., *The British General Election of 1970*, Macmillan (London, 1971).

Butler, D. and Stokes, D., *Political Change in Britain*, Macmillan (London, 1969).

Coupland, Sir Reginald, *Welsh and Scottish Nationalism*, Collins (London, 1954).

Drucker, H. M., and Brown, G., *The Politics of Nationalism and Devolution*, Longman (London, 1980).

Fulton, Committee on the Civil Service (1966–8)(Fulton Committee), HMSO.
1. *Report*, Cmnd 3638, 1968.
2. *Surveys and Investigations*, vol. 3 (1), 1969.

Gilmour, Committee on Scottish Administration (Gilmour Committee), *Report*, HMSO, Cmd 5563, 1937.

Hanham, H.J.
1. *Elections and Party Management: Politics in the Time of Disraeli and Gladstone*, Longman (London, 1959).
2. 'The Creation of the Scottish Office, 1881–7', *Juridical Review* (1965), 205–44.
3. *Scottish Nationalism*, Faber (London, 1969).

Keating, M. and Bleiman, D., *Labour and Scottish Nationalism*, Macmillan (London, 1979).

Keating, Michael and Midwinter, Arthur, *The Government of Scotland*, Mainstream (Edinburgh, 1983).

Kilbrandon, Commission on the Constitution (1969–73) (known as the

Crowther Commission until March 1972, when on Lord Crowther's death,
Lord Kilbrandon became Chairman), HMSO.
1. *Written Evidence 1* (The Welsh Office) (1969).
2. *Written Evidence 2* (The Scottish Office, The Lord Advocate's Department
   and the Crown Office) (1969).
3. *Minutes of Evidence* I Wales (September and November 1969).
4. *Minutes of Evidence* II Scotland (September and November 1969).
5. *Minutes of Evidence* IV Scotland (May and July 1970).
6. Vol. I, *Report*, HMSO, Cmnd 5460, 1973.
7. Vol. II. *Memorandum of Dissent*, HMSO, Cmnd 5460–1, 1973.
8. Research Paper 7, *Devolution and Other Aspects of Government: An
   Attitudes Survey* (1973).
Mackintosh, J. P., *The Devolution of Power*, Penguin (London, 1968).
Madgwick, P. and Rose, R. (Eds.), *The Territorial Dimension in United Kingdom
Politics*, Macmillan (London, 1982).
McCrone, Gavin
1. *Scotland's Economic Progress, 1951–60*, University of Glasgow Social
   and Economic Studies No. 4, Allen and Unwin (London, 1965).
2. *Scotland's Future: The Economics of Nationalism*, Blackwell (Oxford,
   1969).
3. *Regional Policy in Britain*, Allen and Unwin (London, 1969).
Miller, William L., *The End of British Politics? Scots and English Political
Behaviour in the Seventies*, Clarendon Press (Oxford, 1981).
Milne, Sir David, *The Scottish Office*, Allen and Unwin (London, 1957).
Rose, Richard
1. *Politics in England*, Faber (London, 1965). 1980 edition quoted here.
2. *Class and Party Divisions: Britain as a Test Case*, Survey Research Centre,
   University of Strathclyde, Occasional Paper No. 1 (Glasgow, 1969); also
   Sociology II, No. 2 *(1968)*.
3. *The United Kingdom as a Multi-national State*, Survey Research Centre,
   University of Strathclyde, Occasional Paper No. 6 (Glasgow, 1970).
   Also in *Studies in British Politics*, Macmillan (London, 1976).
4. *Governing without Consensus*, Faber (London, 1971).
5. *Class does not equal Party. The Decline of a Model of British Voting*, Studies
   in Public Policy No. 74, University of Strathclyde (Glasgow, 1980).
6. *Understanding the United Kingdom. The Territorial Dimension in Government*, Longman (London, 1982).
SCSA (House of Commons Select Committee on Scottish Affairs)
1. *Report*, HC 267 (1969–70).
2. *Minutes of Evidence*, vol. I, HC 397 (1968–9).
3. *Minutes of Evidence*, vol. II, HC 267–1 (1969–70).
4. *Scottish Aspects of the 1980–84 Public Expenditure White Paper, Minutes
   of Evidence*, HC 689 (1979–80).
5. *Scottish Aspects of the 1981–84 Public Expenditure White Paper, Minutes
   of Evidence*, HC 364 (1980–1).
6. *Scottish Aspects of the 1982–85 Public Expenditure White Paper, Minutes
   of Evidence*, HC 413 (1981–2).
Thomson, Derick C. and Grimble, Ian (Eds.), *The Future of the Highlands*,
Routledge and Kegan Paul (London, 1968).

Toothill, Committee of Inquiry into the Scottish Economy (Toothill Committee), *Report*, Scottish Council (Development and Industry), (Edinburgh, 1961).

Webb, Keith, *The Growth of Nationalism in Scotland*, Penguin Books (London, 1978).

Wheatley, Royal Commission on Local Government in Scotland, 1966–9 (Wheatley Commission), HMSO (Edinburgh, 1969).
  1. *Report*, Cmnd 4150.
  2. *Appendices*, Cmnd 4150.
  3. *Community Survey: Scotland*, Research Studies 2.

Wolfe, J. N. (Ed.), *Government and Nationalism in Scotland*, Edinburgh University Press (Edinburgh, 1969).

Index

Principal references are indicated by bold type.